THE RIGHT TO PRIVACY AND ITS NATURAL LAW
FOUNDATIONS IN THE CONSTITUTIONS OF THE
UNITED STATES AND IRELAND

ABOUT THE AUTHOR

Admitted to the Ohio Bar in 1983, Cynthia Millen served as a clerk in the US District Court and Sixth Circuit Court of Appeals, practiced law at the criminal appellate level and as a guardian-ad-litem in juvenile court. She is most keenly interested in the study of natural law and constitutional rights. She was recently awarded a Masters of Literature (M Litt) in Law from Trinity College, Dublin and plans to continue writing on a variety of topics from her home in Toledo, Ohio – in between visits to the west of Ireland. She is married to Dr James Roberts and they have five children.

The Right to Privacy and its Natural Law Foundations in the Constitutions of the United States and Ireland

This book was typeset by
Gough Typesetting Services for
BLACKHALL PUBLISHING
26 Eustace Street
Dublin 2
e-mail: blackhall@tinet.ie

ISBN: 1 901657 10 8

A catalogue record for this book is available
from the British Library.

Printed in Ireland by
e print.

In memory of the
Honourable Mr Justice Brian Walsh

Contents

PART I

A Common Beginning: the Shared Philosophical Underpinnings of Modern Irish and American Constitutional Rights

PART II

The Fork in the Road

PART III

Finding Privacy: Two Natural Law Liaisons with Unenumerated Rights

Foreword

The subject of Ms Millen's analysis is one that goes to the heart of contemporary public debate in Ireland. The questions it raises are as challenging as any judge will have to face in a long career on the Bench. They require to be addressed at the level of high theory but they are in no sense narrowly academic or removed from the flesh and blood experience of human relationships. Has law a purpose? Is it merely about controls and sanctions or has it a more positive social goal? Whose values should be reflected in law? Is it possible to contemplate a value-free legal order? To what does individual privacy restrict the potential remit of the law?

These questions need to be confronted in particular, sometimes stark, human situations. The best answers will be rooted in human rights. Ms Millen's discussion of the subject is particularly helpful because she takes the long view, placing the issues in a framework of over two thousand years of philosophical reflection. Her analysis of the Irish judicial contribution is strengthened by the fact that, as an American, she can distance herself from the intensity of emotions surrounding public discussion of Ireland and the United States, her sympathetic understanding of the complexity of the issues and of the lonely responsibility of judicial decision-making is obvious.

Anyone who is interested in examining the role of law in society and of the protection of human rights through law will find in Ms Millen's analysis new insights and the impetus for further reflection.

William Binchy
Law School, Trinity College
Dublin
October 1998

Acknowledgements

I would like to acknowledge the kind assistance of the following people during the research of this book.

Mr Gerard Hogan, Trinity School of Law, for his initial encouragement and informative meetings. Professor David Elder, Chase College of Law at Northern Kentucky University, for his help with US and state case law and his great encouragement. The librarians at the University of Michigan Law Library, for their generous assistance. Dr Gerard Quinn, University College Galway School of Law, for his great help and wonderful afternoons of conversation pertaining to the natural law. Professor John McEldowney, University of Warwick School of Law, for his encouragement, suggestions and good Belfast craic. Professor Fergus Kelly, School of Celtic Studies for his guidance with the Brehon Law. My friend and distant cousin, Seamus Haran of Letterkenny, who shared handed-down stories about de Valera, the Civil War and the 1937 Constitution.

Professor William Binchy his patient supervision and for agreeing to write the foreword.

To my husband, Jim Roberts, who along with our wonderful five children, put up with their crazy wife/mother even more than usual over the past six years of work.

Finally, a special thanks to two extraordinary people:

Professor Francis X Beytagh, my outstanding constitutional law professor and one of my favourite Irish-Americans who planted the seeds for this book several years ago and who gave me the impetus to go forward;

The late Honourable Mr Justice Brian Walsh, whose knowledge and eloquence regarding the natural law and the Irish Constitution were only surpassed by his gentility and hospitality. I shall always cherish the several afternoons we spent conversing about the law in his lovely home, along with his kind letters. Thus, it is with great respect and affection that this book is dedicated to him.

Cynthia Millen
September 1998

List of Abbreviations

Harv. L. Rev.	Harvard University Law Review
Amer. J. of Jurisprudence	American Journal of Jurisprudence
Miss. Valley Hist. Rev.	Mississippi Valley Historical Review
Tulane L. Rev.	Tulane University Law Journal
Int'l & Comp. L. Quart.	International and Comparative Law Quarterly
U. Toronto L. J.	University of Toronto Law Journal
S. Tex. L. Rev.	Southern Texas University Law Review
Maryland L. Rev.	University of Maryland Law Review
Hum. Rts. L. J.	Human Rights Law Journal
Psychological Rec.	Psychological Record
Yale L. J.	Yale University Law Journal
S. Ct. Rev.	Supreme Court Review
Cornell L. Rev.	Stanford University Law Review
Eng. Rep.	English Reporter
S. Cal. L. Rev.	University of Southern California Law Review
US	United States Reports
SW2d	Southwestern Reporter 2nd edition
S. Ct.	US Supreme Court Register
U. Chi L. Rev.	University of Chicago Law Review
F. 3rd	Federal Reporter, 3rd edition
E.H.R.R.	European Human Rights Reporter
I.R.	Irish Reports

Table of Cases

Table of Statutes

Introduction

Life is lived once,
and must be lived fully to
justify one's creation.[1]

It could be said that the value which a society places upon man as an individual can be best measured by the intensity of recognition and protection afforded the privacy interests of the individual. Common sense tells us that a person is deemed to be 'valuable' or 'valued' if the exercise of his own decision-making abilities, the exercise of control over himself and his own affairs, in short, the exercise and expression of his own 'uniqueness', is respected and protected by society. Conversely, the strongest proof of a society's disdain for an individual (or a community of individuals) is evidenced by its denial of, or interference with, those privacy interests (assuming, of course, that the individual is otherwise competent). History has provided us with many examples of that denial or interference, and indeed, such malfeasance has proven to be the most effective way to degrade and demoralise the individual.

It is fortunate, therefore, that various privacy interests have been recognised and protected over the past thirty years by the judicial systems of the US and Ireland. This book discusses those protected 'rights of privacy': their philosophical roots or source, their scope, their application via case law and the limitations or qualifications which have been placed upon the enforcement of those rights.

The respective rights of privacy recognised by the US and Ireland have been shaped, more than anything, by their respective historical and philosophical roots. The differences in legal philosophy between the two constitutions are best and most succinctly manifested in the jurisprudence surrounding these respective groups of rights. The rights of privacy in Ireland are, and ought to be, unlike those recognised and protected in the US, and their differences are to be explained by so much more than a simplistic reference to Roman Catholic dogma. It is academically dishonest, to submit that the scope of the right of marital privacy, for example, is qualified or limited, as compared to that of the US, merely because of the Catholic Church's prohibition against abortion and divorce. Rather, there is a long and illustrious history of natural law issues which have come into play with regard to marital and other forms of constitutionally recognised privacy in Ireland. Similarly, one paints with too broad a brush if one contends that there is only natural law on one side of the Atlantic and no natural law on the other. Rather, as the holdings

---

[1] Benazir Bhutto

and dicta in *Griswold*, *McGee*, *Rodrigues*, *Kennedy*, *Norris*, *Roe*, *X* and related cases indicate, the American judiciary continues to wrestle with its own
natural law theories, while Irish legal writers and jurists debate the changing
role of the judiciary and the need for greater legislative guidance in that country.

More fundamentally, and implicit in any discussion of law-making and
judicial decision-making, this book will consider some of the answers to the
age-old question asked by man in society: "What is right and what is wrong,
and how should that be determined for purposes of attaining order and justice?" The words 'good' and 'evil' could just as easily have been used, for it
has been man's ever-present struggle with a non-arbitrary or permanent standard of good and evil within the context of legislating that has created man's
fascinating history of higher law jurisprudence.

And it has been this very human and very personal question which has
made this entire subject matter so enlightening to study. It truly takes one to
the very heart and mind of man through all the course of the ages, in his quest
to govern himself in and with the society around him, according to justice.

Justice Brandeis wrote, in his seminal article about privacy, that: ". . . it
has been found necessary from time to time to define anew the exact nature
and extent of [the rights of the individual]. Political, social and economic
changes entail the recognition of new rights . . ."[2] Although the Irish and
American courts have at times taken paths which are separate, both have en-
ergetically sought to recognise and protect these ever-changing rights if the
individual and thus have preserved the opportunities of each citizen to live the
fullest life possible.

---

[2] Brandeis, "The Right to Privacy" 5 Harv L Rev 193 (1890).

PART ONE

A Common Beginning: The Shared Philosophical Underpinnings of Modern Irish and American Constitutional Rights

CHAPTER 1

The Law before the Law

... In determining what Justice is, we may begin with that Supreme Law which had its origin ages before any written law existed or any state had been established.[1]

All men are by nature equally free and independent, and have certain inherent rights, of which, when they enter into a state of society, they cannot, by any compact, deprive their posterity; namely, the enjoyment of life and liberty, with the means of acquiring and possessing property, and pursuing and obtaining happiness and safety.[2]

[Articles of the Irish Constitution] emphatically reject the theory that there are no rights without laws, no rights contrary to the law and no rights anterior to the law. They indicate that justice is placed above the law and acknowledge that natural rights, or human rights, are not created by law but that the Constitution confirms their existence and gives them protection. The individual has natural and human rights over which the State has no authority.[3]

If one could visualise the constitutions of the United States and Ireland as two fruitful branches, proximate yet separate, of the very old tree of legal theory, the roots would certainly be based in the ancient fertile soil of the Greek philosophers Plato and Aristotle. For from the minds of these men came the food upon which thrived the Stoic theories of natural law. In turn, those grew with the Romans, filled out and became sturdy with the Middle Ages philosophers and theologians, formed bends and curves with the Reformation and Enlightenment eras, and finally branched off into our modern concepts of higher law and fundamental rights. The natural law, first enunciated by the Stoics, but more widely disseminated by Cicero and those Romans who were exposed to and heartily accepted Stoic philosophy, formed the cornerstone for the development of all subsequent democratic legal theories in the Western world, especially those which became the basis for the American and Irish constitutions. But it was Plato, and later, Aristotle, who, exemplifying our view of the ancient Greeks as the first people among whom reflective thought

---

[1] Marcus Tullius Cicero, *De legibus* I.16.9.
[2] Thomas Jefferson, *Virginia Declaration of Rights*, 1774.
[3] *McGee v. Attorney General* [1974] I.R. 269 at 310 *per* Walsh J.

and argument, for its own sake, was exalted by educated men,[4] provided the first raw material for the initial flourishing of the natural law.

"At the root of Plato's theory of legislation", historians throughout time have submitted, "is the idea, developed later by the proponents of natural law, that the legislator through reason alone is able to formulate a set of rules which will be adequate for the needs of the community".[5] The community for Plato was that of the Greek city-state, the polis. Citizenship in the polis was not universal, and the rights and accompanying responsibilities which came with citizenship were treated seriously.[6] The citizen had an active voice in the debates and deliberations pursuant to the enactment of laws within the polis, and those laws were promulgated "in the name of men, not gods. . . ."

> Since Greek religion as far back as we can trace it lacked the components of revelation . . . man had to fall back on himself and his ancestors (tradition or custom) for the answers. At critical moments, the Greeks may have turned to a 'lawgiver' to codify the right answers, but that step was no departure from the rule of human self-reliance.[7]

It was imperative that such a society be ruled by consensus, and that all participants agree to accept and abide by the 'rule of law'.[8] "The general sovereignty of law rather than arbitrary rule was felt as a proud distinction of free Greek cities. Its specific sovereignty over rulers themselves comes through in passages which show them in fact acting subject to it, or which prescribes such subjection as essential to good government."[9]

Adherence to the rule of law was an overriding concern of both Plato and Aristotle. Plato, who so eloquently described Socrates' arguments supporting the rule of law in his *Crito*,[10] pressed the point clearly in his *Laws* as well. "For wherever in a state the law is subservient and impotent, over that state I see ruin impending; but wherever the law is lord over magistrates, and the magistrates are servants to the law, there I decry salvation and all the bless-

---

[4] See, for example, generally Aristotle, *Politics III* and Plato, *Crito*. Also Kelly, *A Short History of Western Legal Theory* (1992) p. 1.

[5] Cairns, *Legal Philosophy from Plato to Hegel* (1948) p. 44. Also Crowe, *The Changing Profile of the Natural Law* (1977) p. 17.

[6] Finley, "Politics" in *The Legacy of Greece* (1977) pp. 22, 25-27.

[7] *Ibid.*, p. 24.

[8] "For such a society to function, not to tear itself apart, a broad consensus was essential, a sense of community and a genuine willingness on the part of its members to live according to certain traditional rules, to accept the decisions of legitimate authorities, to make changes only by open debate and further consensus; in a word, to accept 'the rule of law'..." *ibid.*, p. 24.

[9] Kelly, *op. cit.*, p. 25.

[10] Plato, *op. cit.*, pp. 11-14. In his quest to uphold the laws, Socrates was willing to submit to the unjust sacrifice of his own life.

ings that the gods bestow on states."[11] Aristotle, concerned especially about the pitfalls of men's "appetites" which only "pervert the holders of office" submitted that the law, defined as "reason free from all passion", should govern. "He who commands that law should rule may thus be regarded as commanding that God and Reason alone should rule; he who commands that a man should rule adds the character of the beast."[12] The dichotomy which occurred between the Greeks' adherence to the rule of law, on the one hand, and the later Roman emphasis upon the rule of the magistrate (or monarch) on the other, was crucial to the development of future Western legal theory.[13] But it would be the Greeks' articulation of reason and its instantiation in the law,[14] over the arbitrariness of the rule of men, which would ultimately prevail in the Western world's democracies.[15]

In determining that law, and thus reason, should rule, the Greeks necessarily had to construct standards against which laws should be measured, or in practical terms, standards which men must follow in properly promulgating laws. And once laws were properly enacted, the citizenry had a duty to the polis, the Greek city/state which Aristotle held to be the highest and most natural form of association for mankind,[16] to obey those laws, following the example set by Socrates. In what some have argued was a form of a social contract between the lawgiver and the citizen,[17] the lawgiver had a duty to oppose his own passions and rely upon reason only in enacting laws for the good of the whole polis, in exchange for the obedience and fulfilment of other responsibilities required of the citizen. As Finley discussed:

> Responsibility, not an easily defined concept, has several elements in this context [of the citizen and the Greek city/state]. One is clearly 'obedience to the law' in the sense not merely of general abidance but also of acceptance of all specific decisions taken by the sovereign bodies

---

[11] *Laws* 715d.

[12] Aristotle, *op. cit.*, 5, 1273 a 28-32.

[13] Finley, *op. cit.*, p. 32. See also Kelly, *op. cit.*, pp. 69-70, citing Ulpian, in which Kelly discusses the growth of the notion that the Roman emperor was above or "freed from" the laws, which in turn was to flower into the powerful concept of the divine right of kings, granting "absolute regal power up to the time of Louis XIV and beyond".

[14] Winton and Garnsey, "Political Theory", in *The Legacy of Greece* (1977) pp. 37, 48. "...law is the human embodiment of the divine Reason that governs the universe" and, citing *Laws* 716C, "God is the measure of all things, not, as they say, man".

[15] Kelly, *op. cit.*, p. 70.

[16] Winton and Garnsey, *op. cit.*, pp. 50-51. The authors summarised Aristotle's "evolutionist" argument, of the polis growing out of the village, the village growing out of the household, the household having its roots in the most fundamental association of man and woman; thus the polis is the "highest form of natural association". From that, Aristotle infers that the citizen, like a part of the whole, must be subservient to the state, for the good of both. See Aristotle, *Politics*, 1253 a 19ff.

[17] Kelly, *op. cit.*, pp. 15-17.

through lawful procedures, no matter how painful or objectionable they may be personally.[18]

As inferred by Professor Finley's statement above, one of the standards set up by the Greeks, for the purpose of promulgating the laws which citizens were required to follow under the 'rule of law' doctrine, was an informal system of procedural 'due process', predating the Magna Carta's clause 39[19] by several centuries. There is evidence that the Greeks required the practice of hearing both sides of a case, prohibited more than one prosecution of the same person for the same acts, and had in place regular and impartial judicial procedures.[20] A general predisposition in favour of stability and permanence of the law led the Greeks to establish these rudimentary requirements of procedural due process,[21] and, more importantly for our purpose here, laid the groundwork for the development of what could be termed a 'higher substantive standard' against which a law had to be measured. While it was clear that there was no recognition of inalienable rights[22] or a higher, natural law by our modern definitions,[23] against which a properly enacted law would be measured and held invalid if violative of those rights or that law,[24] there was clearly created by Plato, and later supported by Aristotle, a higher, independent standard for 'good' lawmaking. Plato was the "first philosopher to set up an objective standard of right and wrong independently of individual conscience . . . "[25] In his instructions to lawmakers, Plato insisted that:

---

[18] Finley, *op. cit.*, p. 32 (emphasis added).

[19] "No free man shall be taken, imprisoned, disseised, outlawed, banished, or in any way destroyed, nor will We proceed against or prosecute him, except by lawful judgment of his peers and by the law of the land." (June, 1215)

[20] See, for example, Demosthenes 38. 16.

[21] For an in-depth discussion of procedures surrounding the courts of law in ancient Greece, see Stockton, *The Classical Athenian Democracy* (1990) pp. 96-116.

[22] "Whereas topics such as justice, law, the nature of man, the origins and ends of the state, or constitutions and their decline have always been part of the subject matter of political philosophy [of the ancient Greeks], others of central concern to modern philosophers [such as] the notions of liberty and active rights of the individual are absent in Greek thought." Winton and Garnsey, *op. cit.*, p. 63.

[23] "In political terms, the power possessed by the community [in ancient Greece] was total. That is to say, within the limits imposed by the 'rule of law', however that was understood, and by certain taboos in the fields of cult and sexual relations, the sovereign body was unrestrictedly free in its decision-making. There were areas or facets of human behaviour in which it did not normally interfere, but that was only because it chose not to, or did not think to do so. There were no natural rights of the individual to inhibit action by the state, no inalienable rights granted or sanctioned by a higher authority." Finley, *op. cit.*, pp. 26-27.

[24] "In general, Greek thought knew nothing of the idea that there exists a range of values, which, if human laws should conflict with them, render those laws invalid." Kelly, *op. cit.*, p. 20.

[25] Crowe, *op. cit.*, p. 17, citing *Laws* 705E and *Minos* 314E.

[j]ustice – human justice – must be referred to a supramundane justice, an ideal justice of which it is the pale reflection. The human lawgiver must try to see this justice in order to imitate it in his legislation; he must leave out of consideration all human and variable legislation, all empirical knowledge of laws (which is knowledge appertaining to the world of sense) in order to arrive at the true, intellectual knowledge of justice itself . . . [A] law which is not a good law, in the sense of producing justice, is not a law at all.[26]

It was Plato who would provide the ground for objective morality. "Good and evil", he wrote, "are not the result of any arbitrary distinction or individual experience; they correspond to eternal and unchangeable truths."[27] Indeed, Plato anticipated the fundamental question of natural law when he asked in an early dialogue, *Euthyphro*, whether an act is good because it is commanded, or is it commanded because it is good?[28] The duty of the lawgiver, in order to command that which is 'good', is two-fold under Platonian thought: Utilise reason free from all passions[29] in enacting laws which are "in the interest of the common weal of the whole state".[30] "Keep watch on my present lawmaking – in case I should enact any law either not tending to goodness at all, or tending only to part of it."[31] Justice is achievable through the use of reason; divine Reason is attainable by all humans through empirical means. Human laws need not be imperfect (and less than just) human creations; rather they can and should seek to "correspond to eternal and unchangeable truths" which make up Justice.[32]

While it was Plato who first enunciated an objective standard of right and wrong for lawmaking, independent of personal conscience, which sought to humanly embody 'divine Reason' for the good of the whole community, it was Aristotle who looked to nature, more than anyone before or since, in order to determine what exactly was meant by 'good' or 'for the good of the whole community'. And it was Aristotle who added the element of nature to the natural law (and upon whom Thomas Aquinas relied for the development of his pre-eminent, theologically-based natural law theory). "Aristotle . . .

---

[26] *Ibid.*, pp. 16-17.

[27] *Ibid.*, p. 15.

[28] *Ibid.*, p. 15.

[29] "[T]he task of the legislator is to ordain 'what is good and expedient for the whole polis amid the corruptions of human souls, opposing the mightiest lusts, and having no man his helper but himself standing alone and following reason only'." Winton and Garnsey, *op. cit.*, p. 48, citing *Laws* 835C.

[30] "...[W]e deny that laws are true unless they are enacted in the interest of the common weal of the whole state...[W]here the laws are enacted in the interest of a section (faction)...the 'justice' they ascribe to such laws is, we say, an empty name." *Laws* 715b.

[31] *Laws* 705E.

[32] Crowe, *op. cit.*, p. 15.

consciously used the concept of 'nature' in laying down the fundamental themes of his moral philosophy, his politics and his ethics, including that of an 'intrinsic' morality."[33] He viewed nature teleologically; that is to say that the nature or attributes of a thing could be understood by looking at the end to which it is normally directed. Thus the nature of a baby can be understood by looking at the adult human into which it would normally develop; the acorn by its oak tree; the seed by its flowering plant, etc.[34] This end-based or purpose-based view of the nature and natural phenomena was applied to social phenomena as well. Thus, Aristotle began his *Ethics* with the following: "Every art and every enquiry, and similarly every action and pursuit, is thought to aim at some good; and for this reason the good has rightly been declared to be that at which all things aim." The opening sentence of *Politics* mirrored the same concept, though in the context of the community and how it ought to be governed. "Every state is a community of some kind, and every community is established with a view to some good; for mankind always act in order to obtain that which they think good."[35] Just as a man is the natural 'end' of a baby, or, in other words, the perfected purpose for which a baby is born and develops, 'good' is the natural 'end' of a community, and is the perfected purpose for which any community is established. And achievement of the communal 'good' or 'the good life'[36] is the goal which lawmakers should attempt to attain in the promulgation of their laws. Most of Aristotle's *Politics* dealt with how lawmakers should try to achieve 'good' for the polis, and Plato's element of 'right reason', that is to say, reason without passion, was an absolute necessity in two ways. First, the use of reason without passion was the only way law-givers could attempt to promulgate laws which served the needs of the entire polis rather than any one faction. And Aristotle, even more than Plato, saw the polis as an organic body of which man was only a part,[37] and accordingly, the needs of the whole were much more vital than the needs of any one part in order for the polis to thrive.[38] Second, it was properly within

---

[33] *Ibid.*, p. 19.

[34] *Ibid.*, pp. 19-20. See also Cairns, *op. cit.*, pp. 25-28.

[35] Crowe, *op. cit.*, p. 20. "The end of man is variously described by [both Plato and Aristotle] as the good of man, living well, and happiness, eudaimonia ['fairing well' or 'doing well']." Winton and Garnsey, *op. cit.*, p. 49.

[36] "Deploying [Aristotle's] idea that the nature of everything is to reach always towards its own perfection in the achievement of its purpose, he presented the city-state as the perfected framework for leading the good life..." Kelly, *op. cit.*, p. 13.

[37] "Man's search for the good or happiness is necessarily set in the context of the polis...The polis is...the highest form of natural association. The inference that the individual is subservient to the state is then drawn, with the aid of the doctrine of the whole and parts." Winton and Garnsey, *op. cit.*, pp. 49-50, citing, Aristotle, *Politics* 1253a I9ff

[38] "Even if the good of the community coincides with that of the individual, the good of the community is clearly a greater and more perfect good both to get and to keep. This is not to deny that the good of the individual is worthwhile. But what is good for a nation or a city has a higher, a diviner, quality." Aristotle, *Nicomachean Ethics* 1094b 6ff

man's nature to utilise reason: it was intrinsic to man, and provided man alone with an objective sense of right and wrong, good and evil.[39] This view corresponds with Aristotle's teleological approach to all of nature, and explains why, in Aristotle's world, the man who lives according to reason has the happiest life. "[T]hat which is proper to each thing is by nature best and most pleasant for each thing; for man, therefore, the life according to reason is best and pleasantest, since reason more than anything else is man. This life is therefore the happiest."[40] Just as the acorn becomes perfected in an oak tree; just as the seed's perfected purpose, and thus its nature, is that of the flowering plant; the purpose, the aim, the nature of man is reason. Of all of Aristotle's concepts which would be passed on and mediated by future thinkers, "[t]he role of right reason . . . will be capital".[41] "In these elements [provided by Plato and Aristotle] there is not yet a developed theory of natural law", wrote Professor Crowe in his overview of the natural law. "They are the *disjecta membra* – 'nature' and 'reason', 'good' and 'evil' – features that diverse thinkers will, in their various fashions, form into a profile of the natural law."[42] It will take the Stoics, and the Church Fathers after them, inspired by Cicero, Marcus Aurelius and other Roman writers, to add the form to the Greek's embryonic natural law structure. And later thinkers, upon the rediscovery of Arisotle's 'lost' works in the 9th century by Arab and Jewish scholars, would re-examine and re-shape elements of his work for use in a variety of democratic (and undemocratic, in the case of Marxism[43]) legal theories. All legal theories commonly used in the modern Western world can be said to have originated with Arisotle and Plato. Travelling through the conduit of the early Christian Church, their concepts would pass from Greece and Rome into the High Middle Ages, and into "the secular modern environment of 'higher law' and 'fundamental rights'".[44]

To summarise, the picture which began to develop with the theories of Plato and Aristotle had the following features: one, an objective standard of morality, intrinsic to man yet independent from his individual conscience, which was attainable via reason; two, by utilising this reason, free from human 'passions' or 'appetite', man could promulgate laws which, in order to achieve the greatest justice, served the good of the whole community rather than any one of its individual, subservient parts; and three, a predominating, secular rule of law, with no reliance upon any sort of divine revelation, which subjugated or did not recognise the rights of the individual. Finally, the Greeks

---

[39] "[M]an alone has perception of good and bad and right and wrong and the other moral qualities . . ." Aristotle, *Politics* 8-9, II.

[40] Crowe, *op. cit.*, p. 27. "This view led him to see the function of education and law as instruments for the achievement of the good life. . . ." *Ibid.*, p. 20.

[41] *Ibid.*, p. 27.

[42] *Ibid.*, p. 27.

[43] Winton and Garnsey, *op. cit.*, p. 63.

[44] Kelly, *op. cit.*, p. 104.

had instituted a rudimentary form of due process by maintaining standard judicial procedures and processes within their courts of law. Of all of these features, however, the most important for historical purposes was the notion of an independent standard of justice, one which "everywhere has the same force and does not exist by people's thinking this or that . . ."[45] Indeed, it was:

> [t]his conception, supplemented by the Stoic precept of living according to nature, and connected with a conception of law as a 'rule proceeding from a sort of practical wisdom and reason', which [would] later serve as a resume of almost all that the doctrine of natural law implies. The picture that has begun to emerge is that of a natural law, a standard of moral rectitude connected with human reason. The primitive institutions concerning justice, mythologised or personified, were the first gropings toward this standard . . . [Here], the 'naturally just' was also bound up with reason.[46]

---

[45] Aristotle, *Nichomachean Ethics,* V. 7, 1134b 18-1135 a 5.
[46] Crowe, *op. cit.,* p. 27.

CHAPTER 2

The Law above the Law

... These laws were not ordained of Zeus,
And she who sits enthroned with gods below,
Justice, enacted not these human laws.
Nor did I deem that thou, a mortal man,
Couldst by a breath annul and override
The immutable unwritten laws of heaven.
They were not born today nor yesterday;
They die not; and none knoweth whence they sprang.[1]

For it is not the hearers of the law who are righteous before God, but
the doers of the law who will be justified. When [non-Christians]
who have not the law do by nature what the law requires, they are a
law to themselves, even though they do not have the law. They show
that what the law requires is written on their hearts, while their conscience also bears witness . . .[2]

It was in the second century BC that the Romans conquered Greece militarily,
but, in truth, the Greeks conquered the Romans overwhelmingly. The Romans were completely won over by Greek architecture, literature, performing
arts, visual arts, rhetoric, science, and most importantly for our purpose here,
philosophy. Greek philosophers, making pilgrimages to Rome for a variety of
reasons, left a permanent imprint on the minds of the Roman aristocracy. By
far the most influential school of thought for the Romans, and the one which
they welcomed and absorbed most overwhelmingly into their own culture,
was that of the Stoics. And it was the Stoic concept of man and nature which
provided the foundation for the natural law.

The Stoics, named after the 'painted porch' (*stoa poikile*) upon which
they met with their founder Zeno in the 3rd century BC, presented a philosophy which had an impact on Greece and Rome over five centuries, from Zeno
and his successor Chrysippus (281-208 BC), down an unbroken line to Seneca
(3-65 AD), Epictetus (c.60-100 AD) and Marcus Aurelius (d. 180 AD), through
to Roman writers of the 3rd century AD and the early fathers of the Christian
Church at that time. Unfortunately, much of what was written over those cen-

---

[1] Sophocles, *Antigone* 453-7
[2] St Paul, *Letter to the Romans*, 2:13-15

turies, especially the earlier ones, was lost, either permanently or for several centuries until intermittent 'discovery' during Middle Ages' contacts with the East. In the meantime, however, the essence of Stoicism was observed and recorded by one whose writings were, for the most part, not lost, and it was therefore from Marcus Tullius Cicero (106-44 BC) that we received the earliest and clearest definition of the Stoic natural law, and it was his version which was taken in by the early Christian scholars and passed down. In simplest terms:

> "[f]or the Stoics, the ultimate goal [in life] was the harmony of the individual soul with the universe: 'The virtue of the happy man and a smooth-flowing life consist of this, that all actions are based on the principle of harmony between his own spirit and the will of the director of the universe' . . ."[3]

Rejecting the need for the polis,[4] the Stoics emphasised man's bond with the universe and his fellow man. The world at large possessed a 'soul' with which each man's own soul was connected and by which each man was governed. An individual could learn to abide by the universal laws of life, or frustrate himself in trying to fight them. Either way, man had no choice but to be governed by the universal law which connected him with all other humans and the universe. The dominant power within this 'universal soul', if you will, was reason. The Stoics held that for man to be happy, he must invariably abide by the law of nature as evidenced by reason. The wise man was portrayed as the serene "stoic" who happily lived "in accordance with the reason which is identical with nature."[5] In doing so, the wise man must invariably rid himself of "irrational impulses" (represented by emotions or desires) which only subvert or dilute the law according to nature.[6] In addition, Stoic thought emphasised the natural bond which was held to exist between all men. One must feel a concern or kindness to his fellow man, because all are connected by a common soul and the dominant force of universal reason.[7] "One of the most striking features of the Stoics' teaching in ethics is their universalism, their sense of human unity, their belief that human affairs are governed by rules that hold universally . . . in propositions that are equally true and good in all parts of the world."[8] In summary, the Stoic concepts of a universally applicable and unchanging law which was understandable and attainable by all

---

[3] Winton and Garnsey, "Political Theory" in *The Legacy of Greece* (1977) pp. 57-8, citing *Diogenes*, 7.88.
[4] Crowe, *The Changing Profile of the Natural Law* (1977) p. 35.
[5] Kelly, *A Short History of Western Legal Theory* (1992) p. 47.
[6] Crowe, *op. cit.*, p. 30
[7] *Ibid.*, p. 35. Also, Winton and Garnsey, *op. cit.*, p. 58.
[8] Simon, *The Tradition of the Natural Law* (1965) p. 30.

men through reason, and which controlled events whether or not it was accepted by each individual, lay the foundation for the natural law which would be absorbed, via Cicero, by the early Christian fathers,[9] and handed down to the Medieval canonists. "It is primarily Cicero's account of natural law which represented the Stoic position for Christians like Lactantius and Ambrose and so influenced the Middle Ages . . . [Ambrose and Augustine] took natural law from Cicero, baptised it, and handed it on for preservation to the Church."[10] A perfect example of Stoic thought which begged to be adopted by early Christian thinkers is the well-known gloss by Chrysippus of Pindar's hymn:

> The natural law is king over everything, divine and human alike. It must be the authority that determines what is good and what is evil, the leader of men destined to live in communities; it lays down standard for right and wrong, and it does so by commanding what is to be done and forbidding what is not to be done.[11]

Cicero would record and re-draft the Stoic legacy in the last century before Christ and write the words which would most influence the development of a Christian-based natural law theory.

> True law is right reason in agreement with nature, diffused among all men; constant and unchanging, it should call men to their duties by its precepts, and deter them from wrong-doing by its prohibitions . . . To curtail this law is unholy, to amend it illicit, to repeal it impossible; nor can we be dispensed from it by the order either of senate or popular assembly; nor need we look for anyone to clarify or interpret it; nor will it be one law at Rome and a different one at Athens, nor otherwise tomorrow than it is today; but one and the same Law, eternal and unchangeable, will bind all peoples and all ages; and God, its designer, expounder and enacter, will be as it were the sole and universal ruler and governor of all things.[12]

Cicero contended that merely because a law was enacted by an established legislative method and accepted by the populace, did not mean that the law was 'just' or that it could even be considered 'law' at all. "The most foolish notion of all is the belief that everything is just which is found in the customs or laws of nations. Would that be true, even if those laws had been enacted by

---

[9] Crowe, *op. cit.*, p. 36; and Kelly, *op. cit.*, pp. 57-60, 102-4. The early Christian writer Lactantius (c.250-317 AD) called Cicero's description of God's law "almost divine". Kelly, *op. cit.*, p. 59.

[10] Watson, "The Natural Law and Stoicism" in *Problems in Stoicism* (1971) pp. 228, 235-6.

[11] ab Arnim, *Stoicorm veterum fragmenta*, III n. 354.

[12] Cicero, *De Republica III*, 22.

tyrants? . . . For Justice is one; it binds all human society, and is based on one Law, which is right reason applied to command and prohibition."[13] Herein lies the seed for the notion that all positive law ought to be judged against a 'law above the law' for validation; and if that positive law is contrary to the higher law, it is invalid and indeed not even 'law' at all. By utilising an eternal, unchanging touchstone, as it were, in the form of natural law made available to all men through their divinely granted 'right reason', Cicero had hoped to provide for permanence and security in government, and attain a form of pure justice, not subject to the arbitrary whims of men.[14] In light of the overwhelming dominance of custom, tribal tradition, 'pagan' practices, taboos, and rituals in place throughout the world during Cicero's time,[15] his concept of a higher, universal law, not based upon custom or earthly traditions, was truly revolutionary.

In order to provide for both the necessary permanence yet flexibility needed to effectively operate government, Cicero insisted that the positive law and the natural law had to work in tandem. The positive law ought to further the goals or implement the tenets of the natural law or, at the very least, should not act contrary to the natural law. The positive law could reflect the inevitable variations and developments which occur in society over time or in various situations. Thus a particular law could become more or less stringent or vary in its applicability to provide the flexibility needed to properly reflect a change in knowledge (e.g. a scientific discovery which alters that which was accepted previously as being true) or a particular occurrence. The natural law, however, was and always would be, under Cicero's thinking, unchanging and eternal, and would not vary over time or from place to place. Thus, a system which promulgated its laws based upon and limited by the tenets of the natural law would both have the flexibility necessary for good and effective government, and the permanence needed for stability.[16]

Before looking at the specifics of Cicero's natural law theory, we must ask why Cicero's conception of the natural law is so important. As will be shown, it was his theory, as adopted by the Church fathers of the early Chris-

---

[13] Cicero, *De Legibus I*, 15, 42.

[14] Wilkin, "Cicero and the Law of Nature" in *Origins of the Natural Law Tradition* (1954) pp. 16-21.

[15] Perhaps the finest book ever written on the subject of ancient tribal traditions and rituals, and certainly the most comprehensive, is *The Golden Bough* by Sir James G Frazer, published in 1922. Not only does it provide the reader with a fascinating overview of customs, taboos and practices of most early civilisations, it was also the basis and inspiration for the creative writing in the early part of this century by such masters as T S Eliot and W B Yeats. Discussion of taboos and customs in place in ancient Rome can be found throughout the treatise, and citations are too numerous to list here. For a brief discussion of taboos and customs in place during the time of the reign of the ancient kings of Ireland, see pp. 200-1.

[16] Wilkin, *op. cit.*, pp. 19-24. See generally, Levy, "Natural Law in the Roman Period" in *Natural Law Institute Proceedings II* (1949).

tian Church, which would eventually, via Aquinas, lay the groundwork for
the natural law philosophy underlying the 1937 Irish Constitution. It was also
his concepts, as interpreted by the Roman jurisconsults, via Ulpian and others, which would lay the groundwork for the natural law/natural rights theories upon which the United States' Constitution would be based in the late
18th century. Cicero was the *last common denominator* in the formulation of
both underlying theories.[17] As will be shown, this split in interpretation, occurring during and after Cicero's era, would become the primary cause for the
theoretical differences between the Irish and American Constitutions, which
in turn would be (and continues to be) best exemplified in the recognition and
adjudication of each jurisdiction's constitutional rights of privacy.

> [T]he relation between Cicero's eternal, divinely inspired natural law
> and the practical natural law of the [Roman] jurists somewhat resem-
> bles the relation which was to emerge . . . between the divinely ap-
> pointed natural law of Aquinas . . . and the secular, rationalist natural
> law on which Grotius was to build a law of nations, and which domi-
> nated the legal theories of the seventeenth and eighteenth centuries.[18]

Let us then proceed to examine Cicero's concept of the natural law.

First, Cicero held that the natural law was "something which is implanted
in us, not by opinion, but by a kind of innate instinct".[19] These eternal standards of truth and justice were "revealed to men through right reason according to nature"[20] and were available to all mankind and only mankind, for they
alone had been give the power of reason. Cicero, unlike the secular jurisconsults
who interpreted the natural law as being instinctual in animals[21] as well as
mankind, "had no doubts about the supremacy of man, lifted above the brutes
precisely by his possession of reason".[22] "To those whom reason is given,
there is given also right reason and, in consequence, law which is right reason
commanding and forbidding."[23] Cicero linked the natural law with his concept of the Divine: "[T]he true and primal law, applied to command and prohibition, is the right reason of supreme Jupiter."[24] Christian fathers easily sub-

---

[17] "As all the ages of the world have not produced a greater statesman and philosopher
united than Cicero, his authority should have great weight." John Adams, quoted by,
Wilkin, *op. cit.*, p. 21.

[18] Levy, "Natural Law in Roman Thought", *Studia et Documenta Historiae et Iuris XV*, 7
(1949).

[19] Cicero, *De Inventione II*, 22.65.

[20] Wilkin, *op. cit.*, p. 15.

[21] See, for example, Ulpian's Digest, I,1,1,3.

[22] Crowe, *op. cit.*, pp. 39-40.

[23] Cicero, *De Legibus*, 12, 33.

[24] Cicero, *De Legibus II*, 4, 10.

stituted their own concept of God for Cicero's Jupiter and carried the notion forward.

> Broadly speaking, the Fathers seem to have been content with a conception of the natural law similar to that of Cicero. This conception was, of course, now put into a Christian setting; the impersonal deity or nature of the Stoics gives way to the Christian God, sovereign lord and law-giver; and the knowledge of the natural law and its precepts becomes more intimately a matter of conscience.[25]

Accepting the notion that natural law is revealed to man "through right reason according to nature", the next question must necessarily be: what exactly is, or has been, revealed? Again, said Cicero and the Stoics before him, we must look to man's nature. Based upon the Stoic notion that all mankind shares a "world soul", discussed previously and related to Aristotle's concept of the "whole body" of mankind, combined with Cicero's contention, carried down from Plato and Aristotle's teleological view of nature, that man is necessarily "sociable" in nature, there comes forth the tenet which is paramount and permeates all of the natural law of Cicero and his progeny: The common good is the primary end and purpose for all law.

> Because of the existence of this common tie between all members of the human race, and because man was the object of creation, the obligation rested upon every human being not only to have a care for his fellows but to spare himself no toil or trouble in his efforts to help others. Failure to promote the universal sociability and well-being, he (Cicero) thought a violation of our nature.[26]

In several passages, Cicero emphasised this early rendition of the "golden rule". "We should all therefore have the same end in view, to identify the interest of each with the interests of all; for if each man were to grab for himself, all human society would be disrupted."[27] "Now nothing is more in accordance with nature than for all men to live together as one society, and this will inevitably be disrupted if each member of it is disposed to rob or injure another for his own advantage."[28] And from the same work:

> Moreover high-mindedness, magnanimity, courtesy, justice and generosity are much more in accordance with nature than pleasure, riches or even life itself; to despise all these things and regard them as of no value

---

[25] Crowe, *op. cit.*, pp. 58-59.
[26] Wilkin, *op. cit.*, p. 19.
[27] Cicero, *De Officiis III*, Chapter 6, section 26, 12-14.
[28] *Ibid.* at Chapter 5, section 21, 5-8.

in comparison with the common good is the mark of the highest magnanimity. But to rob another for one's own gain is more contrary to nature than death, pain or any other evil. Similarly it is even more natural to undertake the most difficult and troublesome tasks for the help and preservation of all mankind . . . even more in accordance with nature, I say, than to live in solitude not only without any trouble, but even enjoying the greatest delights and blessed with every conceivable advantage, so as even to excel in beauty and strength . . . [A man] is mistaken [if] he believes that the harm which may happen to his body or estate is more serious than any moral harm [to mankind].[29]

Under Cicero, the common good far outweighed the desires or needs of any one individual.

Just as if each member of our body thought that it could be strong itself by drawing on the strength of the members around it, the whole body would inevitably be weakened and die, so if each one of us were to rob another of what is to his advantage and take all that he could for his own advantage, then the bonds of human society would inevitably be destroyed.[30]

Although Cicero did "present several legally material principles as derived from the law of nature . . . [for example,] the right of self-defence, the prohibition against cheating or harming others, and the precept that one must positively defend others from harm"[31] there was no notion of human or inalienable rights present in any of his writings, nor in any writings related to natural law, for that matter, until the 17th century.[32] Any rights which were enunciated, and they were not rights in the sense in which we currently understand them, were merely incidental to the overall promotion of the common good. Furthermore, there was certainly no concept of privacy, or a sense of the "property which men have in their persons"[33] as defined by John Locke in 1690.

---

[29] Cicero, *De Officiis III*, Chapter 5, section 24; section 25, 1, 2, 6-9; section 26, 9-11.

[30] *Ibid.* at Chapter 5, section 22, 1-6.

[31] Kelly, *op. cit.*, p. 60, citing Cicero, *Pro Milone* 4. 10 and *De Officiis* III, 17. 68, 3. 5. 26, 3. 6. 27, and 1. 7. 23.

[32] See, for example, Weinreb, "Natural Law and Rights" in *Natural Law Theory Contemporary Essays* (1992) p.278.

[33] Locke, *Two Treatises of Government* 2.15 (1690) (Hereinafter *Two Treatises*.) Locke's primary premise, which will be examined more fully below, was that "government, once constituted, has only one function; and that is the protection of the [community] members' property". Property, for Locke, meant more than mere realty or possessions, but extended most importantly to cover the individuals legitimate interests "in their lives, liberties and estates". *Ibid.* at 2.9, 2.11 and 2.19. These concepts, of course, would be reiterated and reflected in Thomas Jefferson's "Declaration of Independence" at the beginning of the American Revolutionary War.

Rather, "Cicero takes the safety and well-being of the public as an interest that overrides the claims of private dignity and the fastidiousness of a personal moral code".[34] This emphasis upon the common good over the rights or interests of the individual would carry over to the Church fathers, to the Medieval canonists and be clearly manifested in the philosophy of St Thomas Aquinas, who "confirmed [man's] personal responsibility while still within and subject to the Providence of an omnipotent God".[35] As will be discussed in Part II, under Aquinas, "duties that defined one's responsibility were for the benefit of other persons [and] any suggestion that, without reference to God, rights are an independent basis of obligations was remote indeed".[36] Clearly, what the Church fathers derived from Cicero was a concept of an idealised community in which the common good was the ultimate aim or end. Before tracing that path of the natural law which led to the Medieval canonists and Aquinas, however, one should first examine the secular natual law concepts of the Roman jurists, who were also influenced and inspired by Cicero. Their view of man and his nature would eventually have a great impact upon the initial development of rights as they came to be understood in the Middle Ages and onward to our present day.

In a nutshell, the Roman jurists were much more 'down to earth' than the Church fathers would be. The jurists could be described as legal technicians who were employed to draft statutes and record various laws and legal customs in the late Roman empire, and they were much more concerned with the day-to-day practicalities of law and government than were the philosophers and theologians. Primarily, they defined the natural law as that which is instinctual to all animals, with man being included in that broad category, and the resulting "instinctive perceptions of what [were] fair and simple rule[s]".[37] They emphasised those facts and attributes which were self-evident to the ordinary man regarding the actual conditions of life and society, and man's activities under those actual conditions. There was no revelatory guidance descending from a higher, divine being. Rather, these were common, universal observations relating to man's nature and the simple rules which arose therefrom. Those 'rules' were understandably very much like those defined by Cicero. The *purpose* of those rules, however, was crucially different. Unlike Cicero and the Church fathers after, who subjugated the interests of the individual in order to serve the common good, the Roman jurists stated that

---

[34] Arkes, "That 'Nature Herself Has Placed in our Ears a Power of Judging' Some Reflections on the 'Naturalism' of Cicero", in *Natural Law Theory, Contemporary Essays* (1992) p. 253.

[35] Weinreb, *op. cit.*, p. 278.

[36] *Ibid.*, also Weinreb, *Natural Law and Justice* (1987) pp. 43-46. Under Cicero's thinking, even if it could be held that men had a legally enforceable duty to help his fellow man, there was no accompanying 'right', if you will, to have such help on the part of others. There was no linking of duties with rights.

[37] Kelly, *op. cit.*, p. 61.

the purpose of the natural law was to provide for the individual needs of each member of a community (as much as possible), for by doing so, the common good would ultimately be served. Hence, Ulpian, the leading Roman jurist of the 2nd century AD, stated that justice is achieved in "the steady and constant will to give each one what is his by law . . . and the fundamental precepts of that law are to live honourably, not to injure others, and to render to everyone what is his".[38]

Ulpian's view of natural law, which will be examined more fully below, focused upon man and the interests of the individual in every respect. And even allowing for the fact that there was indeed cross-fertilisation down through the centuries between Ulpian's secular natural law and that of the Church fathers,[39] *their primary point of divergence occurred in the early centuries AD.*

> There are two distinct schools of thought regarding the natural law: one is the Roman Civil Law and its derivation from the Stoics to the Corpus Juris Civilis and the glosses and comments pertaining thereto; and the Canon law definitions derived from St Paul [and the Church fathers] and carried on through Gratian's Decretum and glosses and commentaries thereto by Medieval theologians.[40]

Though both had their basis in the philosophy of the Stoics as presented by Cicero, each had a unique interpretation of those philosophical concepts which, as we shall see, enormously affected future legal theory. Thus the Stoic notion of the universalism of mankind and the common possession of a world soul translated into the Church father's pre-eminent emphasis on the common good, while the Roman jurists viewed this as justification for "giving each man his due". The Stoic view of natural law as eternal law available to all men through their reason became Divine reason for the Church fathers, and self-evident instinct for the Roman jurists. And eventually, as would develop more clearly in the following centuries and have immense ramifications therein, the Church fathers would infer that all governing power, like the source of reason, descended from God to man, while the civilian jurists would hold that the source of government lay within man himself, with his innate sense, and from there was granted or ascended to its leaders. As will be seen, this latter view died out for several centuries with the decline of the Roman Empire and the loss of the writings of Ulpian and others in the Corpus Juris Civilis. And even though the Corpus was rediscovered in the 11th century, the ascending view of authority would not be resurrected until the 16th century, where it would then have enormous implications for the legal theorists of the 17th and 18th centu-

---

[38] Kelly, *op. cit.*, p. 67.
[39] Crowe, *op. cit.*, p. 88.
[40] *Ibid.*, p. 87.

ries in Western Europe. The descending viewpoint, however, would be carried down uninterrupted by way of the Church fathers to the Medieval canonists and theologians directly to the time of St Thomas Aquinas. This early precursor to the 'divine right of kings', as will be seen, would also have important ramifications for the development of, and conflict among, legal theories in later centuries.[41]

Clearly, the development of the dual concepts of individual rights and due process (procedural and, eventually, substantive) would be tied up in the dichotomy of descending and ascending theories of governmental powers. As the former diminished in its absoluteness and the latter was perceived as having more validity, due process and the recognition of individual rights flourished. Prior to the recognition and development of a right of privacy, obviously, this groundwork had to be laid. But the kind of 'law above the law' which was recognised and utilised by a particular jurisdiction would determine how that groundwork, that basis for rights, would take shape, and, in turn, define the nature and scope of each jurisdiction's right of privacy. Let us now examine those developments separately as each natural law theory grew on its own.

---

[41] See Kelly, *op. cit.*, pp. 60-146 and generally Crowe, *op. cit.*

PART TWO

THE FORK IN THE ROAD

CHAPTER 3

God to Man: the Natural Law Model of Thomas Aquinas

The Natural Law is promulgated by the very fact that God has instilled it in the minds of men so as to be naturally known by them.[1]

Natural law had pushed its way up from cloudy apprehensions of it among early Greeks and Stoics to its position in medieval thought, whereby it was recognised as the end principle of positive laws, the moral limitation of ruling power, and the foundation of free government.[2]

"How lovely it is today! The sunlight breaks and flickers on the margin of my book."[3] So wrote a young monk in Ireland during the 8th century, in the privacy of his monastic cell, as he was transcribing a biblical passage. Like the many monks, priests, nuns and clergy of the Church throughout the Middle Ages, scribes in monasteries throughout Ireland in the 7th and 8th centuries served as the primary conduit through which biblical and ancient scholarly writings were transcribed and thus preserved for future generations and the pages of history. Because the clergy were, for their own needs, necessarily literate in a time when very few people were, and due to the ministerial nature of their profession, it fell to the scholars of the early Church to put into writing the teachings of the Bible, as well as translations of other ancient documents. Hence, it truly can be said that the monks of Ireland,[4] among others in Britain and western Europe, were the 'saviours' of classical western literature, having preserved with awe-inspiring tenacity and beautiful handiwork the writings of the ancients.

Along with preservation, these religious documentarians also inserted their own commentary. Most commonly referred to as glosses, these elaborations

---

[1] St Thomas Aquinas, Summa Theologiae I-II q. 90, a. 4 (reply 1).

[2] McKinnon, "Natural Law and Positive Law" in *Natural Law Institute Proceedings II*, (1949) 85 at 86.

[3] Kinsella (ed.), *The New Oxford Book of Irish Verse* (1989) p. 30.

[4] By the end of the 8th century, there were dozens of monasteries in place throughout the whole of Ireland, and dozens more established by Irish monks throughout continental Europe. See Richter, *Medieval Ireland, The Enduring Tradition* (1988) pp. 50-96.

or adaptations, based upon the original writings, became valuable in themselves. Commentaries concerning the natural law, its definitions and promulgation, provided the link between the lost, natural law writings of Cicero and his contemporaries, and the biblical notion of an eternal, divine law "written in their hearts". The natural law of the Church glossators was, as stated previously, that of Cicero with a Divine adaptation. And it was the aggregate of all of the glosses of Church scholars over several centuries which would lead to the seminal works of the pre-eminent natural law glossator: Aquinas. Let us first examine the contributions of those from Cicero's time to the era of Aquinas.

Irenaeus (c.130-200) was the earliest Christian natural law writer who held that this law found its source in the creator of nature, God, who gave it to man via his reason, and that the Ten Commandments were also handed down by God as a summary and reminder to men of the natural law "written in men's hearts", from the beginning of time.[5]

Origen (c.185-254) was an important contributor because of his discussion of the effect of natural law upon positive law making. He asserted that any positive law which was contrary to the natural law was invalid. This was the first explicit enunciation of the subordinate relationship of positive law to natural law.[6]

Lactantius (c. 300), following Origen's lead, referred to Cicero's writings as "almost divine" and re-emphasised, along with Augustine (354-430) and, later, Isadore of Seville (570-636), that the natural law was that order with which human law must conform.[7] This early higher law standard against which all positive law must be measured did not really have any practical impact upon the political and royal institutions of their day, but its theoretical impact upon our modern concepts of higher law and fundamental rights cannot be underestimated.[8] It would be left to Aquinas and others to elaborate more fully.

Regarding the popular ancient Greek concept of the 'rule of law' and the related notion concerning the source of governmental power (descending versus ascending, mentioned previously), the early Church fathers left a more ambiguous record, which would then be also reflected in the writings of Aquinas. In an ideal world (i.e. that which in the minds of the clergy existed before the fall of Adam and Eve), humans would not need written laws to govern themselves, as each would abide completely by the law placed within

---

[5] Also Kelly, *A Short History of Western Legal Theory*, (1992) p. 103, citing Rom. 2, 14-15 (Letter from St. Paul).

[6] *Ibid.*, p. 103

[7] Augustine, *Diviniae institutiones* 6. 8.

[8] "[T]he early Christian Church was in fact the conduit through which the ancient idea of natural law travelled from classical Greece and Rome into the High Middle Ages, and from there ultimately into the secular modern environment of 'higher law' and 'fundamental rights'. . . " Kelly, *op. cit.*, p. 103.

his heart by the Creator. Because of Man's fall, and his resulting imperfect and sinful nature, it was necessary to institute government to maintain order. Thus, in the early Christian Church, government was viewed as a necessary evil which man brought upon himself. The natural law of God was still available to each individual through his reason, but mankind in general, being flawed, had to be reminded of that law via governmental command and promulgations, or through codification by some authority figure. Thus, that governing authority was viewed as being both mundane in origin, yet God-like also in terms of its avowed purpose. Hence, two apparently conflicting notions were presented in the writings of the early Church fathers in defining the origins of governmental authority. Theodoretus (c. 393-460), for example, wrote that laws and governmental promulgation of them were unavoidable necessities resulting from Man's original sin, and were enacted for the protection of the innocent and the punishment of evildoers.[9] Augustine, on the other hand, wrote that "a state's protective function, however unholy the conditions which had required its exercise, represented a duty laid upon it by God".[10]

> This combination of recognition of the divine origin of political authority with a pessimistic rationalisation of what made it necessary remained standard throughout the early Christian world and into the Early Middle Ages; though it was increasingly overlaid by absolutist doctrine which, by elevating the role of the ruler and prescribing unconditional submission to him, gave emphasis rather to the state's legitimacy than to its origins.[11]

This theocratically-based, descending theory of governmental authority would be supported by the writings of various clergy throughout the centuries, and would accordingly lead to the development of the notion that rulers, though they morally ought to abide by the laws which they had promulgated, were in fact not obligated to do so. Hence, while many writers called upon the ruling authority to "hold his laws binding on all, as soon as he himself showed them respect",[12] the notion which overwhelmingly permeated most of the writings of the Church fathers held that rulers had been "called by God"[13] and entrusted with authority to rule over his subjects. It was in this vein that Gregory the Great, Pope from 590 to 604, contended that "to criticise, let alone to resist, a wicked ruler is sinful; a murmur raised against him is in effect raised against God".[14]

---

[9] *Ibid.*, pp. 90-91.
[10] Augustine, *De civitate Dei* 15. 5, 4. 4.
[11] Kelly, *op. cit.*, p. 91.
[12] Isadore, *Sententiae* 3. 51.
[13] Sedalius Scotus, *De rectoribus christianis*. Scotus was an Irish monk who fled when the Vikings invaded in 848 and served in the court of the bishop of Liege thereafter.
[14] Exposito in librum Job 22, 24.

Though the Church fathers were hesitant to criticise the ruling authority, either due to their recognition of a divine right of kings or as followers of Christ's admonition to "render unto Caesar what is Caesar's",[15] they were adamant in their assertions that government must promulgate laws which serve the common good. And it was the concept of the common good which became the touchstone for determining whether legislation was 'right law'. Isadore's writing on what constitutes 'right law' was representative:

> Now a law will be honourable, just, capable of being obeyed, in accordance with nature and in accord also with ancestral practice, adapted both to its time and to its place; necessary, useful and clear (so as to contain nothing to trip people up through misunderstanding), not framed for the advantage of any individual, but for the common benefit of citizens.[16]

Ignoring the other interesting aspects of Isadore's definition, it was clear that the primary goal of enacting legislation was to benefit the common good. Harking back to Aristotle's teleological examination of the natural end of man's existence, his naturally social inclinations, and the resulting proper aim of the city/state; reviewing the tenet of 'universality' based upon the concept of one universal soul initiated by Plato, defined by Aristotle, and carried on through the Stoics and Cicero; and combining these aspects with the Christian maxim: "love thy neighbour as thyself"; it is plain to see that the culmination of the natural law theory as it entered the Middle Ages was centred upon this paramount notion of the common good. The common good was vital, Ambrose of Milan (c. 340-397) wrote, because it reflected the universality among men, the innate knowledge of the law in all men, and resulted in bringing all men closer together.[17] And Columbanus, also known as Columba the Younger (543-615), an Irish monk born in Leinster who wrote extensively on a variety of theological and scholarly issues, wrote: "Do not believe that we think of ourselves any different than of you: for we are *joint members (commembra) of one body*, whether Gauls, Briton, Irish or any other people."[18]

In sum, what Aquinas was bequeathed in theology and philosophy by his forefathers in faith were all of the elements of the natural law which, by adding the systemic logic of the newly rediscovered Aristotle, he would uniquely put together. One, the natural law was *innate* in all humans, having been placed

---

[15] Matt. 22, 21.

[16] Isadore, *Etymolgiae* 5. 21.

[17] Crowe, *The Changing Profile of the Natural Law* (1977) pp. 61-62.

[18] Richter, *op. cit.*, pp. 56-59 (emphasis added). Columbanus listed the virtue of silence as the second most important attribute after obedience, "as a means of combatting (in Columbanus' own words) 'the greatest Irish failings, the tendency to gossip and to be self-opinionated'". *Ibid.*, p. 59.

within each man by God. Two, the natural law was available to each human by means of his or her reason, again granted by God. Three, the natural law was *universal and unchanging* from place to place and through all time. Four, as God was the ultimate source of the law, it *descended* from Him via His rulers. Five, any positive law which did not conform to the natural law was *invalid*. Six, the paramount aim and end of the natural law was the *common good*: the man-made, positive law must serve the *common good in order to be valid*, in light of mankind's spiritual and rational bond, and the resulting need to benefit the whole rather than any one part.

Thomas of Aquinas (1224-1274) was born to a noble family in Sicily who had hopes that he would become a Benedictine monk, eventually rising to become the powerful and prestigious Abbot of Monte Casino. To the disappointment of his ambitious parents, Thomas chose to enter the Dominican order, accepting its vows of poverty, simplicity, and devotion to study. He remained with the Dominicans until his death, locating himself both in Italy and in Paris, where he wrote voluminously and was recognised for his unsurpassed knowledge of ancient philosophies and literature (having been recently rediscovered and re-introduced into Western Europe by Jewish and Islamic scholars from North Africa and the East). Anecdotes abound extolling Aquinas's brilliance, rapt self-absorption, and ability to undertake several activities at once. His greatest accomplishment, reflected in his writings, was his amalgamation of the works of many classical writers into cohesive bodies of theory and scholarship. By the time of his death in 1274, he had written over one hundred pieces of theological and philosophical scholarship, for which he was canonised and recognised as a Doctor of the Church.[19]

By far, the most celebrated work of Aquinas is the classic *Summa Theologiae*, in which is contained the *Treatise on Law*, covering Questions 90-97. This work was (and continues to be) the clearest statement of the religiously-based branch of the natural law, and, as will be seen, served as the centrepiece for the natural law theory utilised in the creation of the 1937 Irish Constitution. In addition, it is remarkable for the organised, deductive way in which it is presented, and this method of presentation would be mirrored by subsequent writers (e.g. John Locke).

Natural law is merely the participation of the eternal law, created by God, in a rational creature (i.e. mankind).[20] The eternal law is unchanging in all times and all places, and is innate in all humans via reason. Some humans, however, do not observe this law, which is "written in their hearts", and thus government is necessary to remind citizens of the tenets of God's law so that

---

[19] See generally Weisheipl, *Friar Thomas D'Aquino* (1975).

[20] Aquinas, *Treatise on Law* (hereafter *Treatise on Law*), at 91, 2. "Irrational creatures are not ordered to an end higher than the end that is proportional to their own natural powers. Therefore, [one cannot compare rational creatures to irrational ones]." *Ibid.* at 91, 4.

men can attain their ultimate end and purpose: good.[21] All men, held Aquinas, naturally seek the good, for it was for this purpose that they were created, and it is this attainment which ultimately makes mankind happiest and most fulfilled. (Note the teleological echoes of Aristotle here.) Though man has other natural inclinations as well (e.g. the need for sexual union and to nurture and educate one's children, to live in society with others, etc.) first and foremost:

> . . . there is in man an inclination to the good according to nature which he shares with all substances, namely, *inasmuch as all substances desire the conservation of their own existence according to its nature*, and in accord with this inclination, *all those things by which the life of man is preserved and the opposite impeded belongs to the Natural Law.*
> Therefore, *the first principle of the Natural law is this, that good should be done and sought and evil is to be avoided. And on this principle are based all the other precepts of the law of nature. . .* [22]

Once Aquinas established that all men naturally are inclined to the good and wished to be virtuous, for it is by being virtuous that true happiness is attained,[23] he went on to contend that it is the appropriate purpose or end of society to attain the common good.

> Again, since every part is ordered to the whole as the imperfect to the perfect and one man is part of a perfect society, it is necessary that the law properly regard the order to the happiness of society. Moreover, in any genus, that which is called the greatest principle of all the other instances and these others are named with reference to that greatest, just as fire, which is the hottest of all things, is the cause of heat in mixed bodies which are called hot insofar as they have a share of fire. Hence, since law is most of all ordered *to the Common Good, it is necessary that any precept concerning a particular matter (is only considered a law) insofar as it is ordered to the Common Good.*[24]

Men naturally seek to be virtuous, Aquinas held, but some are obviously more receptive to the "law written in their hearts" than others, and even the most virtuous man cannot, single-handedly, "lead another to virtue". Thus, a coercive power is necessary to promote the common good. "This coercive power is vested in the whole people or in some public official to whom it belongs to inflict punishment. . ."

---

[21] *Ibid.* at 91, 4.

[22] *Ibid.* at 94, 2 (emphasis added).

[23] *Ibid.* at 90, 2. Referring back to earlier Questions, Aquinas reconfirms the Aristotelian notion that "[t]he last end of human life is felicity or happiness . . ."

[24] *Ibid.* at 90, 2. Again, we see Aristotle's notion of the organic body of mankind having more importance than any individual part.

As a man is a part of a family, so the family is a part of the state. The state, however, is a perfect society . . . And, therefore, just as the good of one man is not the ultimate end but is ordered to the Common Good; so also the good of one family is ordered to the Common Good of the state . . . [Thus, law] properly speaking, regards first and principally the order to the Common Good. However, to order to the Common Good belongs either to the whole people or to one who represents the whole people. And therefore, to establish law belongs either to the whole people or to a public official who has the care of the whole community, because, as in all other matters, *to order to an end belongs to him to whom that end most properly belongs* . . . We can now gather [from all that preceded] *the definition of a law which is nothing other than a certain dictate of reason for the Common Good, made by him who has the care of the community* . . . [25]

Two important notions are presented here by Aquinas. First, he submitted that man naturally wants and needs to live in society with other people (as did Aristotle). As stated in another writing (which echoes Cicero):

One man alone could not provide himself with all his needs; one man, of himself, could not live an adequate life. It is therefore natural to man, that he should live in the society of many . . . And if it is natural to man to live in the society of many, it necessarily follows that there must be some arrangement whereby those many may be governed. [26]

Second, Aquinas maintained that men have a certain right of self-determination, though there is other writing which makes this assertion appear ambiguous and equivocal. While both Professor Henle[27] and Professor Adler contend that Aquinas enunciated "the first clear statements of the doctrine of popular sovereignty"[28] and Aquinas himself held that the people have the right to depose a king who abuses his power[29] in Question 96, however, he submitted that the ruler is, essentially, above the law.

The prince is said to be freed from the law with reference to the coercive force of the law, for no-one, properly speaking, can be forced by himself. Thus, therefore, the prince is said to be free from the law because no one can make condemnatory judgment against him, for law has its coercive force only from the power of the prince, if he acts contrary to

---

[25] *Ibid.* at 90, 3.
[26] Aquinas, *De regimine principum I*, I.
[27] Henle, *St Thomas Aquinas, The Treatise on Law* (1993) p. 140.
[28] Adler, *The Development of Political Theory and Government* (1994) p.72.
[29] Aquinas, *De regimine principum I*, 6.

the law . . . But with reference to the directive force of the law, the King is subject to it *by his own will*, according to the statement . . . 'Whoever subjects another to a law should observe the same law himself . . .'

Hence, as regards the judgment of God, the prince is not free from the law in reference to its directive force and ought voluntarily, and not through being forced, fulfil the law. And also *the prince is above the law in the sense that, if it is expedient, he can change it or dispense from it according to place and time.*[30]

Hence, while Aquinas held that a ruler ought to abide by his own laws, he was by no means obligated to, and could indeed circumvent the laws if desired. Still, this contention by Aquinas appears to be an aberration in the context of the work taken as a whole and when compared especially with particular sections which emphasised the duty of a ruler to act justly and promulgate laws for the benefit of the common good.

Now, laws are said to be just:

1. from the end, namely when they are ordered to the Common Good;

2. from the lawgiver, namely when the law passed does not exceed the lawgiver's authority;

3. from the form, namely when burdens are imposed on the subjects according to proportionate equality for the Common Good. For since one man is part of the community, whatever any man is and has belongs to the community just as what any part is belongs to the whole; hence *nature also imposes some loss on the part in order to preserve the whole.* And, according to this, laws of this kind, imposing burdens proportionately, are just and oblige in conscience and are legal laws.

However, laws can be unjust in two ways, one way, by being contrary to human good through being opposed to what has just been mentioned:

a. either from the end as when some authority imposes burdens on the subjects that do not pertain to the common utility but rather to his own greed or glory;

---

[30] *Treatise on Law* at 96, 5 (emphasis added). Echoing the Church's commonly held descending view of government authority through the Middle Ages, discussed *above on page 24, 25.* Bishop Richard Fitz Nigel of England wrote in 1179 that "[the actions of sovereigns] ought not to be discussed or condemned by their subjects. For they whose hearts and the motions thereof are in the hand of God, and to whom the sole care of their subjects has been by God himself committed, stand or fall by God's judgment and not by human one". Dialogue of the Exchequer, in Douglas, *English Historical Documents 1042-1189* (1968) preface, ii, p. 491.

    b.   or from the lawgiver, as when someone makes a law that is beyond the authority granted to him;

    c.   or from the form, as when burdens are unequally distributed in the community, even though they pertain to the Common Good.

And laws of this sort are acts of violence rather than laws, as Augustine says, "A law that is unjust seems not to be a law."[31]

Looking ahead to the examination of the 1937 Irish Constitution and Aquinas' influence thereupon, it is interesting to note three points raised in the above quotation which, if applied, would undoubtedly affect the adjudication of that Constitution. First and foremost, all law must be ordered to the common good (and, to do so, it must "do good and avoid evil", keeping in focus that the ultimate good is the preservation of the life of man). Second, a law, *whether or not it is ordered to the common good*, must not exceed the authority of the lawgiver and the burdens of the law's implementation must be equally shared by the community. Third, it is a given that *individuals may have to absorb some loss* "in order to preserve the whole". In terms of the recognition and enforcement of individual rights, i.e. privacy, this last statement is enormously important. Essentially, Aquinas states that when required by the exigencies of the common good, individual rights must be subjugated in order to preserve society. This will be examined more fully in the section pertaining to case law adjudicated under the Irish Constitution, but is important to note here.

    Overall, the most revolutionary aspect of Thomas Aquinas's *Treatise on Law* was its being "the first systemic explanation of human law, which is defined and crucially related to the higher law of nature and of God".[32] By recognising the existence of a higher, permanent concept of law upon which lawmakers can rely for guidance in promulgating human law, Aquinas enunciated an unchanging, non-arbitrary standard of right and wrong in which all men and women can participate via reason, and upon which all positive law can be based. Recognising that circumstances and the needs of a community can change with time, Aquinas allowed for change in particular laws without denying or altering the natural law upon which they were based.

The Natural Law is a certain participation in the Eternal Law as was stated above and therefore it remains unchangeable. This it has from the unchangeableness and perfection of the Divine Reason, the author of nature. But human reason is changeable and imperfect and so its law is changeable. And besides, the Natural Law contains certain universal precepts which endure forever, while law made by man contains certain

---

[31] *Treatise on Law* at 96, 4 (emphasis added).
[32] Kelly, *op. cit.*, p. 134.

particular precepts according to different situations which arise.

A measure ought to be as permanent as possible. But in changeable things, it is not possible for something to be altogether unchangeable. Therefore, human law cannot be altogether unchangeable.

With respect to men, whose acts are regulated by law, law can rightly be changed on account of change in the condition of men to whom different things are useful according to different conditions. . .

[Thus] human law is rightly changed insofar as the Common Good is thereby promoted . . . [However] human law should not be changed unless the damage done thereby to the common welfare is compensated by some other benefit [to the common good].[33]

Again, the focal point here is the common good. When circumstance or proven knowledge changes, then what constitutes 'the common good' can change as well. Examples which immediately come to mind are a scientific discovery which changes society's concept of some formerly held truth, e.g. that quarantine for a particular disease is not necessary; or the studies which indicate that a previously believed concept or prejudice is groundless, e.g. that women are not fit to serve as police officers. As knowledge is gained (i.e. a change in circumstance) then the parameters of what constitutes the common good also changes and new laws are implemented (or old laws repealed). *The outer limits or the parameters of the common good, referring back to previous sections of the Treatise, remained fixed, however. The preservation of the life of man, and "doing good and avoiding evil" toward that end – these define the limits of the common good.* The essence of the natural law lies within these limits and these cannot be altered by man to suit his whims:

The Natural and Divine Laws come from the will of God, as stated above. *Therefore they cannot be changed by a custom coming from the will of man*, but only by Divine authority. Hence it is that no custom can obtain the force of law against Natural or Divine Law . . .[34]

It is this concept of changeable, human-made laws based upon an unchanging, non-arbitrary eternal law which many writers have contended is the strength of Aquinas' thesis. There is permanence coupled with the flexibility necessary for the operation of effective government. There is the recognition of the changing circumstances of human affairs and knowledge, and the need to reflect these changes in laws, yet without acquiesance to the "rudderless sail-

---

[33] *Treatise on Law* at 97, 1, 2 (emphasis added).
[34] *Ibid.*, at 97, 3 (emphasis added).

ing" of purely positive lawmaking, i.e. lawmaking without a higher standard to guide it. Professor Adler, who defined positivism as that legal theory which holds that "there is only positive (man-made) law and that there are no rational grounds for criticism of [that] law", stated that Aquinas established that ". . . there are rules or principles of conduct which are of even greater universality – applying to all men, not merely to one man, and not merely even to one society at a given time and place".[35] Furthermore, "the real meaning of positivism invokes, as St Thomas points out, the notion of the arbitrary, an institution of the will as opposed to something natural, discovered by the intellect".[36] The natural law constitutes "the standard by which all other rules are to be judged good or bad, right or wrong, just or unjust, and in terms of which constitutions and governments are similarly to be judged"[37] and unlike positive law, which must be taught and learned by memory, the natural law is self-evident and deducible. "A legislature declares the law . . . it makes law by fiat . . ." but the natural law is "deduced".[38] Still, Adler maintained that positive law is necessary, in keeping with Aquinas' philosophy. "Positive law without a foundation in natural law is purely arbitrary. It needs the natural law to make it rational. But natural law without positive law is ineffective for the purpose of enforcing justice and keeping peace."[39]

Professor McKinnon similarly submitted that though modern lawmakers and adjudicators do not see themselves as utilising the natural law, and may even find the natural law abhorrent to the process of democratic lawmaking, they unthinkingly do use natural law in promulgating legislation and in adjudicating. "Natural law has survived because men naturally think in terms of it. . . . [A]ny effort to place those values at any point short of the ultimate principles of practical human reason is . . . futile."[40] Adler re-iterated this theme when he stated that "laws made by state or government are not the only directions of conduct which apply to men living in society"[41] and Thomas Davitt compared Aquinas' treatise to a compass for those legislators who "have lost their legal bearing and are foundering and awash in the mountainous seas of uncertainty".[42]

Yet, despite this praise for Aquinas, by the 18th century his theories had all but disappeared from Anglo-American jurisprudence and theories of natu-

---

[35] Adler, "The Doctrine of Natural Law Philosophy" in *Natural Law Institute Proceedings II* (1949) 65-84 at 67.

[36] *Ibid.*, at 67.

[37] *Ibid.*, at 68.

[38] *Ibid.*, at 79 (emphasis in original).

[39] *Ibid.*, at 81.

[40] McKinnon, "Natural Law and Positive Law" in *Natural Law Institute Proceedings II* (1949) 85 at 101.

[41] Adler, *op. cit.*, at 67.

[42] Davitt, "St. Thomas Aquinas and the Natural Law" in *Origins of the Natural Law Tradition* (1954) pp. 26, 40-46.

ral law were not given serious consideration by the majority of legal scholars from the 17th century onward.[43] There are several explanations for this disinterest in Aquinas, most of which will be explored in the next chapter pertaining to growth of secularism and the concept of individual rights. But here it is important to note that Aquinas' failure to address private property, and the rights attached thereto, was probably the single factor most responsible for the demise in popularity of his natural law theory. In the centuries which followed Aquinas, during which urbanisation, industrialisation, the development of capital and its resulting credit and banking industry all flourished and dominated,[44] official recognition and protection of private property, both real and personal, was necessary. Aquinas gives scant treatment to property, in keeping with the Aristotelian basis upon which his theory was built. ("Again, since every part is ordered to the whole as the imperfect to the perfect and one man is part of the perfect society, it is necessary that the law properly regard the order to the happiness of the society."[45]) The Christian tradition of communal use of goods ("[T]he common possession of all things . . . may be said to belong to the Natural Law, since nature has not provided for the distinction of ownership . . . but men have brought [this] in for [its] usefulness in human life."[46]). Any 'rights' an individual may have in a purely Thomistic society are only secondary benefits flowing from the common good. It comes first, and though individuals may benefit uniquely as a result of laws promulgated for the common good, this is not the primary purpose of the lawmaking. "Operations indeed deal with particular matters, but those particular matters can be referred to the Common Good – not indeed as coming under a common genus or species but as sharing a common final cause inasmuch as the Common Good is said to be the common end."[47] And "[a] precept implies application to those things that are regulated by law. However, the ordination to the common good which pertains to law is applicable to singular ends. And, according to this, precepts are given also with regard to certain particulars".[48] Finally, Aquinas summed up this section of Replies by stating: "Just as nothing stands firm according to Speculative Reason unless it is reduced to the first indemonstrable principles (i.e. self-evident principles or the most fundamental principles) so nothing stands firm according to Practical Reason unless it is ordered to the last end which is the Common Good."[49]

In summary, Aquinas presented the most exhaustive and systemic theory

---

[43] For example, there is no reference to Aquinas in Sir William Blackstone's Commentaries on the Common Law of England nor in any of Jefferson's writings.

[44] For a full treatment of these developments, see Braudel, *The Structure of Everyday Life, Civilisation and Capitalism, 15th-18th Centuries, vol. I* (1979).

[45] *Treatise on Law* at 90, 2.

[46] *Ibid.*, at 94, 5.

[47] *Ibid.*, at 90, 2.

[48] *Ibid.*, at 90, 2.

[49] *Ibid.*, at 90, 2.

of the natural law to date. Due to circumstances which will be examined in chapter 4, however, the Thomist theory went out of favour and other theories, reflecting the man-centred focus of the Renaissance and Enlightenment eras, were utilised in developing much of the jurisprudence for the modern western world. Before leaving Aquinas, however, two last points must be made. First, though his emphasis was overwhelming upon the common good as the ultimate end of government, he did recognise the need for equity of a sort in dealing with circumstances which arise unpredictably.

> Dispensation, properly speaking, denotes a measuring out of some common thing to individuals. Hence, the head of a family is also called a 'dispenser' since he distributes to each member of the family, according to weight and measure, work and the necessities of of life. So, in each community, someone is said to 'dispense' because he determines how each member is to fulfil some common precept. *However, it sometimes happens that some precept . . . is not useful for a particular person or in a particular case because it either hinders some greater good or even causes some evil . . .* However, it would be dangerous to leave this judgment to any individual, except perhaps in the case of a clear and sudden emergency . . . *Consequently, he who governs a community has the power to dispense from a human law that rests on his authority, so that, when the application of a law to persons or cases fails, he can grant permission that the law be not observed.* If, however, without such a reason and of his mere will, he grants dispensation, he will be an unfaithful and imprudent dispenser; unfaithful, if he does not act with a view to the Common Good, imprudent if he ignores the reason for dispensing.[50]

This concept of "exceptionality"[51] is vital to the successful and effective operation of government and, as will be shown, is an integral part to the discussion of personal rights and their recognition in modern Irish constitutional thinking. Exceptionality also, however, provides ammunition to those who would find natural law ideology arbitrary or capricious, yet every legal system contains a notion of equity which deviates from the letter of the law. This will be examined in later sections.

The second point which must be made was best summarised by Professor Braudel in his excellent volume (see footnote 44), in which the author submits that "[e]very system of laws must have a principle of exception as a part of its system" and accordingly examines the Epikeia or Equity of Aristotle

---

[50] *Ibid.*, at 97, 6 (emphasis added).
[51] See O'Donoghue, "The Law Beyond the Law", 18 *Amer. J. of Jurisprudence* (1973) pp. 150-164 . In which the author submits that "[e]very system of laws must have a principle of exception as a part of its system" and accordingly examines the *Epikeia* or Equity of Aristotle and the exceptionality of Aquinas.

and the exceptionality of Aquinas. That which:

> . . . made pre-capitalism the source of the economic creativity of the world [was also] the origin or the signal for all major material progress and *for all the most oppressive exploitation of man by man.* Not only because of the appropriation of the surplus value of man's labour, but also *because of those disparities of strength or situation* which meant that there has always been, on a national scale or on a world scale, one stronghold waiting to be captured, one sector more profitable to exploit than the others.[52]

By placing the common good at the forefront of government's goals, Aquinas served to mitigate the severity of exploitation possible by government of individual persons or groups, at least in theory. In comparison, American legal theory, which will be treated next, with its emphasis upon ownership and protection of private property, had left gaping holes through which have fallen, over the past two hundred years, those of lesser "strength or situation", into the abyss of exploitation, or worse. Obviously, the ideal is to somehow provide for the common good without stifling individual human achievement or denying the exercise of fundamental individual liberties. And this is, in a nutshell, the situation facing both the Irish and American judiciaries in the context of modern privacy rights. The approach of Aquinas, however, is a viable and working model for modern times, if utilised to its fullest potential.

---

[52] Braudel, *op. cit.*, p. 562 (emphasis added).

CHAPTER 4

Man to his God: The Protestant Reformation and the Secular Natural Law

[In the Catholic Church, people] do not place their hearts and faith in God, but rather in cowls, special foods, holy water, holy candles, consecrated herbs, indulgences, prized little prayers, precious Friday fasting, confraternities . . . the rosary, and observances, rules, and clothing, none of which God ever commanded . . . Christ's death is the one work of our salvation . . . our heavenly Father has given Christ all power in heaven and on earth . . . we should obey Christ and do what he commands, *[for] in those things which Christ leaves us free to do, no-one in heaven and on earth may forbid us.*[1]

[A]n action is not good because of its correspondence with the essential nature of man, in which God's conception of Man in is essence and potential is reflected, *but because God wills it so.* God's will might equally have willed and prescribed that action's opposite . . . *Thus Law is Will, pure Will, with no foundation in the nature of things.*[2]

It was on the cusp of the 12th century that the writings of Ulpian and other Roman jurisconsults first became available to the Medieval legal scholars of that time, and added substantially to the institution and development of the great university centres. With the westward migration of Byzantine scholars, away from the threatening Turks, came the rich body of legal material known as the *Corpus Juris Civilis* (CJC). Its overwhelming impact and influence upon the legal scholars of that time, down through the Renaissance, cannot be understated. "[I]ts general principles relating to justice, to the concept of law, the division of law, its enforcement, and so on, became central to the medieval concept of law."[3] And it would be the natural law of Ulpian and his contemporaries which would be absorbed, glossed and commented upon by these Medieval legal scholars, and lead to the development, in many ways, of the man-centred, will-powered theories of law exalted by the secular humanists of the Renaissance and Enlightenment eras. As lawmaking became separated from the natural law process enunciated by Aquinas, the *will* of the lawmaker,

---

[1] Taken from Lutheran pamphlets, written in 1524, Germany (emphasis added).
[2] From the writings of William of Ockham (1290-1349) (emphasis in original).
[3] Ullman, *A History of Political Thought: The Middle Ages* (1965) p. 47.

rather than the Divine reason of God, would provide the source and validity for all positive law. Additionally, and most importantly in our journey down the paths to privacy rights, this human-based lawmaking would give birth to the concept of 'rights', reflecting too the influence of Ulpian's discussion regarding the achievement of *ius* as the primary purpose of justice (*ius* being variably defined through the years as "just outcome", "claims" or "rights" in the proprietary sense).[4] Set against the tapestry of intense urban, industrial, and economic development, this 're-born' humanistic emphasis, in the neo-classical spirit of the Greco-Roman tradition, thrived and planted the seeds for revolutions in scientific discovery, the arts, literature, and in the religious world. The Protestant Reformation both added to, and was influenced by, the course of humanism, and the gradual dominance of secular government. Other factors, such as the invention of the printing press, permanently altered man's relationships with others, his view of himself in the world and his conception and relationship with God.[5] In due time, and in varying degrees, "men in some sense confronted God as an equal . . . the free wills of both man and God [were] necessarily matched" and both were seen as having the "arbitrary freedom" to exercise their wills as they wished.[6] Let us begin, however, with Ulpian and the writings of the Roman jurisconsults as they were rediscovered, glossed and commented upon by the Medieval legal scholars.

As discussed previously, the Roman jurisconsults' view of the natural law was a more practical, every day, instinctual conception. "For 'natural' was to them not only what followed from physical qualities of men or things, but also what, within the framework of that system, seemed to square with the normal and reasonable order of human interests and, for this reason, not in need of any further evidence."[7] Thus it was not Divine revelation or participation in the Eternal law via man's reason which accounted for the existence of this law. Rather, it was the self-evident realisation of "the order inherent in conditions of life as the Romans saw it".[8] From these observations, Ulpian and the other jurists drew up laws which, for example, required the care of the property and persons of children and incompetents, allowed for the right of self-defence, provided for intestate succession for blood relatives, and defined the degree of consanguinity at which marriage between a man and a woman was prohibited. *Justinian's Institutes*, one part of the larger, encyclopaedic *CJC*, opened with a statement which could serve as the rallying cry for the secular natural law: "*Justice is an unswerving and perpetual determination to acknowledge all men's rights.*"[9] The word ius, "rights" in this transla-

---

[4] Tuck, *Natural Rights Theories* (1979) pp.13-14.

[5] Ozment, *Protestants: The Birth of a Revolution* (1992) p.46. See generally Eisenstein, *The Printing Press as an Agent of Change* (1978).

[6] Tuck, *op. cit.*, p. 30.

[7] Levy, *Natural Law in Roman Thought* (1949) p. 7.

[8] *Ibid.*, p. 9.

[9] Birks, *Justinian's Institutes* (hereafter *Institutes*) (1987) at 1.1.

tion, has had other meanings over the years, as mentioned previously. According to Tuck, it did not likely signify 'rights' as we know them, but rather a right of use or possession or access. Judging this initial statement within the context of the entire work (which dealt overwhelmingly with issues of commerce and contract[10]), it is more likely that *ius* meant "a just outcome, (including, but not exclusively, giving everyone their *suum* – their own)".[11] After laying down their concept of 'the golden rule' of the natural law, i.e. "live honourably; harm nobody; give everyone his due";[12] the writers of the *Institutes* began with a short discussion of the natural law.

1.2 The Law of Nature, of all Peoples and of the State

The law of nature is the law instilled by nature in all creatures. It is not merely for mankind but for all creatures of the sky, earth and sea. From it comes intercourse between male and female, which we call marriage; also the bearing and bringing up of children. Observation shows that other animals also acknowledge its force. 1. The law of all peoples and the law of the state are distinguished as follows. All peoples with laws and customs apply law which is partly theirs alone and partly shared by all mankind. The law which each people makes for itself is special to its own state. It is called "state law", the law peculiar to that state. But the law which natural reason makes for all mankind is applied the same everywhere. It is called "the law of all peoples" because it is common to every nation. The law of the Roman people is also partly its own and partly common to all mankind. Which parts are which we will explain below.[13]

After discussing the limited applicability of state laws only to that particular state, the text states that:

[b]y contrast, the law of all peoples is common to all mankind. The reality of the human condition led the peoples of the world to introduce certain institutions. Wars broke out. People were captured and made slaves, contrary to the law of nature. By the law of nature all men were initially born free.[14]

Throughout the text, the writers had delineated laws which applied only to

---

[10] While Book One dealt with Marriage, Guardianship and laws pertaining to children and family matters, Books Two, Three, and Four presented the laws pertaining to Wills, Trusts, Estates, Property, Contracts, Partnerships, Pleas and Procedure.

[11] Tuck, *op. cit.*, pp. 12-13.

[12] Another translation of this from the Latin has been, "Live honourably, do not injure others, and render to everyone what is his." *Institutes*, 1.1.3.

[13] *Ibid.*, at 1.2-1.2.1.

[14] *Ibid.*, at 1.2.2.

Romans, and those which were universal to all men. Natural law necessarily applied to all men. But not all universal laws, however, that is to say not all "laws of all peoples" were natural laws. Even though the institution of slavery applied to all people (known to Romans at that time) it was not a law of nature and in fact was contrary to natural law.

1.3   The Law of Persons

The main classification in the law of persons is this: all men are either free or slaves. 1. Liberty – the Latin "libertas" gives us "liberi", free men – denotes a man's natural ability to do what he wants as long as the law or some other force does not prevent him. 2. Slavery on the other hand is an institution of the law of all peoples; it makes men the property of another, contrary to the law of nature.[15]

Confusion arose in Book Two, however, where the writers seemed to say that the natural law and the law of all peoples are one and the same. Under Section 2.1, which describes "The Classification of Things" it was written that:

1. The things which are naturally everybody's are: air, flowing water, the sea, and the sea-shore. So nobody can be stopped from going to the sea-shore. But he must keep away from houses, monuments, and buildings. Unlike the sea, rights to those things are not determined by the laws of all peoples.[16]

And further on in the same section, it was written:

11. Things become the property of individuals in many ways, some by *the law of nature, which as we have said, can be described as the law of all peoples*, and others by our state law. It is easier to begin with the older law. Obviously natural law is earlier. It is the product of the natural order, as old as man himself. Systems of state law did not start to develop until cities were founded, magistracies were established, and law began to be written.[17]

Throughout the remainder of this section, the writers referred to the "law of all peoples" as if it were the same as the natural law.

Why is this an important observation? The Medieval glossators would confuse the "law of all peoples" (*ius gentium*) with the natural law (*ius naturale*) in forming their own theories of natural law. In truth, the *ius gentium* could be derived from either the *ius naturale*, which was unwritten, or the *ius civile*,

---

[15] *Ibid.*, at 1.3-1.3.2.

[16] *Ibid.*, at 2.1.1.

[17] *Ibid.*, at 2.1.11 (emphasis added).

that written or 'state' law which applied to those Roman settlements wherever they were at that time (keeping in mind the vastness and variation of cultures covered by the Roman empire). Instead, *ius civile*, or the civil law, came to be thought of as any positive or statutory law, while *ius gentium* came to be seen as comparable to that natural law espoused by the Church fathers, only more secular in form. The natural law, *ius naturale*, would be subsumed under the *ius gentium*, and "the pedestrian practical working-out of a body of Roman rules suitable for application to foreigners, inflated *post factum* with theory, rose into the rarified atmosphere in which Cicero's philosophy of the law of nature hovered above the earth".[18]

> The only exception from the identification of *ius gentium* with *ius naturale*, or its subsumption in it, was slavery. Although it had to be admitted that by nature men were born free, the universal practice of the ancient world (not merely the Roman) was contrary to this doctrine; and indeed the Romans' use of the word "natural", as opposed to "civil", in describing the quasi-possession or quasi-rights of a contractual type which might be imputed to a slave, gave, as Ernest Levy pointed out, the game away; when natural law and civil law came, as here, into collision, the Roman lawyers were in no doubt that the latter prevailed, and the former went to the wall.[19]

Adding to the confusion between *ius gentium* and *ius naturale* was the question of Ulpian's definition of natural law itself.

> There remains the question of what it was that Ulpian (one of the primary Roman jurisconsults) was trying to express. Perhaps he did have a hankering after Greek philosophy and glimpsed an important truth which he expressed rather ineptly in his formula (i.e. "natural law is the law instilled by nature in all creatures"). Man does share something of his nature with animals – man is, after all, a rational animal. And there ought to be some way of indicating that human patterns of conduct in matters like self-preservation, marriage, procreation and education of children, resemble patterns imposed upon animals by instinct. But here one must tread warily indeed between the metaphors and similes that have misled many besides Ulpian. It may be fruitful to suggest that there is here a confusion not unlike that . . . between the laws of nature like Newton's Law of Gravitation on the one hand, and, on the other hand,

---

[18] Kelly, *A Short History of Western Legal Theory* (1992) p. 63.
[19] Kelly, *ibid.*, p. 63, citing Levy, "Natural Law in Roman Thought" in *Studia et Documenta Historiae et Iuris XV*, 7 (1949) pp. 17-18.

natural laws of morality . . . Ulpian would not be the first nor the last to have been deceived by the resemblence.[20]

As a result of Ulpian's definition and the dominance of *ius gentium*, the natural law of the Roman jurisconsults, as derived from the Stoics and Cicero, came down to the Medieval glossators as a secular, instinctual, man-centred theory which did not depend upon *direct* Divine revelation or implantation, and dealt primarily with everyday commerce. Furthermore, the rationale for the positive law enunciated by the Roman jurisconsults was not, as Aquinas defined it, to help man and society attain the common good, but rather was *to bring order to a chaotic world, by which then the common good is achieved*. As was stated in the *Institutes*: "The reality of the human condition led the peoples of the world to introduce certain institutions."[21] Man-made law, reflecting the "realities" of man's existence, was needed to initiate and regulate contracts, "sale, hire, partnership, deposit, loan . . ." and much more[22] in order to reach the stated goal of "giving everyone their suum". In the jurisconsults' view, by giving everyone "their own", chaos was replaced by order, and the common good was thus achieved. This representation of the law as man's saviour from his savage, chaotic state would be reiterated by legal philosophers centuries later, as would the notion that the common good can only be achieved via the attainment of individual "rights" first.

Another very important notion which was implicit in the writings of the jurisconsults was that of private property.

> At the moment when Roman law first yields historically reliable data, i.e., the era of the Twelve Tables . . . say the late 6th century BC, the institution of private property is already clearly established . . . The picture drawn . . . of the origin of society and laws . . . suggest a primeval condition in which all wants could be satisfied from the bounty of the earth, a condition then disrupted by the effects of greed . . . the order subsequently imposed by men on themselves to avert chaos implies the protection of the individual in the enjoyment of what is "his".[23]

One need only look to John Locke's opening statement in his seminal *Two Treatises* (the purpose of government is to protect citizen's property) to see its striking similarity to the Romans' stated governmental purpose of "giving everyone their own"[24] or "to acknowledge all men's rights (a modern translation of *ius*)".[25] The differences between the natural law theory of the Romans,

---

[20] Crowe, *The Changing Profile of the Natural Law* (1977) p. 51.
[21] *Institutes* at 1.2.2.
[22] *Ibid.*, at 1.2.2.
[23] Kelly, *op. cit.*, p. 76.
[24] *Institutes* at 1.1.3.
[25] *Ibid.*, at 1.1.

and that of Aquinas are never more clear than here, and the distinguishing effects to be had upon the constitutions of the United States and Ireland, respectively, are starkly foreshadowed even at this early juncture.

Two other aspects of the Roman natural law are crucial to note. First, the Romans did, arguably, recognise a kind of a 'right' similar to that which we recognise now. Though typically "the product of agreements or promises made between specific and independent parties. . ." or "possessed as a result of one's relationship with the state, public or the Emperor . . . like a modern right *in rem* . . . against all the world, as distinct from a right *in personam*, available against determinate individuals. . ." it was this concept of *ius* upon which Medieval scholars would rely in recognising 'rights' as we have come to know them – rights independent of contractual or quasi-contractual agreements.[26] "It is among the men who rediscovered the [writings of the Roman jurisconsults] and created the medieval science of Roman law in the 12th century that we must look to find the first modern rights theory, one built round the notion of a passive right."[27]

Second, the Romans contended that the source for all law-making was with Man, not God, though God may have been the ultimate, though distant, origin. In their ascending theory of governmental authority, as opposed to Aquinas' *descending* conception, the Romans clung to somewhat of a legal fiction in justifying Ulpian's well-known axiom, "the emperor's will has the force of statute" ("*quod principi placuit, legis habet vigorem*") with the claim that the people had irrevocably assigned to the emperor and his governors their authority to legislate in exchange for the maintenance of order.[28] Even with this legal fiction, however, the Romans' recognition of the community at large as the source of governmental authority was an important step in the development of democratic legal theory. This *ascending* view, however, would lay dormant for several centuries. "As a result of the overpowering influence of Christianity, the [Medieval] peoples adopted the theory inherent in Christian doctrine – and the ascending view was, so to speak, driven underground, not to emerge again as a theoretical proposition until the late 13th century."[29] And once it did re-emerge, it would do so in quite revolutionary ways.

Before moving forward to examine the contributions of Medieval glossators, it will be of assistance to review, in chart form, the various tenets of the two natural law theories discussed to this point.

It is important to see how each 'school' interpreted the natural law handed down by the Stoics and Cicero.

---

[26] Tuck, *op. cit.*, pp. 7-13.

[27] *Ibid.*, p. 13.

[28] Kelly, *op. cit.*, pp. 68, 91-92. Eventually there would evolve, by the 12th century, the notion of a social compact between citizens and government. *Ibid.*, p. 97.

[29] Ullman, *op. cit.*, p. 13.

Natural Law Element	Aquinas/Church	Roman Jurisconsults
Innateness	Innate via man's participation in Divine reason	Innate via instinct (indirectly from God)
Universal	Yes	Yes
Eternal	Yes	Yes
Personal End	The Good; ultimate happiness within God's plan	Each man achieves his 'due'; his 'rights' (*ius*, *suum*)
Communal soul	Yes, all men part of one 'body'	No communal soul concept
Laws binding on man?	Yes	No
Man's state if he violates Natural law dictates	Ultimate unhappiness	Chaos
Source of Governmental Authority	Descending from God	Ascending from Man
Governmental Purpose/End	The Common Good	Protection of each man's due; Order out of chaos which ultimately serves Common Good
Private property?	No	Yes
Individual rights?	No	Yes, though dissimilar from modern concept of rights
'Touchstone'	Preserve life of man	Preserve life of man
Golden Rule	Do good, avoid evil, and seek the Common Good	Live honourably, do not harm others, and give everyone his due

Though this somewhat simplified chart points out clear distinctions between the two general natural law theories, in reality some 'cross-fertilization' did occur. Just as the Medieval glossators (as will be seen) were aware of the natural law of the Church Fathers, the Church Fathers followed the developments of the secular glossators at the university centres, where much of the study of law was undertaken, and were in turn deeply affected by their commentaries.[30]

---

[30] Crowe, *op. cit.*, p. 8.

The creation and flowering of the university was a uniquely Medieval era development. As the 11th century came to a close, the continent of Europe and the British Isles began to enjoy relative peace and tranquillity. Nurtured by this newly founded stability, populations grew, the economy expanded and became more complex, new industries developed. Urban areas multiplied and became more expansive, and commerce based upon capital and the production and sale of manufactured goods developed rapidly. With this urbanisation, and continually growing commercial interactions, the need grew for educated laymen who could conduct business and efficiently operate the more complex, centralised governmental bodies of the day. That knowledge that had been saved down through the centuries by unworldly monastic scriveners, once thought mysterious and impractical, suddenly became vital to the education of the new urban class. Personnel now needed to be "capable of keeping accurate records, drafting charters and commissions and grants, supplying and serving a judicature, conducting correspondence, [and] in general able to organise and present material in lucid and forceful Latin".[31] The revival of legal studies, relatively unknown since the height of the Roman Empire and the Roman jurisconsults, grew rapidly. Between the 12th and the 14th centuries, dozens of major universities with programmes of legal study emerged and flourished.

The impact upon Medieval society of the birth of the intellectual class cannot be overstated. During the long and dark centuries between the fall of the Roman empire and the Renaissance 'rebirth' of arts and letters, a man typically existed as an illiterate, lowly farmer who lived an average of thirty years in a nameless hamlet from which he and his family never ventured far. He had no surname (only members of nobility had surnames) because he did not need one. His life was irrelevant, just as it was intended to be, for the important life was that which occurred after death, and it was this eternal afterlife that he hoped to attain. In the meantime, he lived day-to-day, in a world he believed to be a flat plane covered with mysterious monster-filled forests and serpent-filled waters, above which hovered heaven, below, hell, and around which revolved the sun.[32] Storms, pestilence, death, ravaging armies, disease, drought, and random calamities were all the result of inexplicable acts of an omnipotent and unfathomable God to whom unceasing prayer should be offered to ensure eternal life. Fasting, sacrifices, and the purchase of indulgences served the purpose of obtaining good favour from God for the souls of deceased loved ones. And it was especially through the intercession of the saints and the Virgin Mary that the dead would rise from the abyss of

---

[31] Kelly, *op. cit.*, p. 119. Also, see generally Braudel, *The Structure of Everyday Life, Civilization and Capitalism, 15th-18th Centuries, Vol 1* (1979).

[32] It is worth recalling that, in 1514, Nicholas Copernicus concluded that the earth, a sphere, rotated on its own axis and orbited around the sun. He was burned at the stake, and Catholics were forbidden to read his writings until such ban was lifted in 1828.

purgatory to the glory of eternal, heavenly life. Religion was not personal or colloquial; it was a mystical and all-powerful control over every aspect of his life, delivered in a language he did not understand. Thus, just as he relied upon the priest to relay his confessions of wrongdoing to God, it was left to the good father to interpret the Scriptures, hand-written in a single and ethereal volume which deserved only to be housed under the sacred dome of the city's cathedral or local monastery. The Holy Bible was not to be touched by common hands, and certainly not intended for common readership. It was sacred, and its interpretation by priests representing the Holy Father was above reproach. It was not necessary, nor was it expected that it ever should be, for the common man to think about or examine its contents himself.[33]

> In the Age of Faith, as Will Durant called the medieval era, one secret of the papacy's hold on the masses was its capacity to inspire absolute terror, a derivative of the universal belief that whoever wore the tiara could, at his pleasure, determine how each individual would spend his afterlife – cosseted in eternal bliss or shrieking in writhing flames below. His decision might be whimsical, his blessings often sold openly, his motives might be evil, but that was his prerogative. Earthly life being 'nasty, brutish and short', in Thomas Hobbes's memorable phrase, only the deranged would invite the disfavour and retribution of the Holy See.[34]

This overwhelming authority of the Pope was based not upon his spiritual superiority, for the papal chair and its subordinates had succumbed to the excesses and greed of men who have enjoyed absolute power for too long. Rather it was upheld because the masses did not know any better, and furthermore did not feel inclined, either out of fear or out of ignorance, to want to know any better. What occurred in the relative calm and prosperity of the late Medieval/early Renaissance era was the flowering of what Leonardo da Vinci would call *saper vedere* (knowing how to see). It would fully bloom at the peak of the Renaissance and Enlightenment eras, but its initial blossoming occurred with the rediscovery and examination of the Roman law texts by university scholars. It is they who would carry down the secular, instinct-based natural law concepts of the Roman jurists to the welcoming minds of the humanists of the Renaissance and Enlightenment, where the concept of the natural law would be complemented by that of natural rights, inalienably possessed by all men (in theory, at least). At the same time, the natural law theory of Aquinas would diminish in strength and authority, just as the Church's

---

[33] A fascinating description of Medieval life and the early developments of the Renaissance can be found in Manchester, *A World Lit Only By Fire* (1993).
[34] *Ibid.*, pp. 91-92.

authority was being questioned by the forces of the Reformation and Intellectualism.[35]

It was Irnerius, a law teacher in Bologna who pioneered, until his death in 1138, the study of *Justinian's Digest* and other sections of the *CJC*. In examining the body of works, he and other glossators focused upon the actual definition of the natural law and its various divisions. Though there were many minor variations on the theme, the glossators overwhelmingly adopted and adapted Ulpian's definition of natural law – that which nature has taught all animals. Natural law was seen as the instinctual touchstone of right and wrong which came from within man, not directly or even necessarily handed down by God, or having a close nexus with the Scriptures. And even though the resulting tenets were often similar to those of Aquinas and the canonists, they were different in origin and scope, and would accordingly have different ramifications on the future rights of privacy.

One crucial difference lay in the common understanding of the source of governmental authority. As discussed above, the Church fathers recognised a *descending* line of authority from God, while the secular jurisconsults contended that authority ascended from the people to the ruling body. Irnerius, accepting the latter view, stated that in consenting to be governed, man made an irrevocable and permanent transfer of his power to that governing body, just as Ulpian had held. Other scholars and events of everyday Medieval life, however, led to the erosion of the notion of an irrevocable transfer of power. The scholar Azo, who was active at Bologna around the year 1200 and died there in 1230 (and who, unlike some other scholars, recognised the biblical law of Moses as being part of the natural law), submitted that "the people had never finally abdicated their authority, and that their enduring lawmaking capacity was to be seen in the legal force attaching to custom, which indeed if universal, could even supersede positive law".[36] Other glossators, Hugolinus, Bulgarus, and John Bassianus, agreed.[37] And in the streets of Medieval cities, popular democratic principles were taking hold. Guilds, instituted by persons working in the same craft or trade, were established as completely self-governing, democratically-operating bodies. Officers were elected by members,

---

[35] "These pioneers established Roman law as the supreme expression of legal and political reason, and set it on a course which would lead to its reception into, and fusion with, the relatively less sophisticated native systems of the medieval states and statelets. Their influence caused the Roman law in its Justinian dress to have the same sort of authority in civil affairs as the Bible had in spiritual." Kelly, *op. cit.*, p. 122. For a general discussion of the Medieval glossators and the growth of intellectuals in that era, see Le Goff, *Intellectuals in the Middle Ages* (1993).

[36] Crowe, *op. cit.*, p. 91-2, citing Azo, *Summa*.

[37] Carlyle and Carlyle, *A History of Medieval Political Theory in the West* (1903-1936) pp. ii, 63, ff. Custom was a very important component in the Medieval concept of law, as noted by the Carlyles, "for even when jurists thought that the Crusaders had to legislate for a new political society, they conceive of them doing so by . . . collecting existing customs". *Ibid.*, pp. iii, 44.

and the activities and common interests of the body were chosen, as well, by a majority vote of the members. This was truly the ascending theory of government at the street level.[38] In religious life, the establishment of new orders was also based upon a democratic model, the most notable of these being the Franciscans (founded in 1209) and the Dominicans (founded in 1216). Ironically, it would be writers and scholars from these orders, especially the Franciscans, who would aid in the development of secularly democratic models of government.

Related to this changing concept of the source of governmental authority was the newly altered notion of the scope of governmental authority, specifically addressing the question whether the king (or other governmental leader) was subject to his own laws. It has already been shown that the Church fathers unanimously agreed that, though a leader ought to abide by the laws he promulgates, he was indeed above the law. Ulpian and other Roman jurisconsults also held that the authority of the lawmaker superseded the rule of law though, as stated above, in theory the community had willingly granted this authority to the lawmaker. It was the Medieval glossators who, in carrying the Roman view of man as the ultimate source of governmental authority to its next step, maintained that the lawmaker must be subject to his own laws. Marsilius, writing in the early 14th century that "the sovereign in the state was the people", held that the leader was only a secondary tool to be utilised to execute the people's mandates.[39] Even more radically, this former rector of the University of Paris maintained that the Church too should be subordinate to the state where temporal matters were concerned, for were not clerics citizens first?[40] For this he was condemned as a heretic, but his teachings "lay like an unexploded mine among Europe's intellectual furniture, to be detonated two centuries later in the age of Reformation".[41]

As further evidence of the cross-fertilisation of secular legal theory with Church tradition, and presenting the logical conclusion of Ulpian's *ascending* theory of governmental authority, the cleric Henry of Bracton wrote in the mid-thirteenth century: "The king should . . . be subject to God and the law, seeing that it is the law that makes the king . . . Let the king accord to the law what the law accords to him, namely sovereign power; for where will and not law is sovereign, there no king can be said to be."[42] In essence, Henry was stating an early version of Abraham Lincoln's popular maxim: "In giving freedom to the slave, we assure freedom to the free."[43] If the king's authority is granted under law created by the people, and the king violates the law, what is

---

[38] Braudel, *op. cit.*, pp. 518-519.
[39] Marcilius, *Defensor pacis I*. 12. 3, 5.
[40] Kelly, *op. cit.*, p. 127.
[41] *Ibid.*, p. 127.
[42] Thorne (ed.), *Bracton* (1968) 3.9.3.
[43] Lincoln, "Annual Message to Congress" 1 December 1862.

there to maintain the validity of that law which created his office, or any law for that matter?

The ultimate expression of the rule of law and the strongest repudiation of the divine right of kings was manifested, however, in an earlier document which had enormous impact upon all western legal theory which followed it: The Magna Carta. Drawn up in 1215, and presented to King John "in the meadow that is called Runnymede", the strength and authority of this Charter has spread, over the centuries, in scope far beyond its original, limited application to the barons and nobles of its day. In particular, Article 39 "expressed[ed] the spirit and principal idea embodied in the Charter"[44] and formed the basis for our modern concept of due process: "No free man shall be taken, imprisoned, disseised, outlawed, banished, or in any way destroyed, nor will We (i.e., the King) proceed against or prosecute him, except by lawful judgment of his peers and by the law of the land."

It was people who thought freely, breaking the bonds of blind obedience to authority, questioning the power of the Church and the exercise of the royal prerogative, who were able to draft the Magna Carta and envision man as the source of governmental authority rather than its hapless subject. If the rediscovery of Aristotle's writings opened up an entirely secular world to the early Medieval scholars exposed previously only to a theocratic view,[45] then the reintroduction of the Roman law served to emphasise the need to live earthly life as fully as humanly possible, and de-emphasised the need to attain the supposed superior life of the hereafter. The Medieval scholars began the initial venture into the exploration of man's 'human-ness' with all of its foibles, longings, experiences and innate desires; the later Renaissance scholars would embrace this humanism (and call themselves *humanists*).

> In the ancient texts Renaissance scholars found an unsuspected reverence for humanity which, without actually dismissing the Bible, certainly overshadowed it. And in the wisdom of antiquity they discovered respect for man in the free expansion of his natural impulses, unfreighted by the corrupting burden of original sin . . .The Christian faith was not repudiated, but the new concept of the cultivated man was the Renaissance *homo universale*, the universal man: creator, artist, scholar, and encyclopaedic genius in the spirit of the ancient *paideia*.[46]

---

[44] Hogue, *Origins of the Common Law* (1966) p.53. For a thorough discussion of the Magna Carta, see Howard, *Magna Carta, Text and Commentary* (1964), and Jones, *King John and the Magna Carta* (1971). "The king was now under law in the constitutional sense." Jones, *ibid.*, p. 105.

[45] Finley, "Politics" in *The Legacy of Greece* (1977) p. 62. "[T]he re-emergence of the...lost works of Aristotle led to the development of a secular conception of society to compete with and gradually erode the dominant Christian theory." *Ibid.*, p. 62.

[46] Manchester, *op. cit.*, p. 105.

Ulpian's natural law, based upon man's innate instincts rather than a Divinely implanted eternal law, was a primary source for this newly developing emphasis upon man's life in the here and now. The Roman jurisconsults accepted man's instinctual needs and mundane desires as that which naturally occurs in all men. Their goal in having men recognise and accept this natural law within themselves was the realisation of happiness and contentment on earth. They, unlike Christian theologians,[47] did not see the ultimate aim of natural law as the enjoyment of eternal life with God. Life was to be relished and lived fully while on earth, with none of the limitations and pressures applied by those who believed in the "burden of original sin". Rather, *the only limitations* upon Ulpian's (and the Roman jurisconsults') natural law theory *were other tenets of the natural law*. In practical terms, therefore, man could only enjoy the dictates of his natural inclinations to the extent that such activities harmed no one else. "Live honourably; harm nobody; and give everybody his due." God's eternal law had nothing to say here.

This discovery by Medieval scholars of this earthy style of law which elevated and revealed in man's instinctual behaviour was perhaps the most important ramification in the development of personal rights and, specifically, the right of privacy. For antecedent to any recognition of personal rights was *the fundamental recognition of personhood* in all of its attributes. This would occur and flourish most fully in the Renaissance and Enlightenment eras, in which man would be the glorified one and not God. Reason would become not that which God implanted in each man, but rather man's own innate ability to understand, explore, test and find answers, independent of Divine intervention.[48] And just as God's will came to be recognised as the power behind all events in the minds of theologians, *man's will* would serve as the determining factor in establishing the validity of a enactment under secular natural law theory. And this is where two Franciscans, William of Ockham and Duns Scotus, both writing in the 14th century, made their ironic contributions to the development of secular positivism and parliamentary sovereignty.

While Aquinas had held that human reason "has to proceed from the precepts of natural law" which is none other than "the participation of eternal law in rational creatures", Ockham and Scotus maintained that God's will was binding upon humans merely because it was *His will*, and not because it had any correlation with a set of natural laws. Every event, every bit of creation, they held, was contingent upon God's will, and God, being omnipotent,

---

[47] "To true Christians, life on earth was almost irrelevant. During it they obeyed the precepts of Catholicism to safeguard their future in paradise, disciplined by the fear that if they didn't, they might lose it. The thought of living for the sheer sake of living, celebrating mortal existence before God took them unto his own, was subversive of the entire structure. Yet that was precisely the prospect humanism offered." *Ibid.*, pp. 112-113.

[48] "[The measure of the Classical world] was man and his reason; its philosophy that which bade him live in accordance with the nature which his reason enabled him to interpret, rather than a personalised God and his revelation." Kelly, *op. cit.*, pp. 165-166.

could exercise His will however He pleased. The results, therefore, of God's exercise of His will were totally arbitrary.[49] Hence, contrary to Thomist theory which held that an action is good because of its "correspondence with the essential nature of man, in which God's conception of Man in his essence and potential is reflected", the good friars' theory led to the following corollary: an action is not willed because it is good (i.e., in congruence with nature/natural law); rather an action is good because it is willed by God. (And, of course, God could have just as easily willed the opposite.)[50]

Though Scotus and Ockham probably did not intend the effect which followed, the ramifications of this new concept were far-reaching in the world of secular legal theory. For combined with the scholars' assimilation of Roman law, as discussed above, the Franciscans' conception of the superiority of God's will over any sort of natural law guideposts, resulted in the notion that man, like God, had an equally powerful and arbitrary will which could be exercised over his earthly realm. The free wills of man and God were "elevated . . . together. The arbitrary freedom of God's will was necessarily matched by a similar freedom of man's will. . ."[51]

> "Natural law . . . ceases to be the bridge between God and man; it affords no indication of the existence of an eternal and immutable order." But by floating off the idea of law from moral imperative lying in nature, and attaching it to the idea of a superior will which cannot be questioned, an intellectual path seemed to have been smoothed out for the advance of will, generally and not with special reference to that of God, as a sufficient basis for legal obligation. This has been pointed to by modern writers as one of the intellectual roots of secular positivism, and the notion – in its modern manifestations so destructive – that the state's will makes law.[52]

In the hands of such writers who did follow, such as the French scholar Jean Gerson, writing in the early 15th century, the notion that "man's relationship to the world is conceptually the same as God's", was a springboard for the development of one of many theories of natural rights.[53] "This was the beginning of a trend which . . . 'the individual . . . becomes the centre of interest for legal science, which henceforth strives to describe his legal attributes, the extent of his faculties, and of his individual rights'."[54]

---

[49] *Ibid.*, p. 145. See also generally Leff, *William of Ockham* (1975).
[50] *Kelly, op. cit.,* p. 145.
[51] Tuck, *op. cit.,* p. 30.
[52] Kelly, *op. cit.,* p. 145, citing D'Entreves, *Natural Law* (1970) p. 69.
[53] Tuck, *op. cit.,* p. 331. Also Finnis, *Natural Law and Natural Rights* (1980) pp. 206-210.
[54] Kelly, *op. cit.,* p. 146, citing Villey, *Le Formation de la pensee juridique moderne: Le Francisanisme et le droit* (1963) p. 210.

As the Renaissance dawned, therefore, there were two clear and distinct concepts of the natural law: one which followed the lines laid earlier by Aquinas and which defined reason as "the participation of Eternal Law in rational creatures"; and the second that portrayed "the law of right reason, which coincides with the biblical law (in some cases) but is not derived from it [and which] part[s] company with Christian morality . . . to form an autonomous department of its own".[55] This latter theory, the secular natural law derived originally from that of the Roman jurisconsults, came to be seen purely as the *law of right reason*, reflecting its perceived man-centred origin. Hooker would describe this "law of nature" as "meaning thereby the Law which human nature knoweth itself in reason universally bound to, which also for that cause may be termed most fitly the Law of Reason [and] being investigable by Reason, without the help of Revelation supernatural and divine".[56] He would be followed by the Dutch scholar Grotius, who would write that "the natural law is the command of right reason . . ."[57] and Samuel Pufendorf who, in maintaining that natural law was free from any connection with divine revelation and was purely the product of reason, altered the "golden rules" of natural law to reflect the relatively new focus of natural rights: "Let no one act towards another in such a way that the latter can justly complain that his equality of right has been violated" and "[T]reat others as having naturally equal rights by reason of the dignity of all men".[58] As Ulpian's rudimentary maxims came into full flower in the 17th and early 18th centuries, it was unquestioned that "'nature' had come to connote, not divine ordinance, but human appetites, and natural rights were invoked by the individualism of the age as a reason why self-interest should be given free play".[59] Man, without any reference to a higher law, was the source and invalidator of this natural law, with its individualistic emphasis upon the natural rights of man, and not, as Aquinas would have had it, the good of the collective body. And, as will be seen, this is the natural law, in particular, which was studied and absorbed by the "founding fathers" of the American Constitution,[60] and which is explicit as well as implicit in the writings of the American Declaration of Independence and US Constitution itself.

Woven throughout the entire history and growth of secularism and man's notion of individualism is, of course, the well-known and much-studied impact of the Protestant Reformation, which was both influenced by the natural law history of the Roman jurisconsults, and subsequently an influence upon

---

[55] *Ibid.*, pp. 142-143.

[56] Hooker, *Laws of Ecclesiastical Polity I*, 8 (1594).

[57] de Groot, *De iure belli et pacis* I.I.10.1-2 (1625).

[58] Pufendorf, *Elementa jurisprudentiae* 2.4.4; and *De officio hominis et civis* I.3.9.6-9 (1661).

[59] Tawney, *Religion and the Rise of Capitalism* (1926) p. 183.

[60] James Madison, Alexander Hamilton, John Jay and Thomas Jefferson are primarily those who influenced the writings surrounding the Revolution and the establishment of state and the national constitutions.

the growth of secularised government. The wealth of information concerning the Reformation, and its eventual effect of temporalizing government and altering man's perceived relationship with God, is vast and well-known.[61] Yet there is one aspect which, until recently, has received scant attention – although it was crucial to the migration and assimilation of *the law of right reason* in the American colonies in the late 17th and early 18th centuries – is the Presbyterian political legacy of those many thousands who emigrated there from the counties of north-eastern Ireland,[62] along with those scholars, teachers, and philosophers of the Scottish Enlightenment[63] who had an important influence upon the education of the founding fathers, most particularly James Madison and Thomas Jefferson.[64] Indeed, as will be seen in the next chapter, their concepts of reason, morality and natural law were shaped to a certain extent by the writings of the Scots Hume and Smith, and the Irish Hutcheson,[65] among others, just as the perceived mood of the young American nation was defined in large measure by the self-sufficient, independent-minded, "radical libertarianism . . . [of] the Scotch-Irish frontiersmen who populated most of the back country from Pennsylvania to Georgia".[66] These variables occurred as a result of the Reformation's revolutionary transformation of the Scots people under the tutelage of John Knox, a contemporary and soulmate of John Calvin, in the middle of the 16th century. The Kirk of Scotland not only emphasised the individualism implicit in all of Protestantism, but strongly encouraged strict morality (often to the point of puritanism), a fierce pursuit of education, and the principles of democracy as evidenced in the governmental structure of the Kirk,[67] all of which transferred with the Scots to Ulster (which is why many Presbyterians were instrumental in the fight for an independent Ireland)

---

[61] See, for example, Tawney, *op. cit.*; Weber, *The Protestant Ethic and the Spirit of Capitalism* (1976); Beard, *The Reformation of the Sixteenth Century in Relation to Modern Thought and Knowledge* (1885); Ozment, *op. cit.*

[62] It has been estimated that between 250,000 to 300,000 immigrants from what is now Northern Ireland arrived between the period from the late 1600s to the year 1800 and settled in the United States and its frontier territories. These were the Ulster Scots-Irish (traditionally called 'Scotch-Irish' in the United States), descendants of the lowland Scots-Presbyterians who settled the plantations in Ulster for Queen Elizabeth I in the early 1600s and left Ireland in search of better land and more freedom. (Second to England, the Ulster Scots-Irish claim more US Presidents as descendants than any other ethnic group.) Leyburn, *The Scotch-Irish, A Social History* (1962) pp.157-183.

[63] See generally Rendall, *The Origins of the Scottish Enlightenment* (1978).

[64] See, for example, Willis, *Inventing America: Jefferson's Declaration of Independence* (1978); Howe, "Why the Scottish Enlightenment Was Useful to the Framers of the American Constitution", 31 Comp. Studies in Society and History (1989) pp. 572-587.

[65] Scottish philosopher and historian David Hume (1711-1776); Scottish economist Adam Smith (1723-90); County Down native Francis Hutcheson (1694-1746), philosopher and writer who taught at the University of Glasgow.

[66] McDonald, *Novus Ordo Seclorum, The Intellectual Origins of the Constitution* (1985) p. 157. See also Leyburn, *op. cit.*, pp. 256-72.

[67] Leyburn, *op. cit.*, pp. 56-61.

and then again across the Atlantic to the colonies.[68] The members of the Scottish Enlightenment, who dominated Europe in the 1740-50s, "adopted the new scientific outlook based upon Newton and Locke" and were well-represented in the 'new' American colleges attended by Jefferson (The College of William and Mary) and Madison (Princeton). The influence of the Scots and the Irish was undeniable.[69]

By the 18th century, the law of right reason, with its emphasis upon natural rights, had fully developed out of the Roman secular natural law roots from which it arose. The secular humanists who subscribed to this form of natural law were explicit about their view that the primary purpose of government was the promotion and protection of individual rights, most notably the right of property and its free exchange.[70] The natural law of Aquinas, in the meantime, lay dormant for all practical purposes. Yet it could still be utilised, as argued in the early 19th century, *to provide protection for personal rights as a logical corollary to attaining the goals of the common good* – "anchored in the moral worth and dignity of the person" as a creation of God, and not, as Pufendorf claimed, merely because reason requires it.[71]

In short, it could be claimed that, like the proverbial house to which many paths lead, the recognition and protection of personal rights could be arrived at by the use of more than one route. What each route looks like, however, and how that route carries one in search of a right of privacy, are two questions which are mapped out more clearly in later chapters.

---

[68] *Ibid.*, pp. 256-281.

[69] Willis, *op. cit.*, pp. 167-80; McDonald, *op. cit.*, p. 55. "Thomas Jefferson, among others, was powerfully influenced by the [Scottish] Common Sense school." See also generally Malone, *Jefferson and His Time vol I*, (1948) pp. 33-98 regarding Jefferson's education and early training.

[70] "[T]he preservation of property [is] the end of government, and that for which men enter into society." *Two Treatises*, section 138.

[71] Kelly, *op. cit.*, pp. 333-334, citing Rosmini-Serbati, *Filosofia del diritto* (1830) p.127. Also Pufendorf, *op. cit.*

CHAPTER 5

Man Glorified: the Enlightened Secular Natural Law exemplified in the Constitution of the United States

[Isaac Newton, t]he architect of the mechanical world view[,] gave [John] Locke every hope that he might discover the relationship between universal physical laws and the workings of government and society, thus bringing the world of men in line with the universe of machine.[1]

The makers of our Federal Constitution constructed a government as they would have constructed an orrery,[2] – to display the laws of nature. Politics in their thought was a variety of mechanics.[3]

Though the legislative . . . be the *supreme* power in every commonwealth; yet . . . it is *not*, nor can possibly be absolutely *arbitrary* over the lives and fortunes of the people. [For just as] no body can transfer to another more power than he has in himself; and no body has an absolute arbitrary power over himself, or over any other, to destroy his own life, or take away the life or property of another . . . but only so much as the law of nature gave him for the preservation of himself and the rest of mankind . . . so [also] the legislative can have no more than this. Their power . . . is limited to the *public good* of the society [having] no other end but preservation, and therefore can never have a right to destroy, enslave, or designedly to impoverish the subjects. . . Thus the law of nature stands as an eternal rule to all men, *legislators* as well as others.[4]

When examining the Constitution of the United States, it is very difficult to limit the scope of examination to only one or two areas. There are literally hundreds of topics and concepts embodied in this truly unique and revolu-

---

[1] Christianson, *In the Presence of the Creator; Isaac Newton and His Times* (1984) p. 337.
[2] An apparatus for representing the planets in the solar system and their orbits, named after the Earl of Orrery (1676-1731) for whom it was first constructed.
[3] Woodrow Wilson, "The New Freedom" (1912) a campaign pamphlet.
[4] John Locke, *Two Treatises* (1690) section 135 (emphasis in original).

tionary document.[5] With an eye, therefore, to the budding recognition and protection of the right of privacy, both explicit and implicit, by the US Constitution, it is proposed to examine more narrowly those truths which are presented here.

First and foremost, the US Constitution, ratified in 1788, was a product of the English and Scottish Enlightenments. It was intended to be a framework for government based upon the 'enlightened' notion that humans can design for themselves as 'apparatus', which, utilising human observation and understanding of nature's laws, would, as much as possible, mimic or complement those laws[6] and would have as its purpose or end the recognition and protection of the individual's inherent and natural rights pertaining to life, liberty and property/the pursuit of happiness.[7] In practical terms, this end was served in the negative rather than in the positive; i.e. government was to be *prevented from* interfering in the exercise of man's natural and inherent rights. Government was to be involved only in those activities which man could not undertake himself or in the context of his own small community. All other activities or 'exercises of rights' were to be left to his discretion, either acting alone or as a member of a group of individuals united by a purpose or common attribute, as is reflected in the Bill of Rights.

The Constitution's concept of inherent and inalienable rights was based in large part upon John Locke's vision of man in the state of nature as described in his seminal *Two Treatises of Government* (1690) of which the *Second Treatise* is the best known and most frequently cited. Locke held that, before there was any sort of formed government, man lived in nature and operated as, if you will, his own legislature, executive and judiciary in order to "*preserve his property, this is, his life, liberty and estate*, against the injuries and attempts of other men . . ." Finding that he alone was unable to adequately exercise these powers, also needing (as Aristotle, Cicero and others had contended) to live together in society with other humans for social and economic reasons, man joined others to create political society, of which its "great and chief end . . . is the preservaton of their property". Man's "*labour, in the beginning, gave [him] a right of property*" which Locke boldly de-

---

[5] General reading on the subject is voluminous. In addition to the legal casebooks and encyclopaediae, a good place to start is with the following, Bowen, *Miracle at Philadelphia* (1966); Kammen, *A Machine That Would Go of Itself* (1986); Levy & Mahoney (eds.), *The Framing and Ratification of the Constitution* (1987).

[6] "[T]he notion of a constitution as some sort of machine or engine had its origins in Newtonian science. Enlightened philosophers, such as David Hume, liked to contemplate the world with all of its components as a great machine." Kammen, *op. cit.*, p. 17. What the founding fathers meant by the law of nature was that defined by Locke, the laws which were "evident to any reasonable person" i.e. the law of right reason as descended from Ulpian. This did not involve any sort of direct divine revelation. Weinreb, *op. cit.*, p. 279.

[7] Locke's "trio" of natural rights contained the former; Francis Hutcheson's contained the latter. Both influenced Jefferson and Madison enormously.

fined, in a precursor to our concept of a right of privacy, "to mean *that property which men have in their persons as well as goods*".

> [N]atural reason . . . tells us . . . that men, being once born, have a right to their preservation, and consequently to meat and drink, and such other things as nature affords for their subsistence: [for] every man has a *property* in his own person; this no body has any right to but himself. The *labour* of his body, and the *work* of his hands, we may say, are properly his. Whatsoever then he removes out of the state that nature hath provided, and left it in [for example, cultivated land], he hath mixed his *labour* with, and joined it to something that is his own, and thereby makes it his *property*. The *labour* that was mine, removing [it] out of that common state [it was] in, hath *fixed* my *property* in [it]. [Thus, f]rom all which it is evident [through the use of man's reason], that though the things of nature are given in common, yet man, by being master of himself and *proprietor of his own person, and the actions or labour of it, had still in himself the great foundation of property . . .*[8]

This recognition and definition of property by Locke was revolutionary for at least three reasons. First, although Grotius had earlier presented a preview in his notion of acquisition of property through means of physical attachment, Locke's theory of labour-based property was the most clear and deliberate statement to date, and is considered by many as his most "influential contribution to jurisprudence".[9] Certainly, its ramifications were enormous. Even the lowliest labourer, who had been traditionally at the very bottom of the social strata beneath the gentlemen and nobles of the land-owning classes, could in theory make rightful claims to the property both within himself and that with which his labour had been mixed. And because this right to one's property was absolute (with the protection of same being the primary purpose of government, according to Locke), no person was allowed to take away or diminish one's property (e.g. via taxation) unless the owner gave his consent.

> *The supreme power cannot take from any man any part of his property without his consent.* For the preservation of property being the end of government, and that for which men enter in society . . . [for without this

---

[8] *Two Treatises*, sections 87, 88, 124, 45, 173, 25, 38, 27, 28 and 44 (emphasis added).

[9] See Tuck, *op. cit.*, p. 61, citing de Groot, *De Iure Praede* (1609) p.216, "[J]ust as the right to use [consumables] was originally acquired through a physical act of attachment, the very source . . . of the institution of private property, so . . . each [one's] private possessions [were] acquired through physical acts of attachment." *Ibid.* As Tuck states, "It was true that there was no private property in the later sense in a state of nature, [however, n]atural man was the subject of rights [and] though not strictly property rights, [they] were not categorically dissimilar." See also, Lloyd, *Introduction to Jurisprudence* (1985) p.120.

protection] they have no property at all. [And while it is] true governments cannot be supported without great charge, and it is fit every one
who enjoys his share of the protection should pay out of his estate his
proportion for the maintenance of it [,] it must be with his own consent
[for without said consent, he who levies taxes] thereby invades the fundamental law of property, and subverts the end of government.[10]

The attractiveness of this theory to colonists eking out a new life in the fertile
soil of the American wilderness, so far away from the taxing, dominating and
class-conscious motherland, was obvious.

A second important ramification of Locke's labour-based theory of property was the implicit and explicit recognition of man having "property in himself". Locke enunciated this in several key sections, such as the two below.

Section 44. From all which it is evident, that though the things of nature
are given in common, yet man, by *being master of himself and proprie-
tor of his own person, and the actions or labour of it, had still in himself
the great foundation of property.* . .

Section 27. Though the earth, and all inferior creatures, be common to
all men, yet *every man has a property in his own person; this no body
has any right to but himself.* . . (emphasis added).

Furthermore, the property man has in himself formed the basis for Locke's
entire labour-based theory. Equally as important, Locke made clear that this
property in one's self (just as with personal or real property) could only be
given up by the consent of the owner.

Section 22. The natural liberty of man is to be free from any superior
power on earth, and not to be under the will or legislative authority of
man, but to have only the law of nature for his rule. The liberty of man,
in society, is to be under no other legislative power, *but that established,
by consent, in the common-wealth; nor under the dominion of any will,
or restraint of any law, but what that legislative shall enact, according
to the trust put in it.* . . (emphasis added).

Yet even the owner of himself could not consent to giving away that which
was necessary for the preservation of that property in himself (i.e. his life or
liberty).

Section 23. *This freedom from absolute, arbitrary power, is so necessary to, and closely joined with a man's preservation, that he cannot*

---

[10] *Two Treatises*, section 11.

part with it... for a man, not having power over his own life, cannot, by compact, or his own consent, enslave himself to any one, nor put himself under the absolute, arbitrary power of another, to take away his life, when he pleases. *No body can give more power than he has in himself; and he that cannot take away his own life, cannot give another power over it* (emphasis added).

Locke is saying that man cannot alienate those things which essentially give him his life, his being, his *personhood*. The natural law seeks the preservation of man; man cannot relinquish those elements of his own preservation. And, as will be seen, it would be these fundamental and inalienable rights of life, liberty and property (recalling Locke's larger definition) which would serve as the limit to the scope of legislative authority and would form the basis for the explicit enunciation of such limits in the American Bill of Rights.

Last, a third ramification of Locke's labour-based theory of property was, as a legacy of the Roman jurisconsults, his presentation of reason as that innate attribute of nature which man utilised in order to deduce the laws of nature around him. By this point in time, as was mentioned in the last section, reason, or *right reason*, as it was commonly called, was cleanly divorced from any divine revelation which so dominated the conception put forth by Aquinas and the medieval canonists. By the 17th century, Locke's understanding of reason and natural law was the logical end result of that which was initiated by Ulpian and handed down by the Medieval glossators to the Age of Enlightenment. Though Locke ultimately recognised the existence of an "omnipotent, and infinitely wise maker", reason was a product of man's own nature, innate and immutable.

Section 6. The state of nature has a *law of nature* to govern it, *which obliges every one: and reason, which is that law, teaches all mankind, who will but consult it,* that being all equal and independent, *no one ought to harm another in his life, health, liberty or possessions:* [for among men,] being furnished with like faculties, sharing all in one community of nature, there cannot be supposed any such subordination among us, that may authorise us to destroy one another, as if we were made for one another's uses... Every one, as he is bound to preserve himself, and not to quit his station wilfully, so *by the like reason*, when his own preservation comes not in competition, ought he, as much as he can, to *preserve the rest of mankind*, and may not, unless it be to do justice on an offender, take away, or impair the life, or what tends to the preservation of the life, the liberty, health, limbs, or goods of another (emphasis added).

Government was instituted to protect the "life, liberty, and property" of those against whom men, who would not use reason, would trespass, and also protect those who were not yet able to utilise their reason.

Section 63. The freedom then of man, and liberty of acting according to his own will, is grounded on his having reason, which is able to instruct him in that law he is to govern himself by, and make him know how far he is left to the freedom of his own will. To turn him loose to an unrestrained liberty, before he has reason to guide him, is not the allowing him the privilege of his nature to be free; but to thrust him out amongst brutes. . .

Section 124 . . . . for though the law of nature be plain and intelligible to all rational creatures; yet men being biased by their interest, as well as ignorant for want of study of it, are not apt to allow of it as a law binding to them. . .

In practical terms, therefore, government was instituted to protect those property interests of the community who formed the government. And while each member of the community had to give up his individual powers of self-governing, Locke held that there were strict limits upon the power which could be transferred to the government, just as there had been limits to what man could give up in the state of nature. Section 135 elaborates upon this very important point and thereby establishes the 'touchstone' of Locke's natural law conception and the limits adopted by the drafters of the American constitution.

Though the legislative . . . be the supreme power in every commonwealth; yet . . . *It is not, nor can possibly be absolutely arbitrary over the lives and fortunes of the people*; for it being but the joint power of every member of the society . . . it can be no more than those persons had in a state of nature before they entered into society, and gave up to the community; for no body can transfer to another more power than he has in himself; and no body has absolute arbitrary power over himself, or over any other, to destroy his own life, or take away the life or property of another . . . so . . . the legislative can have no more power than this. *Their power, in the utmost bounds of it, is limited to the public good of society.* It is a power, that hath no other end but preservation, and therefore can never have a right to destroy, enslave, or designedly to impoverish the subjects. *The obligations of the law of nature cease not in society, but only . . . have by human laws known penalties annexed to them, to inforce their observations. Thus the law of nature stands as an eternal rule to all men, legislators as well as others . . . the fundamental law of nature being the preservation of mankind, no human sanction can be good, or valid against it* (emphasis added).

Not only are there natural law limits, Locke held, on the activities of the legislature, but there are various procedural due process requirements by which the legislature must abide. (Sections 136-142.)

By placing limits on the scope of legislative authority and establishing the way in which legislatures must operate in order to avoid capricious and arbitrary law-making and enforcement, Locke clearly rejected the traditional notion of legislative sovereignty so espoused by, among others, Blackstone: "The legislature, being in truth the sovereign power, is always equal, always of absolute authority; it acknowledges no superior on earth. . . It can, in short, do everything that is not [physically] impossible."[11] No judiciary, held Blackstone, could question or invalidate a properly promulgated law of the legislature; the power and the scope of Parliament was so great that there was "no power in the ordinary forms of the constitution that is vested with authority to control it" and, in his view, setting the judiciary above or over the legislature would be "subversive to all government".[12] Having finally broken the yoke of the royal prerogative, the English view of the absolutely sovereign legislative authority of Parliament was understandable. "[T]he Parliament men are not other than ourselves, and therefore we cannot desert them, except we desert ourselves."[13] The danger of tyranny had come from the monarch, and not from the people: "Kings seduced may injure the commonwealth, but that Parliaments cannot."[14] Reflecting the conflict between Ulpian's view of the people's transfer of authority as total and irrevocable, and Marsilius, who maintained it was not, Locke, adopting the latter's view, differed from the accepted English notion of the day.

> That so infallible a body should be subject to recall or rebuke by those who chose it was unthinkable. Though Parliament might properly withstand the king whom it, acting for the people, had created, the people had no similar right in relation to Parliament because the people and Parliament were identical. The people's act in conferring power on their representatives was one which "once pass'd they cannot revoke". Moreover the power they conferred was total: "The people," according to one of the most ardent Parliamentary spokesmen, "have reserved no power in themselves from themselves in Parliament."[15]

Locke understood that a Parliament unchecked posed as great a danger to the population, especially the minority segments of that population, as did a tyrannical king. But who, or what body, was to determine if the legislature had indeed acted outside of the scope of its authority? As one can imagine, disagreement about the notion of review of legislative activity by a non-legisla-

---

11 Blackstone, *Commentaries*, I, 63, 117 (1765-1769).
12 Blackstone, *op. cit.*, Introduction to Section III.
13 "The Vindication of the Parliament and their Proceedings" (1642) p. 7 (pamphlet).
14 "Reasons why this Kingdom ought to adhere to the Parliament" (1642) p. 7 (pamphlet).
15 Morgan, *Inventing the People: The Rise of Popular Sovereignty in England and America* (1988) pp. 64-65, citing "The Vindication of the Professors and Profession of the Law" (1646) pp. 88-89 (pamphlet).

tive body has been raging since the time of the debates surrounding the enactment and ratification of the US Constitution.[16] The notion of *judicial review* has, and continues to be, a thorny issue. Two of the most important influences upon the Founding Fathers disagreed: Locke was against judicial review (favouring instead a legislative body chosen for such review); and Montesquieu, whose seminal work was *The Spirit of the Laws*, argued in favour of it. More importantly, the Framers themselves disagreed. Supporting those who would argue that the notion of judicial review was intrinsic to the successful workings of the Constitution was Alexander Hamilton. It was in his famous *Federalist no. 78* in which he claimed that "the courts of justice are to be considered as the *bulwarks of a limited Constitution* against legislative encroachments. . . as faithful guardians of the Constitution".[17] Though Hamilton submitted that "the power of the people is superior to both" the legislative and judicial branches, he maintained that it was the courts' "duty . . . to *declare all acts contrary to the manifest tenor of the Constitution void*".[18] Opposing this view was James Madison, who, sharing the concern of many who believed that the power of the legislature would be diluted, submitted that there were great dangers in allowing for judicial review. First, the judiciary would show the effect of their own partisan political views in their deliberations. Second, they would "misconstrue the limits prescribed for the legislative and executive departments . . . " And, finally, "the decisions [of a court] on constitutional questions, whether rightly or erroneously formed, [would not have] any effect in varying the practice" of the legislative or executive branches.[19] Madison, reflecting Locke, held that, in lieu of judicial review, the legislative branch ought to be made up of two separate parts, operated "by different modes of election and different principles of actions" and furthermore held in check by the veto power of the executive.[20] By distributing the power of the legislature among several parts, over which the weaker executive has the power of the veto, Madison aimed to prevent a tyranny of the majority which would infringe upon the fundamental rights of the people. In addition, Madison believed that the pluralistic society of the United States itself, "broken into so many parts, interests and classes of citizens" would guarantee that the "rights of the individuals, or of the minority, will be in little danger from interested

---

[16] There is still disagreement today as to which side dominated in the time surrounding the enactment of the Constitution. While Archibold Cox maintains that "[m]any of the Framers . . . took it for granted that the courts would void unconstitutional acts of Congress," Professor Forest McDonald submits that "the notion that the judges should be so independent as to have power to overrule juries or to pass upon the constitutionality of laws enacted by legislative bodies was alien to American theory and practice." See Cox, *The Court and the Constitution* (1987) p. 55 and McDonald, *op. cit.*, p. 85.

[17] Federalist no. 78, in *The Federalist* (1961) p. 526 (emphasis added).

[18] *Ibid.*, p. 524 (emphasis added).

[19] Federalist no. 50 in *The Federalist* (1961) pp. 344-46.

[20] Federalist no. 51 in *The Federalist* (1961) p. 350.

combinations of the majority".[21]

Both, interestingly, based their respective premises upon the influential writing of Montesquieu, *The Spirit of the Laws* (1748), which had, in turn, been inspired directly by Locke. In it, Montesquieu expressed his recurring theme that power divided was the best guarantee that power would be exercised fairly, for the greatest benefit, and would also serve to avoid tyranny.

> When the legislative and executive powers are united in the same person or in the same body of magistrates, there can be no liberty; because apprehensions may arise, lest the same monarch or senate should enact tyrannical laws, to execute them in a tyrannical manner. Again, there is no liberty, if the judiciary power be not separated from the legislative and executive. Were it joined with the legislative, the life and liberty of the subject would be exposed to arbitrary control; for the judge would then be the legislator. Were it joined to the executive power, the judge might behave with violence and oppression.[22]

Unlike Locke, Montesquieu clearly enunciated the need for an independent judiciary which would lean heavily upon the wisdom of the citizen jury. The jury would come from the community, and, as quickly as its job was completed, melt back into that community.[23]

Judicial review has been touted as a uniquely American phenomenon, yet its development and exercise came about slowly, and it has always been subject to controversy.

> From 1789 until 1869 the Court invalidated only six acts of Congress. Between 1870 and 1873 it swiftly held four acts to be unconstitutional; but after 1890 the procedure began to be utilised far more frequently. Thereafter critics of the Supreme Court made "usurpation of power" a veritable cliché in public discourse; and the phrase remains a standard weapon in the arsenal of those who would attack the Court.[24]

The supporters of judicial review have typically relied upon some variant of Montesquieu's notion, while the opponents of judicial review have, for the most part, "been politically motivated. Jeffersonians attacked the Marshall Court; Whigs and Republicans attacked the the Taney Court; labour advo-

---

[21] *Ibid.*, p. 350. A fascinating volume which discusses the conflict between Madison and Hamilton over the issue of judicial review is Burt, *The Constitution in Conflict* (1992).

[22] Montesquieu, *The Spirit of the Laws XI* (1748) p. 6.

[23] *Ibid.*, p. 6. See generally the discussion in Professor Edward Erler's article "The Constitution and the Separation of Powers" in *The Framing and Ratification of the Constitution* (1987) pp. 151-166.

[24] Kammen, *op. cit.*, p. 31. Writing on the topic of judicial review has been voluminous. See generally Ely, *Democracy and Distrust; A Theory of Judicial Review* (1980).

cates attacked the Fuller, White and Taft Courts; and conservatives attacked the Warren Court".[25] This last Court was criticised for its expansion of civil rights to be protected under the Constitution, either by expanding the scope of those rights already recognised (e.g. the right to a court-appointed attorney even if a defendant could not afford one; the requirement of the recitation of "*Miranda* rights" etc.) or by recognising rights which were not explicitly provided for within the Bill of Rights, including, of course, the right of privacy.

Jefferson had been adamant about the need for an explicit bill of rights, and certainly this was consistent with Locke's thesis concerning the need to preserve certain rights for the pursuance of one's life, liberty and property, and to prevent the infringement of those rights by government. "The best argument in favour of a bill of rights, [Jefferson] told Madison, was 'the legal check which it puts into the hands of the judiciary.' To Madison's charge that it was inadequate to list some rights for fear others would be left out, Jefferson countered: 'Half a loaf is better than no bread.'"[26] It would be Madison who would doggedly pursue that "half a loaf" and succeed in achieving the ratification of the Bill of Rights.[27]

Interestingly, especially for our purposes here, Jefferson's portrayal of a bill of rights as "half a loaf" and his adamance that a recitation of rights be explicitly propounded by Madison in the new Constitution, can lead one to either of two interpretations of the nature of the rights intended to be recognised and protected under the Constitution. "Half a loaf" indicated that there were many other, unexpressed rights against which government could not infringe. On the other hand, Jefferson's insistence and Madison's choice of particular rights for expression could be interpreted to indicate that only those rights were *worth* expressing, as they were most fundamental to man's pursuance of "life, liberty and property". In a letter to Madison, Jefferson had argued strongly against "the omission of a bill of rights providing clearly and without the aid of sophism" for the civil liberties the population ought to enjoy. "[A] bill of rights is what the people are entitled to against every government on earth, general or particular, and what no just government should refuse or rest on inference."[28] Whether the Bill of Rights was a complete expression of *all* the rights intended to be preserved as against governmental intrusion, or whether there were other rights which were preserved, but not enunciated, has long been an issue of contention, especially more recently surrounding those decisions rendered by the Warren Court, and concerning

---

[25] Kammen, *op. cit.*, p. 33.

[26] Rutland, "Framing and Ratifying the First Ten Amendments" in *The Framing and Ratification of the Constitution* (1987) p. 309.

[27] See *ibid.*, pp. 309-316. Also generally Rutland, *James Madison: The Founding Father* (1987) if only because it is fascinating reading.

[28] Letter of Thomas Jefferson to James Madison, 20 December 1787 in Hutchinson (ed.), *The Papers of James Madison* (1962) pp. 10, 336-337.

the right of privacy.

Is privacy one of those rights intended to be recognised and protected by the Constitution of the United States for the preservation of life, liberty and property? Is it implicit in the "half a loaf" already recognised, or was it specifically not intended to be recognised and hence was not explicitly included. This is the crux of the issue here. Based upon Locke's natural law theory which recognises inalienable rights to preserve man's life, liberty and property (with the understanding that property means personal, real and that which one has in oneself), one cannot logically deny the existence and need to recognise a right of privacy. But did the Founding Fathers do so, either explicitly or implicitly? Was privacy contained in the "half a loaf"? And if it were not, was it still a right which the Founding Fathers would have wanted to recognise and protect, but could not specifically enumerate, as reflected in the Ninth Amendment? ("The enumeration in the Constitution, of certain rights, shall not construed to deny or disparage others retained by the people.") And even if the Founding Fathers had not had privacy in mind at all, couldn't 'the people', acknowledging that the needs of a community change with time and what is necessary for the preservation of life, liberty and property changes with it, have since then decreed, or the Court recognised, a right of privacy under the Ninth Amendment? Before proceeding further, let us first examine some of the social conventions existing at the time of the Founding Fathers concerning those areas of life which would fall under a right of privacy conception.

In various colonies/states, sumptuary laws were often enacted to regulate and maintain a certain standard of personal morality. Then, as now, there was a conflict between, in simple terms, those who would advocate a libertarian lifestyle with extremely limited local government, and those who would support the promulgation of these pieces of legislation aimed at curbing so-called 'victimless' crimes.[29] In colonial times, this legislation "related only to restrictions against luxury or extravagant expenditures on clothing, jewellery, and food, which were deemed to be socially harmful. The term later came to designate laws comprehended under the police power, [and dealt with] gambling, alcoholic beverages, prostitution, and the like".[30] Professor McDonald's discussion of sumptuary laws is worthy of further quotation.

> [Although] none of the commentators doubted the justice or prudence of appropriate legislation . . . there was some disagreement over the efficacy of sumtuary laws in the stricter sense. Sir Edward Coke tended to favour them. Blackstone remarked that enthusiasm for them came

---

[29] In the 20th century, a civilised debate on the issue was conducted between Professor Hart and Lord Devlin. See Hart, *Law, Liberty, and Morality* (1963) and Devlin, *The Enforcement of Morals* (1965).

[30] McDonald, *op. cit.*, p. 16.

and went, and expressed his own opinion that they were bad unless they accomplished some useful general purpose ... In America, every colony exercised the power of passing sumptuary legislation, though in their extreme forms such laws were uncommon except in New England and though in all their forms their applicability varied with the social status of the individual. The point here is that in any of its forms, *sumptuary legislation restricted private rights to property, for it required persons to buy some things and prohibited them from buying or selling other things, whether they wanted them or not.*[31]

The New England colonies/states maintained more and stricter sumptuary laws, reflecting the Calvinist background of many of its prominent citizens, and the prevailing notion that the possession of virtue, public and private, was crucial to the ultimate success of government.

The Massachusetts Bill of Rights, for instance, declared that a "constant adherence" to principles of "piety, justice, moderation, temperance, industry and frugality, are absolutely necessary to preserve the advantages of liberty"; and that the people had "the right to require of their lawgivers and magistrates an exact and constant observance" of those principles "in the formation and execution of the laws."[32]

In many writings by prominent citizens of the time, virtuousness was not only considered indispensable to the operation of good government, it was "the directing force of a republic".[33] The references to virtue, however, did not connote virtue in the biblical or deistic sense. Rather, as defined and understood by the Founding Fathers, virtue was a secular concept. Thus while Montesquieu defined virtue as the preference of the common good over one's private interest, echoing Aquinas in his definition of the proper purpose or end of government, Montesquieu's intent was purely mundane: "Virtue in a republic is a very simple matter – it is love of republic."[34] Just as he had "suggested the possibility of a purely secular state . . . authority would come, now, not from religious or regal office but from republic virtue, the disinterested dedication of that modern Cincinnatus, George Washington".[35]

---

[31] *Ibid.*, p. 16 (emphasis added).

[32] *Ibid.*, p. 90, citing Commager (ed.), *Documents of American History* (7th edn, 1963), p. 109.

[33] Wills, *Explaining America: The Federalist* (1981) p. 187, citing Montesquieu, *op. cit.*, at III, 4.3-8. Benjamin Franklin, "[l]ike a scientist undertaking an experiment in a laboratory. . .worked out a scheme of desirable virtues", Temperance, Silence, Order, Resolution, Frugality, Industry, Sincerity, Justice, Moderation, Cleanliness, Tranquillity, Chastity and Humility. It is questionable, however, whether Franklin abided by these himself. Van Doren, *Benjamin Franklin* (1938) pp. 88-90.

[34] Wills, *ibid.*, p. 185.

This is not to say that religious beliefs and organised congregations did not play a role in the birth of the American nation. Rather their effect was acknowledged more by what was avoided or negated instead of what was sought out, as exemplified most clearly in the Establishment Clause of the First Amendment. ("Congress shall make no law respecting an establishment of religion, or prohibiting the free exercise thereof. . . ") First and foremost, as proud products of the Enlightenment Era, the Founding Fathers purposely avoided official reliance upon religious institutions and icons of faith which had dominated the world of politics and government up to that point.

> At the time of the Revolution most of the founding fathers had not put much emotional stock in religion, even when they were regular church-goers. As enlightened gentlemen, they abhorred "that gloomy superstition disseminated by ignorant illiberal preachers" and looked forward to the day when "the phantom of darkness will be dispelled by the rays of science, and the bright charms of rising civilisation". At best, most of the revolutionary gentry only passively believed in organised Christianity and, at worst, privately scorned and ridiculed it. Jefferson[for example] hated orthodox clergymen, and he repeatedly denounced the "priestcraft" for having converted Christianity into "an engine for enslaving mankind . . . into a mere contrivance to filch wealth and power to themselves."[36]

Secondly, the citizens of the new country themselves were overwhelmingly members of various Protestant congregations which, though dissected and separate, all promoted the idea, echoing Locke, that each individual was "considered as possessing in himself or herself an original right to believe and speak as their own conscience, between themselves and God, may determine".[37] This notion, first presented by Martin Luther, of "every man a priest" coupled with the maxim that "God helps those who help themselves" and the fact that most new citizens were fleeing religious persecution in their motherlands, was the perfect religious complement to Locke's labour-based definition of property.[38] Taken together, these conceptions served to create an atmosphere in the new nation which promoted the righteousness of personal gain and capitalism[39] and thus further focused upon the rights and interests of the individual, and the necessary prerequisite of a right to act and think 'privately' as

---

[35] *Ibid.*, p. 186. Cincinnatus was a 5th century Roman patriot who was said to have left his farm to lead the Roman army to victory and then, rather than exploiting his newly earned recognition and power, forfeited his office and returned to his farm. See Wills, *Cincinnatus; George Washington and the Enlightenment* (1984) for a fascinating comparison written about these two equally legendary heroes.

[36] Wood, *The Radicalism of the American Revolution* (1992) p. 330, citing Knoles, "The Religious Ideas of Thomas Jefferson" 30 Miss. Valley Hist. Rev. (1943-44) 194.

[37] Wood, *op. cit.*, p. 332.

[38] See, for example, Kelly, *A Short History of Western Legal Theory* (1992) p. 168.

opposed to emphasis upon the collective good of the state. Though Montesquieu's virtuous leader must maintain a "love of republic" and emphasize the common good in his role as a government lawmaker, his personal life was strictly that. In the end, like Prohibition in the 1920s and 30s, the sumptuary laws of the colonial era were largely ignored and unenforced. The power and interests of the individual were simply too overwhelming and the notion that each person ought to be able to privately determine the course of his life, liberty and property were too ingrained in the culture of the new nation.

The individualistic culture of the new nation was due not only to the absorption of Locke's secular natural law theory, the impact of the Protestant Reformation, and the immigrants' independence-seeking mindset, but also in large part to the interwoven influence of other English and Scottish Enlightenment scholars upon the intelligentsia of the day. The *right reason* of Locke, with which every man was endowed, would be referred to also as the *common sense or communal sense* in the colonial era. Just as with Locke's view, it was *common sense* which allowed each human to perceive and absorb the self-evident truths of the "laws of Nature and of Nature's God" to quote directly from Jefferson's Declaration of Independence. True to the Enlightenment ethos, his concept of reason was based upon the presumption that the world, the universe, and indeed man's own nature were ordered systems which could be observed and, by means of testing and experimentation, understood. And just as nature had imprinted its laws upon physical entities to be reflected in the studies of medicine, astronomy, taxonomy and physics, nature had effected laws by which man ought to govern himself, if only man would allow himself to be open to observing those laws, without any preconceived notions. All men were endowed with the capability or common sense to observe the self-evident truths of nature, and in this way, all men were equal. Indeed, Jefferson believed that the man with the simpler mind was better able to observe and understand nature's laws than the 'educated' man. The latter, he submitted, were too "fond, by a kind of anticipation, to discover [Nature's] secrets. Instead of a slow and gradual ascent in the scale of natural causes, by a just and copious induction, they would shorten the work".[40] In line with the well-known maxim: "Book smart and common sense dumb" Jefferson would maintain: "State a moral case to a ploughman and professor. The former will decide it as

---

[39] Kelly, *op. cit.*, p. 168. "[T]he general psychological and social connection between the ethos of Protestantism, with its emphasis on the individual's direct relationship and answerability to God, and the rise of modern capitalist enterprise, is thought to be well established; the link, roughly speaking, is supposed to lie in the idea that God's favour, the outward mark of his 'election' of an individual for salvation, will be visible in material prosperity here on earth; this transmutes subtly into the idea that God's favour attaches to whatever efforts the individual will make to bring that prosperity about." *Ibid.*, p. 168

[40] Wills, *op. cit.*, p. 187, citing Lipscomb & Bergh, *The Writings of Thomas Jefferson* (1903) pp. 13, 224.

well and often better than the latter, because he has not been led astray by artificial rules."[41] A moral sense was interwoven with common sense.

> It would have been inconsistent in creation to have formed man for the social state, and not to have provided virtue and wisdom enough to manage the concerns of society.

> Morals were too essential to the happiness of man to be risked on uncertain combinations of the head. She [Nature] laid their foundations therefore in sentiment . . . [and t]hat she gave to all, as necessary to all.[42]

Thomas Reid, one of the Scottish Enlightenment philosophers who so influenced Jefferson, stated: "The knowledge that is necessary to all must be attained by all . . . It may therefore be expected, from the analogy of nature, that such a knowledge of morals as is necessary to all men should be had by means more suited to the abilities of all men." And not require special skills or uncommon intelligence. The "means more suited" for possessing "a knowledge of morals" was this *moral sense* innate in all men; the same common sense utilised to grasp those "self-evident truths" to which Jefferson referred.[43] Echoing Reid and others, Jefferson, representing the widely accepted thought of the fathers of American constitutionalism, would maintain time and time again that this ability to comprehend nature's laws of right and wrong, in order to apply them to government, was innate.

> Man was destined for society. His morality, therefore, was to be formed to this object. He was endowed with a sense of right and wrong merely relative to this. This sense is as much a part of his nature as the sense of hearing, seeing, feeling; it is the true foundation of morality, and not [other things] as fanciful writers have imagined.[44]

And again:

> [I do not believe] that justice is founded in contract solely, [not resulting] from the construction of man. I believe, on the contrary, that it is instinct, and innate, that the moral sense is as much a part of our constitution as that of feeling, seeing, or hearing . . .[45]

Truly, justice could not have been based "in contract solely" nor merely in any social compact between governed or the governors, nor merely because it was

---

[41] Boyd, *The Papers of Thomas Jefferson* (1974) pp. 6, 258.
[42] *Ibid.*, pp. 10, 450.
[43] Reid, *Essays 2* (1785-1788) pp. 726-727.
[44] Boyd, *op. cit.*, pp. 12, 15.
[45] Cappon, *The Adams-Jefferson Letters* (1959) pp. 2, 492.

legislated. For, just as envisioned by Locke, the colonists found themselves in a "state of nature" once they had thrown off the structure of British government in declaring their independence in the late 18th century. "[T]o claim rights on the basis of natural law was to go outside the forms and norms of English law and to squint toward independence." This was something which the loyalist representatives were reluctant to do. Yet, finally:

> [w]hen the decision for independence was made, all claims to rights that were based upon royal grants, the common law, and the British constitution became theoretically irrelevant. Independence – the very existence of the United States – was unequivocally justified in the Declaration itself by an appeal to "the Laws of Nature and Nature's God". Quite clearly, it was declared that the rights of Americans arose from the same source.[46]

The colonists did not possess inalienable rights because of a compact between royalty and subject, as with the Magna Carta, because there was no royalty. Nor was there a social compact among citizens, a la Rousseau. Rather, the inalienable rights of the citizenry were reflected in the "construction of man" himself, as stated by Jefferson, and were merely placed on paper in the Constitution and the Bill of Rights. Each person was possessed of an innate moral and common sense, descended from Ulpian's conception of an innate instinct via Locke's notion of innate right reason, to be utilised to maintain society and operate a government for the necessary preservation of man's life, liberty, and property. Locke stated:

> [Since] God has made . . . man in a state wherein they cannot subsist without society and has given them judgment to discern what is capable of preserving that society, can [man] but conclude that [man] is obliged and that God requires [man] to follow those rules which conduce to the preserving of society?[47]

> God having made Man such a Creature, that, in [God's] own Judgment, it was not good for him to be alone, put him under strong Obligations of Necessity, Convenience, and Inclination to drive him into Society, as well as fitted him with Understanding and Language to continue and enjoy it.[48]

Accordingly, men are free "to order their Actions, and dispose of their Pos-

---

[46] McDonald, *op. cit.*, pp. 58-59.
[47] Tully, *A Discourse on Property: John Locke and His Adversaries* (1980) p. 48.
[48] *Two Treatises* at section 77.

sessions, and Persons as they think fit, within the bounds of the Law of Nature, *without asking leave, or depending upon the Will of any other Man*".[49] And as discussed previously, government is also limited by the law of nature, for, *per* Locke, no positive law can be valid unless it "be conformable to the Law of Nature"[50] and government cannot take away from man that, which by nature's law, he is unable to part with himself (i.e. his life, and those things which promote and maintain the preservation of his life – liberty and property).[51]

As can be surmised from all of the above, a right of privacy, though not explicitly listed in the Bill of Rights of the US Constitution, was most definitely an integral and basic part of its underlying theory and the norms and thought of the day. All of the factors contributing to the formation and eventual realisation of the constitutional democracy created by the Founding Fathers in the late 18th century [i.e. the Protestant Reformation, The English and Scottish Enlightenments, the secular Natural Law theory of John Locke (ultimately derived from the Roman jurisconsults and Ulpian)] and the independent, individualistic mindset of the colonial-era immigrants (most notably the large body of Scots-Irish from North-eastern Ireland) seeking freedom in the new land, point to a common element: the drive of man to shape and control his own life. Surely this is the essence of privacy: the defining of one's own person and the path of one's life, without intrusion or coercion from an outside source. As will be elaborated upon in Part Three, the framers of the Bill of Rights, most notably James Madison and Thomas Jefferson, referred to these rights collectively as pertaining to the freedom of conscience. In addition, those rights listed were not, by the clear admission of Madison and Jefferson, the exhaustive list of rights to be recognised and protected by the US Constitution, and, for that reason, the Ninth Amendment was included. Clearly, privacy was an integral part, indeed a touchstone, of the total collection of rights to be protected.

In summary, in the American Declaration of Independence and Constitution, we have reached the culmination of the development of the secular natural law, the seeds of which were first planted by Ulpian and the Roman jurisconsults. Reason, or the innate common sense possessed by all people, and of which all people are equally endowed, is the vehicle through which Nature's laws for mankind and society are observed and understood, to in turn be applied to preserve that which man himself cannot by Nature's law alienate: his life, and those things which preserve and maintain his life – his liberty and property. And, echoing Locke, the most integral property to preserving man's life, is the property he, and each person, has in himself.

---

[49] *Ibid.*, at section 4 (emphasis added).
[50] *Ibid.*, at section 135.
[51] *Ibid.*, at section 23.

CHAPTER 6

The Resurrection of Thomistic Natural Law: The 1937 Irish Constitution

As long as I live anyhow, it will always be a matter of great pride for me that I was the head of the Government that was able to get a majority of the Irish people to support and pass that Constitution.[1]

I do not think that a further Constitution – an unwritten one – was intended by the People of Éire to exist side by side with this written Constitution or even – perhaps it would be more correct to say – outside and beyond the present Constitution.[2]

Nearly 400 years after Shakespeare's Macmorris asked the question "What is my nation?"[3], the answer would become clear. It would be de Valera who would provide that answer by means of a Constitution drafted by him and enacted in 1937. More than any other figure in modern Irish history, Eamon de Valera defined the concept of Irish statehood and shaped the nation of Ireland as it exists today.[4]

Ironically, de Valera's thoughts and underlying legal philosophy upon which the 1937 Constitution was based are less well-known than those of Jefferson and Madison regarding the US Constitution, primarily because his goal in drafting a constitution was very different from theirs. Though dead for 150 years, the US statesmen had disseminated a virtual cornucopia of letters, pamphlets, articles and documents concerning their theories of law and government as justification for the colonist's revolution and formation of a new government, from which their intentions and purposes can be easily discerned. De Valera, though essentially rebelling against the same country, was making a far different statement: his 1937 constitution would serve as the "ultimate vindication of de Valera's brand of Irish republicanism"[5] and the crowning rebuke to hundreds of years of subjugation and denigration of the Irish cul-

---

[1] Eamon de Valera, as quoted in *The Irish Press*, 13 October 1937.
[2] *State v. Lennon* [1940] I.R. 136 at 179 (Johnson J).
[3] *Henry V*, Act 3, Scene 2, spoken by the Irish Captain Macmorris when questioned about the Irish nation's loyalty to the English king.
[4] Tuathaigh, "The Irish Nation-State in the Constitution" in *De Valera's Constitution and Ours* (1988) pp. 46-59 provides a concise discussion.
[5] Fanning, "Mr de Valera Drafts a Constitution" in *ibid.*, p. 34.

ture and people at the hands of the English hierarchy and government.[6] Hence, the elevation of Irish as the national language,[7] the effective recognition of Roman Catholicism as an integral part of Irish republican statehood,[8] the deletion of the Oath of Allegiance and any mention of the King or Governor-General, and the explicit establishment of sovereignty over the entire island in Articles 2 and 3, were all intended to declare Ireland's final and complete separation from all things colonially British, and its resurrection, if you will, as the State of Ireland. Typically, therefore, the focus of the scholarship concerning the Irish constitution has revolved primarily around these issues[9] and not the philosophical underpinnings or de Valera's theories pertaining to natural law and rights. We must, therefore, look at what does exist concerning de Valera's philosophical basis for the 1937 Constitution and study the Articles themselves to determine the underlying legal theories.

First, it is important to note that much has been 'borrowed' from the US Constitution and various Anglo-American notions of justice; several articles of the 1937 Constitution clearly reflect these origins: the separation of pow-

---

[6] See, for example, Gay, *The Cultivation of Hatred* (1993) p. 81, in which the author describes how "English cartoonists had caricatured the Irish as alcoholic, childlike, relatively innocuous Paddy" or "as a ferocious Frankenstein's monster, a gorilla-like . . . masked Caliban wielding a wicked knife" from the late 18th century onward. See generally Foster, *Modern Ireland, 1600-1972* (1988) for an outstanding overview of modern Irish history and interaction with the British empire.

[7] Article 8. de Valera's mastery of Irish later in life "had transformed [his] sense of Irishness . . . he sought the future by rekindling an ancient fire". Edwards, *Eamon de Valera* (1987) p. 39.

[8] Article 44. De Valera "was to admit later that Article 44 gave him more anxiety than anything else" in the drafting of the Constitution. Originally, Article 44.1.2°. recognised a "special position" of the Church "as the guardian of the Faith professed" by most citizens, and also recognised the other religious denominations to, what seemed to be, the satisfaction of all of the clergy at that time. In fact, the Church had sought even stronger language recognising its role, but de Valera demurred. Chubb, *The Politics of the Irish Constitution* (1991) pp. 28-29, 33-34.

[9] The two most recent biographies of de Valera deal with the time surrounding the drafting and enactment of the 1937 Constitution in very brief passages, and focus primarily upon its relationship to the Church, and the sovereignty of Northern Ireland. In every biography of de Valera, the major focus has been upon his activities during the civil war, his dealings with Britain during World War II and his promotion of Irish language and culture. See, for example, Coogan, *De Valera, Long Fellow, Long Shadow* (1993) pp. 486-498; Dwyer, *De Valera, The Man and the Myth* (1991) pp. 197-201. For a more specific discussion of the role of the Roman Catholic Church in the drafting of the constitution, see Nolan, "The Influence of Catholic Nationalism on the Legislature of the Irish Free State", Irish Jur. 120, 157-169 (1975); McWhinney, "The Courts and the Constitution in Catholic Ireland", 24 Tulane L. Rev. 69 (1954); McDonagh, "Philosophical-Theological Reflections on the Constitution" in *The Constitution of Ireland, 1937-1987* (1988) p. 192. This article provides a much more balanced view of de Valera's independent stand against the Church than the two articles cited immediately previous; Keogh, "Church, State and Society" in *De Valera's Constitution and Ours* (1988) p. 103 and Chubb, *op. cit.*, pp. 22-59.

ers,[10] the concept of judicial review of legislative enactments,[11] habeas corpus,[12] procedural due process[13] and various enumerated personal rights echoing those contained in the Bill of Rights.[14] That having been established, however, the differences between the two constitutions are much greater and more significant than the similarities. The Irish Constitution is first and foremost a product of the Thomistic natural law tradition. And though it is submitted that the role of the Catholic Church in the drafting of the Irish Constitution has been greatly exaggerated and oversimplified by friends and foes alike,[15] it is imperative to any balanced understanding of the natural law basis of the Irish Constitution to examine the impact that the Roman Catholic Church and its leaders did have in the drafting and enactment of the document.

Three points will be asserted. First, de Valera staunchly maintained his independence in the face of those clergy who would attempt to make the Irish Constitution a completely 'Catholic apologia'. Second, rather than viewing the 1937 Constitution as a 'Catholic Constitution', it is more accurate to view both the Irish Constitution and the Roman Catholic Church as having adopted the same *modus operandi*, centred on the natural law theory of Aquinas[16] with the 'borrowings' noted above. Third, there is a right of privacy contained explicitly and implicitly in the 1937 Constitution, but that right is different from that contained in the context of the US Constitution in both scope and applicability, due to its different philosophical origin and purpose.

It is well-known that de Valera's early life and education were largely moulded by his contacts with the Roman Catholic Church and this was re-

---

[10] See Casey, "The Judicial Power Under Irish Constitutional Law", 24 Int'l & Comp. L. Quart. (1975) 305.

[11] Article 34. See also Article 15.4.2°; Heuston, "Personal Rights under the Irish Constitution", Irish Jur 205 (1976); Quinn, "Legal Change, Natural Law and the Authority of Courts", 45 Doctrine & Life (January 1995) 97.

[12] Article 40.4.2°-6°.

[13] Article 40.4.1°.

[14] Article 40.5-6°.

[15] Several commentators have laid little emphasis on the fact that de Valera disagreed with Roman Catholic Church leaders and Fine Gael members, among others, with regards to Article 44. The latter groups had wanted a more religious, confessional bent, contending that de Valera was taking a far too secular approach. Dwyer, *op. cit.*, pp. 199-200. See also Keogh, "Church, State and Pressure Groups", 45 Doctrine & Life (January 1995) 42. Cf. Article 44.2 non-discrimination based upon religious beliefs and a non-establishment clause, among other guarantees. The Constitution of Ireland is much less overtly sectarian than, for example, that of Britain, which has an established religion and explicitly condones discrimination against Catholics and members of other religious groups. The Prince of Wales, for example, is prohibited from marrying a Catholic.

[16] After Aquinas was canonised in 1323, and proclaimed a Doctor of the Church in 1567, his natural law system was formally adopted as the form of government of the Roman Catholic Church.

flected in his personal life,[17] and, ultimately, in his drafting of the Constitution of 1937. As a student, attending only Catholic institutions, he excelled in Greek, Latin, English, French and Mathematics, achieving honours in all of these subjects at Blackrock, a college opened in 1860 outside of Dublin by the French Holy Ghost Fathers. Indeed, "Blackrock became not just an academy for him but a home, and after he married he chose to live, and ultimately to die, as near to the College as possible".[18] And when it came time to draft the 1937 Constitution, de Valera turned not only to the legal advisor of the Department of External Affairs, John Hearne, but also to John McQuaid, a Holy Ghost Father from Blackrock and a well-known Jesuit writer, Father Edward Cahill. In addition, he personally consulted with all of the leaders of the other major denominations in Ireland.[19] Yet, ultimately, it was de Valera, and de Valera alone who drafted the end product and made his stand on the controversial articles and issues involved.[20] For, contrary to commonly accepted representations, de Valera rejected the advice of many of those clergy he did seek out.

> Among those who pressed de Valera to adopt a wording [in Article 44] more fully consonant with the teaching of the Catholic Church were Cardinal Joseph MacRory, the Archbishop of Armagh, and Dr John Charles McQuaid, the President of Blackrock College, and later–from 1940 until 1972–the Archbishop of Dublin. So determined was de Valera to resist wording that would exclude all references to other churches or religions that he sent the Secretary of his Department of External Affairs, Joe Walshe, on a special mission to the Vatican to argue his case.[21]

De Valera prevailed, and though the original Article 44 strikes modern-day readers as favouring the Church's position too much, in fact, from de Valera's perspective and those of other contemporaries, it was "a compromise that denied the Catholic Church the kind of exclusive recognition it would have preferred".[22]

Perhaps the best argument against those who would maintain that the 1937 Irish Constitution is an entirely Roman Catholic document is to speculate upon what de Valera *could* have drafted. From a practical standpoint, he

---

[17] At one time, de Valera had seriously thought of becoming a priest. He remained a devout, practising Catholic until the end of his life. Coogan, *op. cit.*, p. 23.

[18] *Ibid.,* p. 23.

[19] *Ibid.*, p. 489.

[20] Fanning, *op. cit.*, p. 39, citing de Valera's newly released papers at Killiney.

[21] *Ibid.*, p. 40.

[22] *Ibid.*, p. 41. See also Keogh, *op. cit.*, pp. 43-46. "Despite [pressure from religious extremists], Ireland remained a liberal democracy, and the 1937 Constitution, framed in difficult times, did not bear the hallmark of extremist confessional influence." *Ibid.*, p. 45.

could have *established* Catholicism as the State religion of Ireland, or required an oath of loyalty to the Catholic Church as the English had done with the Anglican church. In light of the long history of penal laws and subjugation imposed upon Roman Catholics over previous centuries,[23] and the preferential treatment afforded members of the Church of Ireland, in both public and private sectors, it is feasible to imagine that de Valera would wish to 'turn the tables'. This, however, he did not do, and instead took great pains to recognise the other organised religions in Ireland, much to the chagrin, as stated earlier, of Catholic clergy and conservative leaders.

Some would argue that, even if Catholicism is not the established religion *de jure*, then it certainly is *de facto*.[24] Indeed, just as in the United States, where the vast majority of citizens profess certain beliefs, the practices of that majority will be evident in the operation of daily life in that country. In theory, because the United States has enunciated a clear separation of church and state in its first amendment, holidays such as Christmas and Easter should not be granted governmental recognition. Yet practicality dictates that Christmas be recognised as a bank and federal holiday in the United States, and all public schools close around the Easter week. Yet neither the Muslim celebration of Eid after the fasting month of Ramadan nor the sacred Jewish holiday of Yom Kippur are not afforded the same recognition, although students and workers of those religions are allowed to stay home during those times. Such preferences exist even though the society in the United States is much more pluralistic than that of Ireland. Furthermore, statistics bear out the fact that Protestants in the Republic typically enjoy a higher standard of living than the average Catholic.[25] Moreover, there are no legal restraints on the exercise of their religion.

As will be discussed more fully in chapter 7, the arguments which maintain that the strict laws concerning abortion and divorce (before November 1995) in Ireland are proof of Catholic domination are somewhat simplistic. Rather, in order to correctly understand the implication of de Valera's constitution, and its general notion of privacy, one must view them as results of the

---

[23] Presbyterians and others were often discriminated against as much as Catholics; hence, many of Ireland's first and most ardent fighters for independence were Presbyterians, and hundreds of thousands of Presbyterians emigrated to the American colonies. See for example, MacDermot, *Wolfe Tone and His Times* (1968) and Leyburn, *op. cit.*, pp. 157-183. See also generally, Foster, *op. cit.*, pp. 259-286.

[24] See, for example, Nolan, *op. cit.*, p. 157, *et seq.* Nolan, like others, incorrectly refers to the natural law aspects of the Constitution as "Catholic social teaching". Though similar, the Irish interpretation of Thomistic natural law and the Church's interpretation are two separate and distinct entities, as will be shown.

[25] "Fitzgerald, Republic's Protestants sitting pretty in top professions" in *Irish Echo*, (17-23 January 1996), p. 4. Former Taoiseach Dr Garret Fitzgerald's study of the 1991 census indicated that Protestants enjoy a higher standard of living than Catholics in the Republic of Ireland, and are proportionally better represented in 'white-collar' jobs, land and business ownership and in all top professions.

application of Thomistic natural law to Irish republican society, and not simply the imposition of Catholic doctrine. For though the two are both based
upon the same legal theory, each enunciates its own unique and distinct interpretation. Only the method used is the same; not necessarily the results.[26]

If de Valera celebrated the Catholic religion in the 1937 Constitution, he
glorified the Irish language. The goal in utilising both, however, was the same:
to establish the republican and distinctly Irish nature of the new nation and
government. Language, even more than religion, played a paramount role in
forging a new identity for Ireland.

> It is the bond that kept our people together throughout the centuries, and
> enabled them to resist all the efforts to make them English. It would be
> useful to us in that way today, when we have poured in upon us, from
> every direction, influences which are contrary to the traditional views
> and hopes of our people. The biggest thing that could be done for our
> people is to restore the language.[27]

All Irish men and women, Catholic, Protestant and non-Christian, could be
united under the banner of the Irish language and the shared history which de
Valera emphasised repeatedly in many of his speeches and which had formed,
early on, his concept of Irishness.[28] It would have been disingenuous of de
Valera to promote Catholicism as the sole unifier of Ireland, for he would
have been denigrating the memories of those Protestant republicans who fought
for Irish freedom. Language and culture served as far better common denomi-
nators in drawing together the people from two different traditions. His choice
of Douglas Hyde as first president of the Republic was a clear statement by de
Valera to this end: Hyde was a Protestant, a fluent Irish speaker, and an activ-
ist for Irish language and culture.[29] And de Valera's documentation to the

---

[26] "[Rather than viewing the Constitution as a Catholic one], it is better to view it as de
Valera's effort to grapple with the fundamental problems that faced him and to bring and
hold together the two traditions that were reflected in Ireland." Chubb, *op. cit.*, p. 39.

[27] Coogan, *op. cit.*, p. 12, citing a speech delivered by de Valera on 30 October 1955.

[28] Cf. *ibid.*, p. 12, citing Joyce, "Eamon de Valera, Bruree Man", *The Capuchin Annual*
Apart from the Irish language the child [de Valera] heard stories that caught the secret
voice of the nation. He shared the traditions of the people, their music and their songs.
By winter firesides, where crickets chirped, and where the kettle hung conawning on the
crook, he heard with pride of the gallant Sarsfield; of Emmet and Tone; of the Bruree
Feniens who fought at Kilmallock in '67, and left one of their number dead on the bullet-
swept street. He heard of the Great Famine, and of the Land War and its evictions and
clearances . . . He heard about the hurling matches and race meetings and matchmakings;
about the feats of great mowers and spadesmen, about all those things that are warp and
woof of Irish life in the countryside.

[29] Hyde was instrumental in fostering governmental requirements for instruction of the
Irish language in elementary schools. See Dunleavy & Dunleavy, *Douglas Hyde* (1991)
pp. 124-126.

Vatican of his rationale for including all religions in the original Article 44 supports the notion that de Valera did not wish the 1937 Constitution to be a 'Catholic constitution'.

> If the attempt were to be made to embody in the new Constitution the full Catholic ideal there would be an immediate outcry from the Protestant section of the population, and a bitter religious controversy might easily ensue. [Not only would the Government be charged with needlessly causing this controversy, and providing provocation for bitter-attacks on our fellow-countrymen in Belfast, it] would further be charged with having raised a new barrier to the reunion of our country, and with having recklessly caused offence to a section of our countrymen whose ancestors produced many patriots whose names are revered in many a Catholic home: Wolfe Tone, Emmet, Parnell, etc.[30]

In consulting with the heads of various denominations prior to drafting Article 44, de Valera generated enormous goodwill, and helped to "face up to the latent sectarianism and basic intolerance in sections of Irish society".[31] And though he made great gains with the minority religious groups in Ireland, his conflict with the Catholic Church leaders and conservatives remained acute. The only complaints with the final version came from those wanting it to be more strongly worded in favour of the Church.[32] De Valera, as stated before, held his ground, and ultimately, even when the Article was further secularised in 1972 by the deletion of sections 2 and 3 under part 1, the Catholic Church wholeheartedly agreed.[33]

   How then did the Catholic Church influence de Valera's drafting of the 1937 Constitution? Primarily and most importantly, it served to create the environment in which de Valera would be predisposed to choose the Thomistic natural law system and tenets over other forms of government available to him at that particular time in the early 20th century. And though de Valera maintained that there were clearly secular considerations as well,[34] the natural law aspects dominate and dictate the tenor of the document.

---

[30] Keogh, "The Irish Constitutional Revolution, An Analysis of the Making of the Constitution" in Litton (ed.), *The Constitution of Ireland 1937-1987* (1988) pp. 45-46.

[31] *Ibid.*, p. 39. See also discussion pp. 32-39.

[32] See Chubb, *op. cit.*, p. 41.

[33] Consider the words of Bishop Cathal Daly spoken at the New Ireland Forum in May 1994, "We have not sought and do not seek a Catholic State for Catholic people. We believe that the alliance of Church and State is harmful for [each]. We rejoiced when that ambiguous formula regarding the special position of the Catholic Church was struck out." See generally Hogan, Whyte and Kelly, *The Irish Constitution 1094-1099* (3rd edn, 1994); Forde, *Constitutional Law of Ireland* (1987) pp. 524-537; Casey, *Constitutional Law in Ireland* (2nd edn, 1992) pp. 553-572.

[34] "Certain of the fundamental rights are couched in language of secular nationalist nature while others are clearly and strongly inspired by the Christian view of natural law."

Setting aside the republican and nationalist aspects of the constitution, one is struck immediately by the paternalistic and almost familial tone of the language, especially when compared with that of the US Constitution.[35] Partially, this is due to de Valera's own cultural biases, just as the American writers brought their own prejudices to the writing table, many of which were not corrected or alleviated for well over one hundred years after the document's ratification, and which were far more heinous than de Valera's shortcomings.[36] Beyond de Valera's view of typical Irish society as a rural, male-dominated, church-centred, tradition-based network of communities, the protective nature of the Irish Constitution properly reflects the role of the state under a Thomistic natural law system: the state is *supposed* to take a greater role in "guarding the common good", especially as compared with the role of government under the US Constitution.

Under the Thomistic natural law system, as discussed in a previous section, the end of government is the common good, and the role of the individual is subjugated and second to the needs of the common good. Just as Aquinas saw society as an organic body (re-iterating the thinking of the earlier Greek philosophers) in which the interest of the whole was paramount to those of its individual parts, government's end ought to be the promotion of the interests of the whole of society: the common good. Implementing Aristotle's teleologic notions, and formalising the concept of a "law written in their hearts", Aquinas held that the natural end or 'perfection' of man was the good, and that one found the good in abiding by the eternal law of God, in which all humans can participate via his or her reason. That eternal law has as its 'touchstone' the notion of doing good and avoiding evil and, because man needs to live in society with others to survive and prosper, seek the common good. Under Thomistic notions, the purpose and definition of law was "none other than a certain dictate of reason for the Common Good".[37] And the responsibility for seeking and promoting the common good "belongs either to the whole people or to one who represents the whole people[38] [under]some ar-

---

Costello, *The Natural Law and the Constitution*, 45 Studies 414 (1956). "As well as the influence of the political teaching of St Thomas Aquinas ... there is also the philosophical influence of the tradition of liberal democracy, as well as the impact of the practical turn of mind of the English constitutional lawyers ..." Newman, *Studies in Political Morality* (1962) p. 417.

[35] The paternalism of the US Constitution, however, was hidden and much more damaging than that of Article 41.2. The rights expounded in the American "Bill of Rights" only applied to white male property owners. Slavery was legal well into the 19th century. Women were denied a wide variety of civil rights into the 20th century and racism and sexism in the application of the laws continued well into the mid-1960s and 1970s.

[36] Article 41.2 has essentially been made moot by Articles 40 and 45.2.1° and related laws.

[37] *Treatise on Law* at 90, 3.

[38] *Ibid.*, at 90, 3.

rangement whereby those many may be governed".[39] The common good, in
Aquinas's view, was the pinnacle; the ultimate focus for society.

> Again, since every part is ordered to the whole as the imperfect to the
> perfect and one man is part of a perfect society, it is necessary that the
> law properly regard the order to the happiness of society . . . Hence,
> since the law is most of all ordered to the Common Good, it is necessary
> that *any precept concerning a particular matter [is only a law] insofar
> as it is ordered to the Common Good.*[40]

> As a man is part of a family, so the family is part of the state. The state,
> however, is a perfect society . . . And, therefore, just as the good of one
> man is not the ultimate end but is ordered to the Common Good; so also
> *the good of one family is ordered to the Common Good of the state . . .
> [Thus, law] properly speaking, regards first and principally the order
> to the common good.*[41]

> Operations indeed deal with particular matters, but those particular mat-
> ters can be referred to the Common Good–not indeed as coming under a
> common genus or species but as sharing a common final cause inas-
> much as the Common Good is said to be the common end.[42]

De Valera mimicked Aquinas' wording in effectively implementing his theories in the context of a modern-day, working and effective constitution. The
theme which runs through the entire text of the document is that individual
rights, individual privileges, and personal protections are all "subject to", "limited by", "guided by" and implemented "according to" the dictates of the
common good. Aquinas' submission that the preservation of society, being
crucial to man's survival and realisation, is paramount to all other considerations was effectively carried over by de Valera. Clearly, the rights of the individual are qualified by this dictate, and, according to Thomistic dogma, they
correctly ought to be.

What is the common good? Or, in more practical terms, what 'guideposts' ought one use in determing whether a particular law is consistent with
the dictates of the common good, or at least not antithetical to the common
good? Again, relying upon that natural law which is "merely the participation
of the eternal law, created by God, in a rational creature",[43] we see that:

---

[39] Aquinas, *De regimine principum I.* I.
[40] *Treatise on Law* at 90, 2 (emphasis added).
[41] *Ibid.*, at 90, 3 (emphasis added).
[42] *Ibid.*, at 90, 2.
[43] *Ibid.*, at 91, 2.

> . . . inasmuch as all substances desire the conservation of their own existence according to its nature, and in accord with this inclination, *all those things by which the life of man is preserved and the opposite impeded belongs to the Natural Law* . . . Therefore, the first principle of the Natural Law is this, that good should be done and sought and evil is to be avoided. And on this principle are based all the other precepts of the law of nature . . .[44]

Before examining further the application of these aspects of the common good, and the arguments of 'arbitrariness' which immediately arise whenever such seemingly nebulous concepts are discussed, let us look at the other aspect, that of the secular natural law, which de Valera also included in the 1937 Constitution. In two areas specifically, Article 40, which deals with personal rights, and Article 41, which discusses the rights of the family unit, de Valera either implicitly or explicitly declared that there are rights which are "inalienable and imprescriptible" and "antecedent and superior to all positive law".[45] Echoing the words of the American drafters of the Constitution and the Declaration of Independence, de Valera stated what has been recognised as the focal point of secular natural law: live honourably, harm no one, and, most importantly, give everyone his due.[46] The last tenet of the secular natural law is what makes it so clearly distinct from its Thomistic counterpart. Secular natural law seeks to preserve the life of the individual by protecting the interests of the individual; Thomistic natural law, on the other hand, seeks to protect the life of the individual by promoting that which all individuals, as part of society, rely upon for life: the common good. We will return to this point momentarily.

Similarly, de Valera drew upon the secular natural law to enunciate a right to private property in Article 43. Again, this was the focal point of Locke's *Treatise* and the establishment of government under the US Constitution. Aquinas, however, though recognising that private property existed, did not maintain that it was a natural law right, just as he did not recognise the inalienable rights of the individual to liberty.[47]

> As Aquinas said, the natural law is neutral in the areas of personal servitude and private property, and that cuts both ways. There is no *prima facie* right to either servitude or liberty, either private property or common possession. It is the essence of a natural rights theory that it attributes *prima facie* rights to natural men; Aquinas explicitly avoided doing so . . . The most important area which his theory left out, and

---

[44] *Ibid.*, at 94, 2 (emphasis added).
[45] Article 41.1.1°.
[46] See discussion in Part II Chapter 4.
[47] See Part II Chapter 3.

which was left unconnected with any rights theory . . . was the area of natural liberty. In Aquinas, men do not have a *prima facie* natural right to liberty any more than they have a *prima facie* natural right to dominate other men.[48]

So here we have in the 1937 Irish Constitution a collection of eclecticisms: Anglo-American notions of due process, habeas corpus and civil liberties, coupled with the secular natural law tenets of natural rights to liberty and private property, qualified by the Thomistic natural law 'end' of attaining/ protecting the common good, all falling under a system of government which separates the powers of governing (as did Montesquieu) while allowing for judicial review and the invalidation of legislation found to be unconstitutional (as did Jefferson). The question then becomes this: which element of the Constitution takes priority when cases present situations in which one element must be weighed against another (e.g. cases involving a right of privacy)? Or, getting more to the heart of the matter, which is more important in the scheme of things under the Irish Constitution: individual rights (whether or not they are enumerated) or the maintenance of the common good? Clearly, in reading the document, the common good prevails. De Valera was not ambiguous on that point. While individual rights are an integral part of the successful operation of democratic society, under de Valera's design, the common good is paramount.

Walking through nearly every section and Article which deals with the rights of citizens or the purpose of government, one cannot help but trip over the common good at every turn. Article 6 states that the primary purpose of the government, the powers of which "derive, under God, from the people"(another echo of the Thomistic approach), is ultimately to "decide all questions of national policy, according to the requirements of the common good". Article 40.6 recognises a series of individual rights, yet each one is qualified by the State's duty to protect the common good (or, using other words, the public interest or rights of the general public). Article 42, dealing with the right of the family to education its children, allows under section 3.2 that "the State shall, however, as guardian of the common good, require . . . certain minimum education, moral, intellectual and social". Article 43, which recognises the "natural right, antecedent to positive law, to the private ownership of external goods", a clear enunciation of the secular natural law, qualifies that right by its own section 2.2: "The State, accordingly, may as occasion requires delimit by law the exercise of the said rights with a view to reconciling their exercise with *the exigencies of the common good.*" Freedom of religious worship, protected by Article 44, also is subject to "public order and morality". And, relating back to Article 43, the Directive Principles of Social

---

[48] Tuck, *op. cit.*, p. 20.

Policy places a specific limitation (though Article 45 in itself is not an enforceable 'law' but only a directive) upon private property ownership by directing the State to insure that ownership is distributed among "private individuals and the various classes" so as to "best . . . subserve the common good", thus preventing concentration of ownership in a few "individuals to the common detriment".

Finally, the Preamble itself, after referring to the Holy Trinity "as our final end" and to whom "all actions both men and States must be referred", states that the first purpose of enacting the Constitution is to seek to "promote the common good", while, secondarily, "with due observance of Prudence, Justice and Charity, so that the dignity and freedom of the individual may be assured . . ." This statement, in a nutshell, defines the hierarchy of interests to be protected under the Irish Constitution. The rights of the individual are secondary to, and are to be protected by means of, the common good. Thus, it can be said that, under the Irish Constitution, the rights of the individual are protected via the promotion of the common good. Yet, if the protection of an individual right is contrary to the promotion of the common good, then it ought not to be protected. Clearly, "[t]he Irish constitutional provisions tend to be more qualified than those in the US Constitution"[49] and that which they are qualified by is the Thomistic notion of the common good.[50] Indeed, framed in another way, it can be said that, under the US Constitution, reflecting its secular natural law basis, the rights of the individual are paramount, to be limited only when the exercise of those rights infringes upon another's exercise of his/her rights; collectively, such infringements are harmful to the general welfare (or common good) of the community. Under the Irish Constitution, reflecting its Thomistic natural law basis, the common good is paramount and individual rights are protected only when they serve to promote, or are not contrary to, that common good. While both constitutional fabrics have as their common thread the preservation of man's life (and things necessary for that preservation), the way in which each fabric is woven reflects each one's distinct philosophical warp, and are thus different.

Where does this leave two very important sections of the Irish Constitution, for our purposes of discussing the right of privacy, that is, Article 40.3

---

[49] Beytagh, "Individual Rights, Judicial Review and Written Constitutions" in *Human Rights and Constitutional Law* (1992) 150.

[50] The discussion of the common good limitation upon constitutional rights is large and interesting. In addition to the standard casebooks and constitutional law books, see, for example, Delany, "The Constitution of Ireland, Its Origins and Development", 12 U. Toronto L. J. 1 (1957); Costello, "Limiting Rights Constitutionally, Human Rights and Constitutional Law" in *Human Rights and Constitutional Law* (1992) p. 175; Keane, "Property in the Constitution and Courts" in *De Valera's Constitution and Ours* (1988), p. 137; Walsh, "The Constitution and Constitutional Rights" in Litton (ed.), *op. cit.* and, Crowe, "The Irish Constitution and the Courts", 47 Notre Dame Lawyer (1971) 281.

and Article 41? And, secondly, as asked before, how does one practically define the scope of the common good?

Article 40.3.1°, in particular, lays the groundwork for the recognition of rights which are not explicitly enumerated, especially when read in context with the subsection which follows, which specifies particular rights to be protected. This recognition of unenumerated rights under the Irish Constitution, which will be discussed more fully in the next section, has been a flashpoint for heated disagreement concerning the validity and applicability of the Thomistic natural law and natural rights. Article 41, similarly and especially prior to the introduction of divorce in November 1995, clearly enunciated the Thomistic (and Aristotelian) tenet that the family is "the natural primary and fundamental unit group of Society, and . . . a moral institution possessing inalienable and imprescriptable rights, antecedent and superior to all positive law". For it, as well, has been at the centre of the natural law/natural rights arguments. And even though there is not a clear expression qualifying these sections, are the rights defined within subject to the limitations of the common good? Yes.

> It is not just in the field of property and parental rights that the exigencies of the common good may justify legal restrictions. The Constitution contains an article (Article 40.3) of wide import for it declares that the States is to guarantee to respect, defend and vindicate the 'personal rights' of the citizens. This article does not, however, mean that only those specified in it obtain the benefit of the guarantee – all the citizens' personal rights must be respected, defended and vindicated by the State. The Supreme Court has concluded that it is for the courts to decide what these rights are and the courts have fulfilled this task by declaring, for example, that the right to privacy is a 'personal right' within the meaning of the article. But obviously laws may interfere with the enjoyment of personal rights . . . and questions arise as to the constitutional validity of such laws. Here again the concept of the common good is a relevant consideration for unless the personal right involved is an absolute one whose exercise can in no circumstances be restricted then there has been no unconstitutional failure on the part of the State to respect, defend or vindicate the right in suit if the impugned restriction is one reasonably necessary in order to promote the common good. *The exigencies of the common good may therefore justify laws restricting the exercise of constitutionally protected rights.*[51]

---

[51] Costello, *op. cit.*, pp. 178-79 (emphasis added). At a formal level, this proposition has not been altered as a result of the introduction of divorce. From a substantive philosophical standpoint, however, there is a difficulty in articulating a coherent justification for regarding a relationship based upon a revocable commitment in such fundamental, natural law terms.

While the particulars of Judge Costello's declaration will be discussed in Chapter 8, he makes it clear that it is up to the judiciary to prevent the legislature from having "untrammelled power over the fundamental rights in the constitution",[52] whenever the legislature restricts constitutionally protected rights for the "exigencies of the common good". In short, it is for the court to decide what rights are protected, which rights are *absolutely* protected, what defines the common good, and how far the legislature can go in restricting individual rights in the name of the common good.

> . . . the power of the State to act for the protection of the common good or to decide what are the exigencies of the common good is not one which is peculiarly reserved for the legislative organ of government, in that the decision of the legislative organ is not absolute and is subject to and capable of being reviewed by the Courts. In concrete terms that means that the legislature is not free to encroach unjustifiably upon the fundamental rights of individuals or of the family in the name of the common good, or by act or omission to abandon or to neglect the common good or the protection or enforcement of the rights of individual citizens.[53]

There is a double-edged limit upon the legislature: it may not "encroach unjustifiably" upon individual (or family) rights under the guise of protecting the common good, nor may it "abandon or neglect the common good" in its attempt to protect or enforce individual (or family) rights. Thus, the obvious tension which exists between the judiciary and the legislature,[54] just as in the United States, is further complicated under the Irish Constitution by the need to balance the individual or familial exercise of "natural and human rights" with the "duties and obligations to consider and respect the common good of that society".[55] The common good, while similar in effect to the notions of *parens patriae* and police powers in the United States, is vastly different. And herein lies a crucially defining point. In the United States, the police powers, which protect public health, safety and morals,[56] and *parens patriae*, a con-

---

[52] Crowe, *op. cit.*, p. 292.

[53] *McGee v. Attorney Generel*, [1974] I.R. 284 at 310 (*per* Walsh J.).

[54] Just as in the United States, this conflict is a recurring theme. See, for example, Clark, "The Constitution and Natural Law, A Reply to Mr Justice O'Hanlon" 11 Irish L.. Times 177 (August, 1993); Clark, "The Role of Natural Law in Irish Constitutional Law" Irish Jur. 187 (1982); Hogan, "Constitutional Interpretation, The Constitution of Ireland, 1937-1987" in Litton (ed.), *op. cit.* For the American perspective, see, for example, cf. Meese, "The Supreme Court of the United States, Bulwark of a Limited Constitution", 27 S. Tex L. Rev. 455 (1986) and Cox, "The Role of the Supreme Court, Judicial Activism or Self-Restraint", 47 Maryland L. Rev. 118 (1987).

[55] [1974] I.R. 284 at 310 (*per* Walsh J.).

[56] See generally Kauper and Beytagh, *Constitutional Law, Cases and Materials* (5th edn, 1980) pp. 705-710, 720, 726-34 and cases cited therein, most notably the majority opinion for *Meyer v. Nebraska*, 262 *US* 390 (1923).

cept which allows the State to protect those who are unable to protect or speak for themselves,[57] are typically *reactive* powers of the state in response to an exercise or infringement of a right which has already taken place or immediately threatens to take place. The police power or *parens patrie* notion do not have a causal effect upon the formation of the right in question. Rather they come into play only after the right has been exercised or infringed. Although the Irish notion of the common good at times operates this way, it is altogether a different animal. And this difference must be recognised and accepted in order for there to be a proper understanding of the nature of rights under the Irish Constitution and their proper adjudication.

The common good, under Thomistic natural law philosophy, is a proactive concept. As discussed previously in our examination of Aquinas' *Treatise on Law* and its natural law formation, the common good is the perfect end and purpose of government, and, as such, it is not to be viewed as a mere parameter outside of which individual rights may not trespass, but rather as *the means by which individual rights are to be recognised, protected and, if necessary, modified (with the exception of the absolute right all persons have to life, which is, just as in the secular natural law, the raison d'etre of the natural law)*. De Valera, recognising this, stated that the purpose of the Irish government is to "promote the common good . . . so that the dignity and freedom of the individual may be assured".[58] If the primary purpose of a government is to "promote the common good", then it only follows that *the first and most important consideration in any adjudication concerning fundamental rights ought to be the common good.*

In reality, however, the common good is often the final consideration in an adjudication dealing with limitations on fundamental rights. This is a questionable approach. For when "the exigencies of the common good are called in aid to justify restrictions on the exercise of basic rights, it has to be borne in mind that the protection of basic rights is one of the objects which the common good is intended to assure".[59] *It is from and because of the common good, and the drive to attain it[60] that basic rights under the Irish Constitution ensue and are recognised.*

> The notion of the common good is derived from the concept that a political community exists to provide a whole range of conditions (material, social, moral, cultural) so that each of its members can realise his or her development as a human person. Thus the common good is the whole

---

[57] It is as the *parens patrie* that the State terminates parental rights in cases of child abuse.

[58] Preamble of the Irish Constitution.

[59] Costello, *op. cit.*, p. 178.

[60] Costello specifically makes the distinction that the common good is "derived from the scholastic philosophy and differs fundamentally from the utilitarian concept of the greatest good of the greatest number; [the latter providing flawed] justification for the restriction on the rights of members of minorities". *Ibid.*, p. 178.

ensemble of conditions which collaboration in a political community brings about for the benefit of every member of it. This point is made clear in the preamble . . . for the common good is not the good of the political community as such (which is a concept inherent in the totalitarian State and inimical to the protection of human rights) but *is an end to be promoted for specific purposes, which include the furtherance of the dignity and freedom of every individual in society.*[61]

Costello's statement echoes Aquinas: "Operations indeed deal with particular matters, but those particular matters can be referred to the Common Good – not indeed as coming under a common genus or species but as sharing a common final cause . . ."[62]

Costello's definition of the common good as "the whole ensemble of conditions which collaboration in a political community brings about for the benefit of every member in it", is as thorough a definition as one could find. More practical, however, is Mr Justice Walsh's view of the common good as "the satisfaction (in so far as possible) of the greatest proportions of interests of all persons with the least sacrifice, the least friction, and the least waste".[63] This also mirrors Aquinas's quite modern definition of just legislation:

Now, the laws are said to be just:

1. from the end, namely when they are ordered to the Common Good;
2. from the lawgiver, namely when the law passed does not exceed the lawgiver's authority;
3. from the form, namely when burdens are imposed on the subjects according to proportionate equality for the Common Good.[64]

Returning to Mr Justice Walsh's definition, as well as relying upon our own abilities to reason, however, it is plain to see that "the interests of all persons" are bound to vary from generation to generation, and thus that which best serves the common good is altered. The explicit recognition and protection of implicit rights of privacy, more necessary in modern times when intrusions into one's private life and the infringement upon one's private interests are so much more prevalent and frequent, is an example of this occurrence. Aquinas recognised this:

[T]he Natural Law [as the participation of the eternal law, created by God, in a rational creature], contains certain universal precepts which

---

[61] Costello, *op. cit.*, p. 178 (emphasis added).

[62] *Treatise on Law* at 90, 2.

[63] Walsh, "Existence and Meaning of Fundamental Rights in the Field of Education in Ireland", 2 Hum. Rts. L.J. 319 at 327 (1981).

[64] *Treatise on Law* at 96, 4.

endure forever, while law made by man contains certain particular precepts according to different situations which arise . . . [L]aw can rightly be changed on account of change in the condition of men to whom different things are useful according to different conditions . . . [Thus], human law is rightly changed insofar as the Common Good is thereby promoted . . .[65]

Mr Justice Walsh also spoke directly on this issue (extra-judicially):

The Constitution always speaks in the present tense, and therefore, it is to be interpreted in the light of current circumstances and standards, bearing in mind the fundamental principles upon which it is founded. . . In so far as the future is concerned, there is . . . bound to be considerable development in the constitutional jurisprudence. When one bears in mind that the Constitution contains moral beliefs and philosophical concepts derived from natural law and enacts these fundamental beliefs and concepts in terms of positive law, it is impossible to set any limits to the possibilities for new developments.[66]

Thus, as long as the attainment of the common good is the ultimate end and purpose, new laws can be enacted, old laws can be repealed, and rights can be recognised, which reflect the current "greatest proportion of interests of all persons". And the recognition and enforcement of various collective rights under the general concept of the right of privacy serves both to attain the common good, by the definitions given above, and to promote the common good, in its "furtherance of the dignity and freedom of every individual in society".[67]

By fully accepting Aquinas's definition of 'good': "inasmuch as all substances desire the conservation of their own existence according to its nature, [the good consists of] *those things by which the life of man is preserved and opposite impeded*"[68] and applying it to protect the "greatest proportion of interests of all persons" as is possible, the Irish judiciary, in interpreting the Irish Constitution, has at its disposal a non-arbitrary, eternal standard of the common good upon which "the dignity and freedom of the individual may be assured" at this time, and down through the ages. Herein lies the beauty and brilliance of Aquinas's natural law theory as applicable via the Irish Constitution: the reliance upon eternal truths for permanence, stability, and predictability, coupled with the flexibility necessary to reflect the variances in human needs and occurrences.

---

[65] *Ibid.*, at 97, 1.2.
[66] Walsh, *op. cit.*, pp. 325, 327.
[67] Costello, "Limiting Rights Constitutionally, Human Rights and Constitutional Law" in *Human Rights and Constitutional Law* (1992) p. 178.
[68] *Treatise on Law* at 94, 2 (emphasis added).

PART THREE

Finding Privacy: Two Natural Law Liaisons with Unenumerated Rights

The Secular Natural Law Model: the American Judiciary's Fickle Courtship via Fourteenth Amendment Substantive Due Process

What is a man,
If his chief good and market of his time
Be but to sleep and feed: a beast, no more.
Sure he that made us with such large discourse,
Looking before and after, gave us not
That capability and god-like reason
To fust in us unus'd.[1]

The state of nature has a law of nature to govern it, which obliges every one: and reason, which is that law, teaches all mankind, who will but consult it, that being all equal and independent, no one ought to harm another in life, health, liberty, or possessions.[2]

State a moral case to a ploughman and a professor. The former will decide it as well and often better than the latter, because he has not been led astray by artificial rules.[3]

Today, there are issues and controversies arising nearly every day which involve in some way an individual's right to privacy and liberty interests, and which the Framers of the US Constitution never could have imagined. During 1996 and 1997, various legislative bodies and courts in the United States have faced the topics of *divorce*; (Should no-fault divorce laws be repealed in favour of the earlier fault-based laws so that the soaring rate of divorce and family break-up can be reversed?) *child custody*; (Should joint custody be mandated by the courts, except where one parent is found unfit, so that each parent can have an equal voice in the child's upbringing?) *paternity*; (Does the unwed father who never knew about the birth of his child have the right to nullify the mother's termination of parental rights and subsequent adoption of

---

[1] *Hamlet*, Act III, Scene 4.
[2] John Locke, *Two Treatises* at section 6.
[3] Thomas Jefferson.

that child?) *surrogacy*; (Whose rights are paramount: the contracting parents
or the woman who agreed to bear the child?) *frozen embryos*; (Who do these
belong to, especially after the donors have been divorced?) *gay marriages
and adoption*; (Is there a civil right to same-sex marriages and adoption?)
school choice; (Does a taxpayer have the right to assign his tax dollars to a
private school for the education of his child?) *withdrawal of medical treatment*; (Does an individual have the right to request that medical treatment be
withdrawn? Does he have the right to withdraw medical treatment from his
child?) *euthanasia*; (Does one who is terminally ill, though not imminently
so, have the right to have his life taken? Does one who is in permanently
chronic pain have the right to have his life taken?) *competency*; (Does the
next of kin have the right to terminate the life of an incompetent who is terminally ill, in permanently chronic pain, or has a poor quality of life? Can an
incompetent be forced to undergo sterilisation or any other physically-intru-
sive procedure?) and last, but never least, issues relating to *reproduction* (Can
the government prevent the 'morning-after-pill' from being imported? How
far can government infringe upon the recognised right of a woman to have an
abortion? Does the father have the right to prevent an abortion? When does
the foetus' right to life vest? Is there a foetal right to privacy?).

The list could go on, without even touching upon issues relating to criminal search and seizure, libel and defamation of character, the right to travel,
the rights of citizen versus aliens, or the newly developing privacy issues
surrounding what constitutes a family, the use of computers and the internet,
among many others. Further complicating such issue resolution in the United
States are the tensions between the judiciary and the legislature and between
the state and federal governments. Who is the arbiter? Who is the appropriate
legislator? Who is the appropriate guardian and protector of the rights of citizens? [4]

It is submitted that the acceptance, indeed the embrace, of the secular
natural law by adjudicators of these difficult conflicts touching the heart of
privacy would serve as a greatly needed stabilising influence in those
adjudications, bringing enormous predictability to the jurisprudence surrounding the rights of privacy through reliance upon a concrete, independent standard of right and wrong. Non-arbitrary standards, contrary to what some writers have maintained, are not achieved either through legislation or any sort of
consensus-based/representation-reinforcing mode of judicial review.[5] Legis-

---

[4] Writing on the topic of privacy has been as varied and immense as the subject itself. See,
for example, Miller, *Assault on Privacy* (1971) regarding the breach of privacy in the
computer age where information stored in data banks can be used without consent; Miller,
"Comment and Queries, Concerning the Principle of Psychological Privacy" 31 Psychological Rec. 101 (1981).

[5] See, for example, Ely, "Toward a Representation-Reinforcing Mode of Judicial Review"
37 Maryland L. Rev. 451 (1978); Ely, "The Supreme Court 1977 Term, Foreword, On
Discovering Fundamental Values", 92 Harv L Rev 5 (1977); but cf. Brest, "The Funda-

lation is subject to repeal at the next election, and, as will be discussed more fully later, judicial decisions based upon the latest poll or the political leanings of the current majority in the Congress or State House are hollow and eventually meaningless. Rather, it is only through the acceptance and utilisation of a timeless standard, against which all decisions pertaining to individual rights can be judged, that arbitrariness can be avoided and a notion of consistent justice can be achieved. And this is no more important than in the area of privacy, where the lives and life plans of individuals can be literally written off by the pen of the adjudicator or legislator. The secular natural law, with its eternal standard of justice, as defined by John Locke and upon which the US Constitution is based, is a proverbial treasure-trove lying just beneath the surface of our written Constitution, just waiting to be exposed by anyone "who will but consult it". Taking a cue from the Irish approach to natural law, it is time to dig it up and use it openly.

Unfortunately, this entire area of discussion has been so obfuscated by the writings of 'professors' who, unlike the 'ploughman', add their own 'artificial rules'. It is ironic that any good reader with a secondary education can clearly understand the words of Jefferson and Madison pertaining to the issue of explicit and implicit rights, written in such a straightforward manner in the letters between them or in drafts of documents, while that same reader would be befuddled by many of the legal profession's articles pertaining to same.[6] Whatever opinion one has for the Court's opinion in that case, Justice Blackmun's simple statement in *Roe v. Wade*[7] that a right of privacy can be found either in the Fourteenth Amendment's concept of personal liberty, or in the Ninth Amendment's reservation of rights is soundly based upon the understanding intended by the creators of that document, consistent with the secular natural law basis of the US Constitution, as discussed previously. The Ninth Amendment, written by Madison, was inserted at his insistence because he and Jefferson did not want the enumeration of some rights to indicate that there were no other rights to be protected.[8] Conversely, the Tenth

---

mental Rights Controversy, The Essential Contradictions of Normative Constitutional Scholarship", 90 Yale L. J. 1063 (1981); Berns, "Judicial Review and the Rights and Laws of Nature", [1982] S Ct. Rev. 49.

[6] "Of course, there was in the beginning, as there is now and, as Ely shows, as there has been throughout the course of our history, a good deal of confusion as to what is meant by natural right and natural law. But what matters is the Founders' understanding and not that of Thomas Hutchinson, John C Calhoun, or the host of modern writers quoted by Ely. And the Founders were not confused." Berns, *op. cit.*, at 76.

[7] *Roe v. Wade* 410 *US* 113 at 153 (Blackmun, J.).

[8] In Madison's original draft of the Bill of Rights, dated 8 June 1789, and sent to Jefferson for his comments, Madison stated what would become the Ninth Amendment as the following, "The exceptions here or elsewhere in the constitution, made in favour of particular rights, *shall not be so construed as to diminish the just importance of other rights retained by the people*; or as to enlarge the powers delegated by the constitution; but either as actual limitations of such powers, or as inserted merely for greater caution."

Amendment was inserted so that the federal government could not claim any unenumerated powers, i.e. those powers which were not explicitly listed in the Constitution for exercise by the federal government, were reserved for the states or the people themselves to exercise. Hence, rights still existed even if they were not enumerated; powers of the government over the people and their rights did not.[9] Jefferson, furthermore, made clear that the Constitution, like any law, belongs to the generation currently living, and that "one generation of men [did not have] a right to bind another".[10] Finally, it was the belief of both Madison and Jefferson that the purpose of enunciating a bill of rights was to protect the rights of the minority in the face of the power of the legislative majority. It was the tyranny of the majority, they believed, on both the federal and the state level, which posed the greatest threat to the rights of the individual.[11] In fact, Madison feared that the states would trample more upon the rights of the individual than the federal government, and sought to include an amendment which would specifically apply to the states. It was passed by the House, and narrowly defeated by the Senate, but it gives us,

---

Madison's "Draft of the Bill of Rights" 8 June 1789, cited in *The Republic of Letters, vol. I*, (1995) p. 623. (Hereafter *Republic of Letters*.) As will be discussed more fully, Berger, in "The Ninth Amendment", 66 Cornell L. Rev. (1980) misconstrued Madison's intent in drafting the Ninth Amendment. Clearly, based upon the letters of Madison and Jefferson, the Ninth was intended to recognise the existence of other protected rights. Even though Madison originally believed that there was no need to add a bill of rights, as the Constitution had "never placed basic rights in jeopardy" because such rights did not depend upon "parchment" for their existence, he came to agree with Jefferson that, in enumerating at least some rights, "[h]alf a loaf is better than no loaf at all. If we cannot secure all our rights, let us secure what we can". *Republic of Letters*, pp. 587, 596.

[9] In a letter to Jefferson dated 8 December 1788, Madison underscored this point in his discussion of the proposed amendments to the Constitution, "The friends of the Constitution . . . wish the revisal to be carried out no farther than to supply additional guards for liberty, without abridging the sum of power transferred from the States to the general Government" *Republic of Letters*, p. 579.

[10] *Ibid.*, p. 631. "[I]t may be proved that no society can make a perpetual constitution, or even a perpetual law. The earth belongs always to the living generation. They may manage it then, and what proceeds from it, as they please, during their usufruct. They are masters too of their own persons, and consequently may govern them as they please." *Ibid.*, p. 634.

[11] "In our Governments the real power lies in the majority of the Community, and the invasion of private rights is *chiefly* to be apprehended, not from the acts of Government contrary to the sense of its constituents, but from acts in which the Government is the mere instrument of the major number of constituents . . . I am sure that the rights of conscience in particular, if submitted to public definition would be narrowed much more than they are likely ever to be by an assumed power. One of the objections in New England was that the Constitution by prohibiting religious tests opened the door for Jew Turks and infidels." *Ibid.*, p. 564 (emphasis in original). Jefferson agreed in a subsequent letter to Madison, "The tyranny of the legislatures is the most formidable dread at present, and will be for long years." *Ibid.*, p. 588.

once again, a view of the philosophy upon which the enumeration of some rights was based.

> In addition to the Bill of Rights' limitations on federal power, Madison proposed an amendment of his own, one found nowhere in the extensive debates in the ratification conventions or in the pamphlets of the period: "No State shall violate the equal rights of conscience, or the freedom of the press, or the trial by jury in criminal cases." This was Madison's final attempt to write the federal veto on state laws into the Constitution and underscored his view that the principal threat to individual rights came from unjust majority factions in the states "operating . . . against the minority". "I think there is more danger of those powers being abused by the state governments than by the government of the United States. The same may be said of other powers they possess, *if not controuled by the general principle, that laws are unconstitutional which infringe the rights of the community*." [12]

In short, the Framers intended that the Constitution acknowledge that rights existed which were not necessarily enunciated in the document itself, that said rights were not to be determined or protected by a legislative majority as the rights and interests of the minority would invariably be abused or unrepresented and that each generation would bring its own interpretation to the Constitution.

The primary purpose of the Constitution, as can be read in the Preamble to Madison's 8 June 1789 Draft of the Bill of Rights, was to declare:

> That government is instituted, and ought to be exercised for the benefit of the people [in whom all power originally vested and from whom all power is derived]; which consists in the enjoyment of life and liberty, with the right of acquiring and using property and generally of pursuing and obtaining happiness and safety.

> That the people have an indubitable, unalienable and indefeasible right to reform or change their government, whenever it be found adverse or inadequate to the purpose of its institution. [13]

The overwhelming emphasis, reiterated from Locke and the basics of the secular natural law, is upon the rights of the individual to seek 'his due' in a way he deems most fitting. And truly, this is the essence of privacy, which lies at the very core of rights' recognition and protection.

---

[12] Madison's Draft of the Bill of Rights, 8 June 1789 as enclosed in a letter to Thomas Jefferson dated 30 June 1789, as cited in *Republic of Letters*, p. 597 (emphasis added).

[13] *Ibid.*, p. 622.

But who ought to be the arbiters, the ones to ascertain that the rights of the people are being duly protected? How is the secular natural law applied in a practical way? And what are the parameters, the limits, if any, upon the recognition and protection of individual rights? Are there natural law guideposts which the arbiter may utilise in addressing rights issues? Finally, what is the role of the legislature in view of the paramount nature of personal rights? Let us examine each one of these questions individually, then apply their answers to several of the most important privacy cases and issues in American constitutional jurisprudence.

According to the Framers, and consistent with the need for independence from the oppressive influence of the majority, an independent judiciary is the only appropriate arbiter of individual rights guarantees.

> [Madison] had concluded that a bill of rights would be useful in laying down "fundamental maxims of free Government" and setting up defences against "usurped acts of the Government". These views gave Jefferson great satisfaction, but to Madison's arguments in favour of a bill of rights, he added a third: "the legal check which it puts into the hands of the judiciary. This is a body, which if rendered independent, and kept strictly to their department merits great confidence for their learning and integrity." [14]

Jefferson, in his letter to Madison on this topic, continued his support and praise for an independent judiciary by quoting, in Latin, a phrase from Horace's *Odes*, which states: "The man tenacious of his purpose in a righteous cause is not shaken from his firm resolve by the frenzy of his fellow-citizens bidding what is wrong."[15] Later that year, in arguing for the ratification of the Bill of Rights, Madison would state before Congress that "independent tribunals of justice will consider themselves in a peculiar manner the guardians of those rights".[16] And "those rights" included the unenumerated rights as well.

Professor Thomas Grey elaborated further:

> For the generation that framed the Constitution, the concept of a "higher law", protecting "natural rights", and taking precedence over positive law as a matter of political obligation, was widely shared and deeply felt. An essential element of American constitutionalism was the reduction to written form – and hence positive law – of some of the principles of natural rights. But at the same time, it was generally recognised that written constitutions could not completely codify the higher law. Thus

---

[14] *Ibid.*, pp. 524-525.
[15] *Ibid.*, p. 587, fn. 70.
[16] Gales and Seaton, 1 Annals of Congress (1834) 457.

in the framing of the original American constitutions it was widely accepted that there remained unwritten but still binding principles of higher law. The Ninth Amendment is the textual expression of this idea in the federal Constitution.

As it came to be accepted that the judiciary had the power to enforce the commands of the written Constitution when these conflicted with ordinary law, it was also widely assumed that judges would enforce as constitutional restraints the unwritten natural rights as well. The practice of the Marshall Court and of many of its contemporary state courts, and the writings of leading constitutional commentators through the first generation of our national life, confirm this understanding.[17]

In a subsequent article,[18] Professor Grey provided detailed scholarly and historical proof in support of the fact that, in addition to clearly accepting the existence of unwritten, natural rights, the colonists and the Framers viewed the role of the judiciary as requiring it to hold void any positive law which was contrary to those unwritten, natural rights. After laying out the development of the unwritten, natural law in England through the 16th century scholar, Christopher St Germain,[19] to the 17th century legal master, Sir Edward Coke,[20] Grey examined several English cases in which the judiciary declared void various acts of parliament based upon unwritten law, noting the impact that these had upon the thinking of American legal scholars of the next century. *Dr Bonham's Case*[21] was most notable for Coke's holding which stated that "when an act of Parliament is against common right and reason, or repugnant, or impossible to be performed, the common law will control it, and adjudge such act to be void".[22] This holding would be upheld in later English cases[23]

---

[17] Grey, "Do We Have an Unwritten Constitution?" 27 Stan. L. Rev. 703, 715-716 (1975).

[18] Grey, "Origins of the Unwritten Constitution, Fundamental Law in American Revolutionary Thought", 30 Stan. L. Rev. 843 (1978).

[19] St Germain noted that "the common lawyer's resort to what was considered 'reasonable' as a source of law was the English equivalent of the natural law arguments of the scholastics and the Roman and canon lawyers". Grey, "Origins of the Unwritten Constitution, Fundamental Law in American Revolutionary Thought" at 853, citing St Germain, *Doctor and Student* (n.p. 1580) pp. 4, 9.

[20] Coke declared that "the law of nature was part of the law of England and took precedence over earthly law, since it was of Divine origin, eternal and unchanging". Later, Sir Henry Finch submitted that "positive laws contrary to natural law 'lose their force, and are no laws at all'". Grey, *ibid.* at 853, citing Calvin's Case, 77 Eng. Rep. 377, 391-392 (K.B. 1609); Finch, *Law, A Discourse Thereof* (4th edn, 1759) p. 75.

[21] Eng. Rep. 646 (C.P. 1610). See other cases cited in Grey, "Origins of the Unwritten Constitution, Fundamental Law in American Revolutionary Thought" at 854.

[22] Eng. Rep. at 652. The case dealt with an act of Parliament which would allow a person to be both a party and judge in an action. This was held to be void.

[23] See, for example, *Day v. Savadge*, 80 Eng. Rep. 235 K.B. 1614.

and relied upon by early colonial writers[24] and early colonial case law as well.

> Although during the colonial period Americans had not been much given
> to debate over issues of constitutional theory, their few pronouncements
> reflected their intellectual debt to 17th century England, and its idea of
> fundamental law. Thus, for example, when the dissident freemen of
> Massachusetts Bay Colony attacked the sovereignty of the governing
> magistrates, they did so in the name of the traditional legal rights of
> Englishmen. And when in the case of *Giddings v. Browne* a Massachu-
> setts court invalidated a town meeting's appropriation of public money
> for a minister's house as an impermissible confiscation of taxpayer's
> property it held that the appropriation was "against the fundamental law
> and therefore void".[25]

And while the notion of parliamentary sovereignty was transplanted to the
colonies, it "made less headway against traditional notions of fundamental
law in America", where circumstances and the population made for a reality
different than that in England. Overall, in the early 18th century, "the traditional view that legislative authority was legally confined by fundamental law
continued to predominate over the new notion of parliamentary supremacy"[26]
and this view would later be reflected by the newly established US Supreme
Court in several of their early cases. While *Marbury v. Madison*[27] has traditionally been accepted as the seminal enunciation of the doctrine of judicial
review, there are two other cases which better exemplify judicial review based
upon the recognition and utilisation of unwritten, fundamental law.

Both *Calder v. Bull*[28] and *Fletcher v. Peck*[29] dealt with property rights of
citizens. In *Calder*, the Supreme Court held that *ex post facto* laws, explicitly
prohibited under Article I, section 10 of the Constitution, applied only to criminal laws and not civil statutes, thus finding that there was not an issue to
adjudicate concerning a change in Connecticut's property laws which had
adversely affected the appellant. In writing for the majority opinion, however,

---

[24] Grey, "Origins of the Unwritten Constitution, Fundamental Law in American Revolu-
tionary Thought" at 865, citing Otis, "The Rights of the British Colonies Asserted and
Proved" in Bailyn, *1 Pamphlets of the American Revolution* (1965) pp. 409, 476; Haskins,
Law and Authority in Early Massachusetts (1960) pp. 36, 56-57.

[25] Grey, "Origins of the Unwritten Constitution, Fundamental Law in American Revolutionary Thought" at 865-866, citing *Giddings v. Browne*, 2 Hutchinson Papers 1-25 (1st
edn, 1769). See also the discussion surrounding the unpopular Sugar, Stamp, Townshend
and Quartering Acts, and the legal arguments against their validity, relying again primarily upon their violation of fundamental law. *Ibid.* at 869-884.

[26] *Ibid.*, at 867, citing Leder, *Liberty and Authority* (1976) pp. 80-94.

[27] 5 *US* (1 Cranch) 137 (1803).

[28] 3 *US* (3 Dall.) 386 (1798).

[29] 10 *US* (6 Cranch) 87 (1810).

Justice Chase expounded upon the limitations which were placed upon the legislature by fundamental law, and enunciated the Supreme Court's earliest recognition of the unwritten law implicit in the Constitution.

> I cannot subscribe to the omnipotence of a state legislature, or that it is absolute and without control . . . There are acts which the federal, or state legislature cannot do, without exceeding their authority. There are certain vital principles in our free republican governments, which will determine and overrule an apparent and flagrant abuse of legislative power; as to authorise manifest injustice by positive law; or to take away that security for personal liberty, or private property, for the protection whereof the government was established. An act of the legislature, contrary to the great first principles of the social compact (to establish justice, to promote the general welfare, to secure the blessings of liberty, and to protect their persons and property from violence), cannot be considered a rightful exercise of legislative authority.[30]

Chase then went on to offer further examples of legislative abuse which would be void, continuing to reflect much of the theory laid out in the writings of Locke, Montesquieu and others (e.g. Pufendorf and Burlamaqui), and fundamental law notions of the English courts.

> A law that punished a citizen for an innocent action, or . . . for an act, which, when done, was in violation of no existing law; a law that destroys or impairs the lawful private contracts of citizens; a law that makes a man judge in his own cause; or a law that takes property from A and gives it to B: it is against all reason and justice, for a people to intrust a legislature with such powers; and therefore, it cannot be presumed that they have done it. The genius, the nature and the spirit of our state governments, amount to a prohibition of such acts of legislature: and the general principles of law and reason forbid them . . . To maintain that our federal, or state legislature possesses such powers (as described above), if they had not been expressly restrained; [is] political heresy, altogether inadmissible in our free republican government.[31]

The Court, through Justice Chase, reiterated two crucial concepts here. First, just because a legislative body has not been expressly prohibited from enact-

---

[30] 3 *US* (3 Dall.) 386 at 387-388.

[31] *Ibid.*, at 388. But see Justice Iredell's separate concurring opinion in which he submitted, that "the ideas of natural justice have no fixed standard" and thus all the court could really say was that a legislative act, "in the opinion of the judges, was inconsistent with the abstract principles of natural justice" but that the Court did not possess the power to declare the act void just because it violates natural justice. *Ibid.* at 398-99.

ing certain types of legislation does not mean that they are allowed to do so. There are unwritten "fundamental principle[s] flow[ing] from the very nature of our free republican government"[32] which serve as limits to the exercise of legislative authority. Here is natural law thinking written clearly into the case law of the US Supreme Court. Moreover, here is the affirmation that there exists an independent measure of right and wrong, not subject to the omnipotent whims of the legislature, and the touchstone for what is right and wrong lies in those core principles which Locke and Jefferson declared: the preservation of life, liberty and property.

Second, in outlining those areas into which legislative bodies may not tread, Chase essentially defined a zone of privacy which must be protected. In stating that the legislature may not "take away that security for personal liberty, or private property, for the protection whereof the government was established",[33] Chase summarized that it is the realm of private actions and the exercise of private rights into which a legislature may not enter.

These twin tracks of thought are re-affirmed by Justice Marshall in another property case, *Fletcher v. Peck*.[34] In that case, the state of Georgia had enacted a bill allowing the sale of over thirty million acres of public land in 1795. That land was accordingly sold, divided and resold many times thereafter to various private parties. In 1796, it came to light that there had been much underhanded dealing with regards to the enactment of the previous year's bill, and many legislators and businessmen had illegally benefited or had conflicts of interest. The legislature thus passed a new law, essentially voiding the act of 1795. Were, therefore, the subsequent re-sales of land invalidated because now there was no clear title? The Court held that even though the law had been repealed, those who possessed a vested, absolute ownership of the land they had purchased could not be divested of same merely because the legislation had changed. In so ruling, Justice Marshall attempted to tie the case to Article I, section 10, which prohibits the states from passing any law which impairs the obligations of contracts, even though it was clear that these were not contracts currently being executed, but completed conveyances of real property. Marshall went on, therefore, to find the statute invalid because it violated "general principles which are common to our free institutions".[35] In addition to its somewhat tenuous violation under the Contract Clause. Other statements in the Court's opinion are noteworthy for their explicit references to and reliance upon the unwritten, natural law:

> The legislature of Georgia was a party to this transaction; and for a party to pronounce its own deed invalid, whatever a cause may be assigned

---

[32] *Ibid.*, at 388.
[33] *Ibid.*, at 388.
[34] 10 *US* (6 Cranch) 87 (1810).
[35] *Ibid.*, at 139.

for its invalidity, must be considered as a mere act of power which must find its vindication in a train of reasoning not often heard in courts of justice . . . If the legislature of Georgia was not bound to submit its pretensions to those tribunals which are established for the security of property, and to decide on human rights, if it might claim to itself the power of judging in its own case, *yet there are certain great principles of justice, whose authority is universally acknowledged, that ought not to be entirely disregarded* . . . The principle is this: that a legislature may, by its own act, divest the vested estate of any man whatever, for reasons which shall, by itself, be deemed sufficient . . . It may be well doubted whether the nature of society and government does not prescribe some limits to the legislative power; and, if any be prescribed, where are they to be found, if the property of an individual, fairly and honestly acquired, may be seized without compensation? [36]

Here we have the reiteration of several well-accepted legal maxims arising either from the unwritten common law or the Lockean notions of natural law. In this early American constitutional law holding, however, it is important to note that the Court found that it must go outside the expressly written elements of the Constitution in order to fairly adjudicate the case at hand. The Contract Clause, as would be shown in subsequent cases,[37] could never adequately encompass all of the conflicts which would occur between individuals and government concerning economic and property rights. Similarly, other pieces of the Constitution which seek to protect the rights of individuals also can never entirely accommodate all of the controversies which would arise. Over the course of constitutional adjudication, the Court has attempted to appropriately protect unexpressed individual rights by attaching that right to a

---

[36] 10 *US* (6 Cranch) 87 at 130-36.

[37] See, for example, *Home Building & Loan Association v. Blaisdell*, 290 *US* 398 (1934) in which emergency legislation during the Depression which allowed a moratorium for mortgage payments was held not to impair "the Obligations of Contracts" under the Contract Clause. The majority there stated that "the question is no longer merely that of one party to a contract as against another, but of the use of reasonable means to safeguard the economic structure upon which the good of all depends" and placed reliance upon Justice Marshall's earlier statement in *McCulloch v. Maryland*, "'We must never forget that it is a constitution we are expounding, a constitution intended to endure for ages to come, and consequently, to be adapted to the various crises of human affairs.'"*Ibid.*, at 415, citing (4 Wheat.) 316, at 407. In an angry dissent by Justice Sutherland, however, the minority argued that the majority had gone far outside the limited inquiry presented to the Court, and that the Contract Clause was indeed written expressly to prevent government from interfering with contractual obligation during times of trouble. See also *Trustees of Dartmouth College v. Woodward*, 17 *US* (4 Wheat.) 518 (1818) whether the granting of a corporate charter constituted a contract subject to the Contract Clause; *New Orleans Gas Co. v. Louisiana Light Co.*, 115 *US* 650 (1885) whether a franchise grant of a monopolistic privilege to a utility was a contract subject to the Contract Clause, among others.

related one written in the body of the document or an amendment,[38] often resulting in an obviously far-reaching, result-oriented opinion of the Court, and subjecting it to divisiveness and controversy. Avoidance of controversy or the employment of these contrivances are not a reasons enough, in and of themselves, for adopting the method recommended here of openly recognising and utilising unwritten natural law elements in adjudications involving constitutional rights, however. Rather the secular natural law principles upon which the US Constitution are based ought to be openly utilised because, as will be shown, justice, via a more predictable and substantive manner, is better attained and the inalienable rights of the individual to life, liberty and property, are better protected. Finally, the Court could openly and freely, without having to forage for an explicit vehicle in the Constitution by which to perform its purpose, protect those individual rights such as privacy which are necessary to the preservation of the life, liberty and property of the individual. This, after all, was the stated purpose of government for which the Constitution was written.

What about Justice Black's firm and consistent dissenting contention that the amendment process was the way, and the only way, in which the Framers intended that new constitutional rights be recognised?[39] What of his and Justice Iredell's recurring argument that the natural law has "no fixed standard" and thus its contents are subject to the opinions of the justices currently sitting on the bench?[40] Justice Black, who has been one of the most consistent and straightforward writers in the history of the Supreme Court, makes strong arguments in support of his contentions. But they are unfortunately, shortsighted views based upon inaccurate premises which serve primarily to dodge the important issues at hand. While they may observe the letter of the law, they certainly do not serve the spirit.

---

[38] Thus the "freedom of association" has been recognised as implicit in the First Amendment's freedom of expression clause and the due process clause of the Fifth and Fourteenth Amendments (see, for example, *NAACP v. Alabama*, 357 *US* 449 (1958)); 'academic freedom' under the First Amendment (see, for examle, *Keyishian v. Board of Regents*, 385 *US* 589 (1967)); 'right to travel' under the due process clause of the Fifth Amendment, the privileges and immunities clause and the commerce clause (see, for example, *Kent v. Dulles*, 357 *US* 116 (1958)); 'right to vote' under the equal protection and due process clauses of the Fifth and Fourteenth Amendments (see, for example, *Louisiana v. United States*, 380 *US* 145 (1965)); among others.

[39] See, for example, *Harper v. Virginia Board of Elections*, 383 *US* 663, 670 (1966) (Black J. dissenting) held poll tax to be unconstitutional.

[40] See, for example, *ibid., Adamson v. California*, 332 *US* 46, 69-91 (1947) (Black, J. dissenting). Fifth Amendment privilege against self-incrimination held not applicable to the states via the Fourteenth Amendment in this seminal case which outlined four theories of "incorporation" of the bill of rights as applicable to the states via the Fourteenth Amendment; *Griswold v. Connecticut*, 381 *US* 479, 507-527 (1964) (Black, J. dissenting) Connecticut statute prohibiting use of contraceptives held unconstitutional as a violation of the constitutional right of privacy.

In arguing that the amendment process or legislative enactments are the only means by which new rights ought to be recognised, Black ignored the Framers' rationale for enunciating the Bill of Rights guarantees in the first place. The Framers, as stated previously, understood that the minority faction in each community needed to be protected *most of all* from the actions, or inertia, of a majority-backed legislature. The Framers knew that the minority can never fully depend upon whatever sense of goodwill or righteousness the majority may have for the recognition and enforcement of the rights of the minority. And the majority, as such, will seek to retain its level of power so as to continue to influence events in the community and best maintain its level of comfort, through economic and social authority. One only needs to look at the history of African-Americans in the United States to see just how ineffective the amendment process is, when relied upon solely, in protecting the rights of minorities. For even after the Civil War amendments were adopted (and it took a Civil War to do so) states routinely denied African-Americans the right to vote, to attend school or to run for office; in short, the right to live their lives as fully accepted citizens of the United States. But for the coerced enforcement of opinions of the Supreme Court which recognised the various ways in which states attempted to circumvent the Fourteenth Amendment, African-Americans would still be living as second class citizens. But under Black's thinking, African-Americans could still be required to use separate drinking fountains, separate schools, separate train cars and be denied the right to vote because of the inability to pay a poll tax, and yet the Constitution would not be infringed, in his view, because there is nothing which expressly prohibits such treatment. As Professor Grey noted, "it should be clear that an extraordinarily radical purge of established constitutional doctrine would be required if we candidly and consistently applied the pure interpretative model" of Justice Black.[41]

Ironically, it was Justice Black who first supported the notion that all of the Bill of Rights were incorporated into the due process clause of the Fourteenth Amendment and as such are applicable to the states.[42] While he was a staunch supporter of the Bill of Rights, his failure to look inside of them (and not beyond them, as he would claim) for their fundamental natural law meaning and purpose (i.e. the preservation of life, liberty and property), made his understanding of them incomplete. Without meaning any disrespect to Justice Black and his brilliance as an adjudicator,[43] it seems that he had based his arguments upon the same incorrect premise that others have accepted and still do accept (e.g. Professor Ely), that the United States is, as Professor Murphy has stated it, "a representational democracy rather than . . . a constitutional

---

[41] Grey, "Do We Have an Unwritten Constitution?" at 713. Also *ibid.* at 710-714 and cases cited therein.

[42] See *Adamson v. California*, 332 US 46, 69-91 (1947) (Black, J. dissenting).

[43] See, for example, *New York Times Co. v. United States*, 403 *US* 713 (1971) (Black J.).

democracy".[44] The Framers, as discussed previously, favoured constitutionalism over purely representational democracy, clearly rejecting the notion of
legislative supremacy.

> These two theories make competing and sometimes conflicting demands
> on governmental institutions. As an abstract model of political organi-
> sation, democracy stresses equality and popular rule, at least to the ex-
> tent that legislators and the chief executive officer are regularly, if indi-
> rectly, accountable to the public at contested elections. As an abstract
> model, constitutionalism emphasises that certain rights of the individual
> citizen are protected against government, even against popular govern-
> ment and majority rule. If one takes Madison at his word and accepts his
> view as authoritative, the Philadelphia Convention mapped a system
> that was to contain much more of constitutionalism than of democracy.[45]

In addition, Black, reflecting Iredell's earlier argument in *Calder v. Bull*,[46]
and Ely have both been critical of the utilisation of the natural law, or any
concept which they view as being outside of the Constitution, in the adjudication of the right of privacy.[47] In general, both view the reliance upon "extra-
constitutional" law as merely reflecting the opinions of the current members
of the bench, having no connection with the expressed elements of the Constitution, and in particular, both were critical of the Court's "finding" of a
constitutional right of privacy, either as "emanations" from other expressed
rights, as described by Justice Douglas in the Griswold majority opinion,[48] or
as a right arising out of the Ninth Amendment, as Justice Goldberg declared
in his concurrence.[49]

> Professor Ely charges that in those decisions, based on a right of "pri-
> vacy" drawn by no imaginable arts of construction or interpretation from
> the constitutional test, the Court has violated its "obligation to trace its
> premises to the charter from which it derives its authority". He goes on:
> "A neutral and durable principle may be a thing of beauty and a joy
> forever. But if it lacks connection with any value the Constitution marks

---

[44] Murphy, "An Ordering of Constitutional Values" 53 S. Cal. L. Rev. 703 at 706-9 (1980),
citing Ely, *Democracy and Distrust* (1980).

[45] Murphy, *op. cit.*, at 708, citing Madison, *The Federalist Nos. 10, 37, 39, and 51, 11* in
Lipscombe (ed), *Writings of Thomas Jefferson* (1905) pp. 50-51.

[46] "[T]he ideas of natural justice [have] no fixed standard." 3 *US* (3 Dall.) 386 (1798) at
398-99.

[47] See, for example, Ely, "The Wages of Crying Wolf, A Comment on *Roe v. Wade*", 82
Yale L. J. 920 (1973); and *Griswold v. Connecticut*, 381 *US* 479, 507-527 (1964) (Black,
J. dissenting). See especially *ibid.*, at 511, fn. 4, for Justice Black's compilation of "catch-
words and phrases invoked" under notions of natural justice.

[48] 381 *US* at 479-486. (Douglas J.).

[49] *Ibid.*, at 486-499. (Golberg J., concurring).

as special, it is not a constitutional principle and the Court has no business imposing it."[50]

Once again, it is submitted that there is a failure to recognise the purpose and origins of the Bill of Rights and the entire rationale for enacting the Constitution. In particular, though his articles never lack for articulate footnotes, Professor Ely's reliance upon preconceived notions is made evident by the citations which are *not* present. In his forewords for the 1977 Supreme Court Term,[51] for example, Ely somewhat cynically denigrated the entire realm of natural law and its influence upon the founding fathers by claiming that, firstly, no-one, including the Framers, can really understand what is meant by the natural law;[52] secondly, even though the Framers (Jefferson) did explicitly rely upon the natural law (i.e. what has been referred to in this book as the secular natural law) in the Declaration of Independence, these references were only included because the writer of this "brief" needed "references to anything that seemed to help" his argument,[53] thirdly, the drafters of the Constitution, having made their case for revolution in the Declaration, omitted, "in anything resembling explicit form", any references to natural law doctrine in the document;[54] and fourthly, the natural law, since it has been invoked incorrectly throughout history in support of various "nefarious" causes, including slavery and gender discrimination, is a concept which "is a discredited one in our society".[55] It is true that the 'natural law' has been the stated basis for

---

[50] Grey, 3 *US* (3 Dall.) at 398-99 at 704, citing Ely, *op. cit.*, at 949.

[51] Ely, "On Discovering Fundamental Values" 92 Harv. L. Rev. 5 (1978).

[52] *Ibid.*, at 23 and fns. 83 and 84.

[53] Ely, *op. cit.*, at 24. See also *ibid.*, fn. 88. But see Berns, *op. cit.*, at 55. "[Ely] denies the existence of natural rights and natural law. What was self-evident to the authors of the Declaration of Independence is not at all evident to Ely."

[54] *Ibid.*, at 25. But see Ely's remarks at the end of fn. 89, "The fact that many persons at the time, following one variant of natural rights theory, would have held that our natural rights had been "merged in" and therefore superseded by, the written guarantees of the Bill of Rights (citations omitted), seems in one sense irrelevant to the present discussion. For the task before us is the location of a source of values with which to give content to such open-ended provisions as the Ninth Amendment, *whose clear implication seems to be that the class of protected rights is not exhausted by those that are explicitly set down in the document.*" Ely then, after citing to his own work, eclipses anymore discussion along this line by the following curt ending, "It does remain true, however, that the adoption of a written Bill of Rights constitutes some evidence of a less than wholehearted commitment to a natural rights philosophy." Yet a quick review of the letters between Jefferson and Madison, as discussed above clearly supports the contrary view. The Bill of Rights, with its Ninth Amendment, was a declaration of some of the most crucial rights in the natural law scheme to preserve man's life, liberty and property, in order to explicitly secure those rights against governmental infringement, coupled with the understanding and indication that all of the rights which ought to be secured could not be expressed, either for that time or for times to come.

[55] *Ibid.*, at 28.

such heinous assertions as the inferiority of African-Americans or that women should be subservient to men. Rather than discrediting the natural law, however, one ought to discredit those who misinterpret or misuse the natural law for their own purposes. To argue that the natural law is discredited in our society because some have misused it for their own benefit is similar to stating that the teachings of Jesus are no longer useful because some have twisted them for their own evil purposes. Shall we not listen to Wagner because Hitler made his music a part of the Third Reich propaganda? Rather, what is needed is a clearer understanding of the natural law which was relied upon by the founding fathers so that it can be effectively and consistently utilised, in order "to give content to such open-ended provisions as the Ninth Amendment", as Ely requested.[56] As noted above, Ely did not fairly examine the elements of the secular natural law, nor its effect upon the Framers, nor its influence in the drafting of the Constitution, nor the scholars who have written in praise of the natural law,[57] then chose to condemn it because it has been misused and misinterpreted.[58]

The secular natural law continuously referred to in this book, with its primary tenet of preserving the life, liberty and property of each individual (and its secondary maxim: Live honourably, do not harm others, and give everyone his due), could not rationally or reasonably be used as the basis for slavery or subservience of one group of persons to another. Indeed, slavery, or the subjugation of one group to another, has long been recognised as not being part of the natural law, or as contrary to the natural law.[59] And philosophers from earliest Greek times forward have contended that one's own "appetite", "passions", "prejudices" or "opinions" must be kept out of any rational application of the natural law.[60] Rather, what is needed is a clear and

---

[56] See fn. 51 above.

[57] See, for example, Murphy, *op. cit.*, and Grey, "Origins of the Unwritten Constitution, Fundamental Law in American Revolutionary Thought". Ely refers to one of Grey's articles in his foreword to the 1997 Supreme Court term, but it is only used to support Ely's contention that "there were a good number of people (in Colonial times) who espoused the existence of a system of natural law principles". Ely, *op. cit.*, at 22-23, fn. 82. Grey's article, of course, stands for much more than that, and in fact, Grey disagrees with Ely's natural law notions in that article. Grey, *ibid.*, at 846, *et seq.*

[58] *Cf.* Grey, "Do We Have an Unwritten Constitution?" "I do not think that the view of constitutional adjudication outlined by [Professor Ely and other commentators] is sufficiently broad to capture the full scope of legitimate judicial review." *Ibid.*, at 705; Brest, *op. cit.* "I shall argue that none of [Professor Ely's and other's] affirmative theories can withstand the force of his own criticisms." *Ibid.*, at 1089; Murphy, *op. cit.*

[59] In *Justinian's Institutes*, discussed in Chapter 4, it was clearly stated that slavery was "contrary to the law of nature" *Institutes* at 1.2.2. And Aquinas maintained that slavery was not a part of the natural law. Tuck, *Natural Rights and Theories, Their Origin and Development* (1979) p. 20.

[60] "[T]he task of the legislator is to ordain 'what is good and expedient for the whole polis amid the corruptions of human souls, opposing the mightiest lusts, and having no man his helper but himself standing alone and following reason only'." Winton and Garnsey,

simple understanding of its tenets, without being "led astray by artificial rules".

The natural law tenets of Locke ought to be utilised by adjudicators in recognising and protecting those rights not expressed in the US Constitution through the Ninth Amendment. Reliance upon Locke's notion of preserving the life, liberty and property (understanding that Locke intended to include "one's property in himself" in the definition of property) of the individual, which is, after all, the stated purpose for the institution of government and the enactment of a constitution for the United States, coupled with the adoption of his secular natural law limitations to the exercise of these rights (i.e. the infringement upon *another's* exercise of his/her recognised rights), not only would allow for the broadest protection of individual rights possible, but, if applied without prejudice or the insertion of one's "passions" or "appetites", would also provide for the most consistent and predictable standard against which future adjudications and legislation could be measured. Let us examine how this would play out in various privacy cases already decided.

Let us begin with *Griswold v. Connecticut*,[61] involving the right of a married couple to obtain and use contraceptives. This has been recognised, both in the United States and Ireland,[62] as the seminal marital privacy case. Because most writers, and indeed all of the judges who heard the case presented at the Supreme Court, agreed that government ought not to be allowed to intrude on the intimate decisions of man and wife, the controversy surrounding Griswold (unlike *Roe v. Wade*) was limited to how the Court arrived at its decision. Justice Douglas delivered the opinion of the Court, holding the Connecticut statutes unconstitutional as violative of a right of privacy implicit in the "penumbras" in various of amendments of the Bill of Rights, "formed by emanations from those guarantees which give them life and substance".[63] Chief Justice Warren and Justice Brennan joined with Justice Goldberg in his concurring opinion in which he submitted that the statutes in question were unconstitutional as violative also of a right of privacy under the Ninth Amendment.[64] Justice Harlan wrote an opinion concurring in the judgment in which he submitted that the statutes were unconstitutional as violative alone of the due process clause of the Fourteenth Amendment "because the enactment violates basic values 'implicit in the concept of ordered liberty'".[65] Justice White also concurred in the judgment in a separate opinion in which he submitted that the statute was unconstitutional, again relying solely upon the due

---

"Political Theory" in *The Legacy of Greece* (1977) p. 48, citing Plato, *Laws*, 835C. See also Aristotle, *Politics*, 5, 1273a, 28-32. Law is "reason free from all passion".

[61] 381 *US* 479 (1964).

[62] See generally *McGee v. Attorney General* [1974] I.R. 284.

[63] 381 *US* at 478-486.

[64] *Ibid.*, at 486-499.

[65] *Ibid.*, at 499-502.

process clause of the Fourteenth Amendment, because it deprives the parties of "'liberty' without due process of law . . ."[66]

Justices Black and Stewart filed the case's dissenting opinions. Let it be noted, however, that both deliberately made it clear in those opinions that they disagreed with the Connecticut statutes, finding them "offensive"[67] or to be "uncommonly silly law".[68] Their dissents were based upon their submission that the statutes did not violate any portion of the Constitution.

In Black's lengthy dissent, interestingly, he admitted that "[t]here are, of course, guarantees in certain constitutional provisions which are designed in part to protect privacy at certain times and places with respect to certain activities"[69] citing, as an example, to the Fourth Amendment. And he agreed that if the defendants had only been "convicted for doing nothing more than expressing opinions to persons [about certain contraceptives], [he] could think of no reasons at this time why their expression of views would not be protected by the First and Fourteenth Amendments, which guarantee freedom of speech".[70] And he stated that he was in complete agreement with "the graphic and eloquent strictures and criticisms fired at the policy of [the statutes in question]"[71] by the majority. Yet, he maintained that the statutes were not unconstitutional. "I like my privacy as well as the next one, but I am nevertheless compelled to admit that government has a right to invade it unless prohibited by some specific constitutional provision. For these reasons I cannot agree with the Court's judgment and the reasons it gives for holding this Connecticut law unconstitutional."[72] In summary, Black admitted that the statutes were bad law (although he was correct to contend that this has no bearing on the adjudication), invasive of privacy, *beyond* being violative of the First Amendment (since the defendants did more than talk about contraceptives: they sold them to women whom they were treating in the context of a doctor/patient relationship) and not quite specific enough in the time and place of their violation of privacy to warrant coverage by the Fourth or any other amendment, yet they were not unconstitutional because they did not violate a specific constitutional guarantee expressed by the Framers. And those who did find these statutes to be unconstitutional were merely invalidating them "on the basis of their own appraisal of what laws are unwise or unnecessary".[73]

This is a perfect case in which the theory proposed here could have been applied. Here are statutes which do not clearly violate an express provision of the Constitution or the Bill of Rights, so the Court must look to something

---

[66] 381 *US* at 502-507.
[67] *Ibid.*, at 507. (Black J., dissenting).
[68] *Ibid.*, at 527. (Stewart J., dissenting).
[69] *Ibid.*, at 508. (Black J., dissenting).
[70] *Ibid.*, at 507-8.
[71] *Ibid.*, at 507.
[72] 381 *US* at 510. (Black J., dissenting).
[73] *Ibid.*, at 512.

else. Secondly, there never would have been an express provision in the Constitution or Bill of Rights which covered this situation because the Framers could have never possibly anticipated that, nearly two hundred years after ratification, there would exist the technology to prevent pregnancy, nor would it ever have been appropriate in that time and culture to even discuss such matters. ("Congress shall make no law infringing upon the free exercise of a married couple to engage in sexual activity . . ."?) Rather, as the concurring opinion indicated, and Parts 1 and 2 of this book support, the relationships between a husband, wife, and their family have served as the core element in the overall scheme for the preservation of the individual since time immemorial,[74] a notion which the Framers understood and accepted.

This, in and of itself, via application through the Ninth Amendment of the secular natural law theory as discussed here, would be enough to find the statutes unconstitutional. Rights surrounding personal relationships which substantiate the preservation of a person's life, liberty and property would be secured and protected *prima facie* as against governmental intrusion, subject to the limits mentioned previously, i.e. infringement upon another's rights to preserving his life, liberty and property. In a case such as *Griswold*, the decision is easy. There is a married couple who both desire to use contraceptives in order to plan their family as they wish and they are both legally competent. Their doctors are acting with their consent and otherwise in a legal manner. The question which would be brought before the Court, therefore, would be whether the Connecticut statutes serve to protect the rights of others in preserving their life, liberty or property. The answer here is clearly no. By exercising their rights of privacy in procuring and using contraceptives, the parties here are not infringing upon the rights of others. The government, therefore, does not have any interest in intruding upon the parties.

But what of the morality argument? Could it not be argued, in this or other privacy cases which will be re-evaluated here, that the government has an interest in promoting moral well-being in the community it serves? This argument is more relevant in the cases involving the privacy of non-married couples, same-sex couples and the cases involving the viewing of obscene material in one's home. Are seemingly victimless crimes truly that? Last, in light of the parameters used here (i.e. a person may only exercise his rights to the extent that it does not infringe upon another's exercise of rights in the preservation of life, liberty and property), is there a new view of the abortion cases? Does the foetus gain more importance under our application of Lockean natural law via the Ninth Amendment? Would end of life issues also be examined differently and possibly have a different result?

Under Lockean natural law theory, as mentioned above, the only limitation to the recognition and enforcement of one's rights effecting the preserva-

---

[74] 381 *US* at 495-6. (Goldberg J., concurring).

tion of one's life, liberty and property via the Ninth Amendment would be the infringement upon another's exercise of the same rights. As Locke stated:

> Every one, as he is bound to preserve himself, and not to quit his station wilfully, so be the like reason, when his own preservation comes not in competition, ought he, as much as he can, to preserve the rest of mankind, and may not, unless it be to do justice on an offender, take away, or impair the life, or what tends to the preservation of the life, the liberty, health, limbs, or goods of another.[75]

Government itself has no protected interests. The only interests it may protect are those of others and, as stated many times before, it was for this reason that government was instituted. Hence, government may promulgate laws in order to preserve the life, liberty or property of its citizens. Government, in this scheme, may not pass legislation which merely has some generalised nexus with the common welfare of the people, or promotes some notion of morality. As discussed in Chapter 5, under the secular natural law, the common good is achieved by allowing everyone, as much as possible, his due. By protecting the rights of the individual, as much as is feasible without infringing upon another's rights, the government best attains the common good. Here is the difference, pointed out before, between the secular natural law and Thomistic natural law. In the latter, the government and its citizens are bound to promote and protect the common good even if individual rights are sometimes compromised, as Aquinas predicted and as will be examined more closely in Chapter 8. Under the former, the rights of the individual are paramount, and through this protection of individual rights, it is contended, the common good is ultimately served.

Hence, under the secular natural law, the government may only infringe upon the perceived right of an individual (in preserving life, liberty or property) in order to prevent the clear infringement upon another's rights. In the course of an adjudication in which plaintiff is claiming infringement by government (in its execution of a law which has affected plaintiff) the government's only argument could be that the express purpose of the law is to prevent infringement upon another's rights, with specific proof that, without enforcement of that particular law, another's life, liberty or property would be in danger. Thus, in such cases in which the government prohibits a particular activity for generalised reasons of morality or majority consensus (e.g. under various state sodomy, prostitution, or obscenity statutes), the evidentiary burden on the government would be greater, and most likely, impossible to uphold. Preventing particular sexual activity or prohibiting the viewing of certain obscene materials at home or a particular establishment for that purpose

---

[75] *Two Treatises*, section 6.

would be unconstitutional.[76] In attempting to prohibit or regulate private activities between two consenting and competent adults, it would be nearly impossible for the government to point to explicit examples in which another's rights are being infringed. The mere fact that a majority may find such activity immoral or distasteful would not be sufficient ground for its prohibition.[77] Rather there must be palpable evidence, under the theory proposed here, of infringement upon another's rights touching upon his preservation of life, liberty or property.

Would the outcome of *Roe v. Wade* be affected under this line of thinking? Without considering the amount of scientific knowledge which now exists concerning the viability of foetuses, and the ability of the medical community to maintain the life of a baby born after only twenty-two weeks gestation, knowledge of which Justice Blackmun did not have in 1973,[78] it could

---

[76] Thus *Bowers v. Hardwick*, 478 *US* 186 (1986), in which the Supreme Court held that homosexual sodomy was not protected under a constitutional right of privacy, would have had a different result under the scheme proposed here. *Stanley v. Georgia*, 394 *US* 557 (1969), in which the Court protected an individual who read obscene materials in the privacy of his home under the First Amendment, could theoretically be expanded upon to protect activities as well under the view proposed here. Government, of course, would be able to enact time and place legislation to protect the rights of children and others, via zoning ordinances and other legislation, but again, it would have to show that such legislation was enacted to prevent specific harm to others and the time and place legislation would have to be as narrowly written as necessary. *Cf. Shelton v. Tucker* 364 *US* 479 (1960) in which the Court, in invalidating a statute requiring teachers to report all association memberships, stated that "even though the governmental purpose be legitimate and substantial, that purpose cannot be pursued by means that broadly stifle fundamental personal liberties when the end can be more narrowly achieved". *Ibid.*, at 488.

[77] See, for example, *Commonwealth of Kentucky v. Wasson*, 842 SW 2d 487 (Ky. 1992), in which the Supreme Court of Kentucky found a sodomy statute unconstitutional under the state constitution as violative of its right of privacy. The court there stated that the government's argument centred upon "the level of moral indignation felt by the majority of society against the sexual preference of homosexuals" in justifying criminalisation. The court held that "[d]eviate sexual intercourse conducted in private by consenting adults is not beyond the protections of the guarantees of individual liberty in our Kentucky Constitution simply because 'proscriptions against that conduct have ancient roots'". *Ibid.*, at 493, citing *Bowers v. Hardwick*, 478 *US* 186 (1986) at 192. See also *Eisenstadt v. Baird*, 405 *US* 438 (1972) in which the Court invalidated a Massachusetts statute prohibiting distribution of contraceptives to single persons, although such distribution was allowed for married persons. The Court, in holding that this violated the equal protection clause of the Fourteenth Amendment, maintained that the stated goals of the statute, deterring premarital sex and regulating the distribution of potentially harmful articles, were not reasonably related to the effects of the statute, nor was the distinction between married (referring back to the holding in *Griswold*) and unmarried persons rationally based.

[78] See 410 *US* 113 (1973). In a normal, full forty week gestation period, twenty weeks would fall approximately at the halfway point, or at five months into the pregnancy, which is clearly within the second trimester. Under *Roe's* reasoning and today's medical advancements, a clearly viable foetus may be legally aborted in the United States.

be strongly argued that, under the adoption of the secular natural law limitations proposed here, the government could have prevailed if it could show that it was acting on behalf of the life, liberty and property interests of the unborn foetus. Clearly, by aborting the foetus, any opportunity that it may have to "preserve its life" is dashed forever. In *Roe*, the Court examined three reason why the statute prohibiting abortion should be upheld. The first two, i.e. the discouragement of illicit sexual conduct and concern over the health of the women undergoing the abortion, were quickly dismissed as no longer being applicable. Only then did the Court arrive at the third argument, that the State has a valid interest in protecting pre-natal life.[79]

Under secular natural law theory, the last argument for the State would be paramount. Clearly, Locke recognised the preservation of life as the most important tenet, the *raison d'etre* of the natural law, and the legislature had a duty to uphold this tenet, most of all.

> [N]o body can transfer to another more power than he has in himself; and no body has absolute arbitrary power over himself, or over any other, to destroy his own life, or take away the life or property of another . . . so . . . the legislative can have no more power than this . . . It is a power, that hath no end but preservation, and therefore can never have a right to destroy, enslave, or designedly to impoverish the subjects. The obligations of the law of nature cease not in society, but only . . . have by human laws known penalties annexed to them, to inforce their observations. Thus the law of nature stands as an eternal rule to all men, legislators as well as others . . . the fundamental law of nature being the preservation of mankind, no human sanction can be good, or valid against it.[80]

The Court discussed at length whether the foetus could be considered a 'person' for purposes of protection under the liberty clause of the Fourteenth Amendment, but quickly dismissed that argument by stating that all of the other Constitutional discussions of 'persons' indicated that that was meant was 'post-natal' life.[81] Then the Court discussed the claim by the state that life began at conception, and hence the state's interest in protecting the foetus commenced at that time as well. After a review of various legal treatments of the unborn child under tort and property law, however, concluded that "the unborn have never been recognised in the law as person in the whole sense".[82] The Court then, holding the Texas statute unconstitutional under the Fourteenth Amendment, recognising a woman's qualified right to an abortion as coming within her constitutional right of privacy, concluded that the state

---

[79] 410 *US* at 147-150.
[80] *Two Treatises* at section 135.
[81] 410 *US* at 157.
[82] *Ibid.*, at 162.

may, only after the end of the first trimester, "regulate the abortion procedure in ways that are reasonably related to maternal health . . ."[83] "in promoting its interest in the health of the mother".[84] Secondly, the Court held that, only after viability of the foetus, may the state, "in promoting its interest in the potentiality of human life" regulate or proscribe abortion, except when the life of the mother is at risk.[85] Hence, what arose from *Roe* was the trimester rule: unlimited abortion in the first trimester; some state regulation to protect the life of the mother in the second trimester (because the woman is at greater risk for physical injury during a second trimester abortion and the state has an interest in protecting her life); and, during the third trimester, the state may regulate or prohibit abortions pursuant to its recognised interest in the now viable foetus, but the state may never prohibit an abortion when the mother's life, in "appropriate medical judgment" is in danger. In sum, a woman in the United States is free to have an abortion at any time during her pregnancy.[86]

Under application of the secular natural law, it is submitted, the outcome would have been entirely different because much more weight would have been given to the life or 'potential life' of a foetus. When weighing the preservation of a life, which, all semantics aside,[87] the embryo/foetus is human life, as distinguished from a tree or a diseased gallbladder,[88] one cannot logically argue that the inconvenience to a woman in any way could outweigh the

---

[83] Thus various state statutes which require waiting periods, counselling or lengthy informed consent prior to obtaining an abortion have not been upheld because they were found not to be reasonably related to maternal health, but rather as barriers to obtaining an abortion. See, for example, *Planned Parenthood of Missouri v. Danforth* 428 *US* 52 (1976). But see *Planned Parenthood v. Casey*, 112 S. Ct. 2791(1992) (informed consent upheld).

[84] 410 *US* at 164.

[85] *Ibid.*, at 165.

[86] Roughly 17,000 third-trimester abortions are performed each year in the United States. "Foster's appointment is good news" *Detroit News* (9 January 1995). The US Congress failed to override President Clinton's veto of a bill which would prevent "partial-birth" abortions, in which the foetus/child is aborted as it comes out of the birth canal. The President claimed that to ban this procedure deny a woman access to a medical treatment which could be life-saving to her. Yet most women obtained "partial-birth" abortions for reason of convenience, since the vast majority of health problems for the mother would have been ascertained at a much earlier time in the pregnancy. "Senate upholds veto of ban on late abortions" *USA Today* (27 September 1996) p. 4A.

[87] "Pro-choice groups call themselves 'pro-choice' because they cannot bring themselves to admit that they are pro-abortion. They have had terrific success, thanks to a sympathetic press, in keeping the focus of discussion on the exceedingly rare instances of rape and incest rather than on the roughly 1.5 million abortions for convenience each year that this society tolerates." "Foster's appointment is good news" *Detroit News* (9 January 1995). Note that groups which oppose abortion refer to themselves as 'pro-life' while they are referred to as 'anti-choice' by those who oppose them.

[88] See Dworkin, "Unenumerated Rights, Whether and How Roe Should Be Overruled" 59 U. Chi. L. Rev. 381, 400-401 (1992); Wellington, "Common Law Rules and Constitutional Double Standards, Some Notes on Adjudication" 83 Yale L. J. 221 (1973).

death of another's life. If *Roe* were decided today, under the scheme proposed here, there would be much greater attention given to the protection of foetal life by the state, especially now that a foetus is able to live outside the womb as early as twenty-two weeks, and contraceptives are universally available to men as well as women to prevent pregnancy, thus offering a solution to the problem of unwanted pregnancy which is much less intrusive upon everyone's rights, and completely legal. More than likely, under application of Locke's secular natural law, the court would prohibit all abortion except in cases where the life of the mother is in danger.[89] The state would argue that it is acting to protect the life of the foetus in infringing upon the mother's less compelling liberty interests of having to carry a baby to term, and most likely would succeed. The presumption under the secular natural law would be in favour of the life, even potential life, of the foetus at any time in its gestation.

There would be another effect from applying the secular natural law to the abortion issue, and that would be a resulting end to arbitrariness in determining when a foetus is a human being for purposes of legal actions concerning loss of foetal life. As it stands now, the foetus only has as much value as the mother places upon it. Unlike any other human life, it derives its 'standing' in the court of law based upon the opinion of its mother. Thus, if the foetus is merely an unwanted pregnancy, then the mother may abort it. If, however, a foetus of the same 'age' is a wanted baby, and it dies due to an illegal act of another, then the woman has a cause of action for wrongful death or, under acts currently in force in twenty-four states, the perpetrator can be prosecuted for homicide of the foetus that dies, even if, at the time, the foetus would not have been viable outside of the womb.[90] By adopting the view that any foetus or embryo, no matter how 'young' is considered human life for legal purposes,[91] much of the controversy surrounding time of viability would

---

[89] Pregnancies by rape are extremely rare because typically a 'morning-after' pill or a procedure in which the contents of the uterus are scraped out for evidence is performed in the emergency room immediately after a rape victim reports the crime. In those cases where unreported incest or rape results in a pregnancy, it has been recognised, as in the *X* case in Ireland, that such a pregnancy, in itself, is harmful to the health of the mother. Every state in the United States allows for abortion after rape or incest.

[90] "Abortion Laws, A Report From the States" *Wall Street Journal* (9 August 1995) p. 9A. It is interesting to note that the National Organisation for Women, the most ardent advocate for abortion on demand, has condemned the practice of female infanticide in India and selected abortion of female foetuses in India and China.

[91] The Court has recently taken a turn toward the natural law approach, though not in so many words, in the case of *Planned Parenthood v. Casey* 112 S. Ct. 2791 (1992). There the Court, in upholding an informed consent procedure promulgated by the state of Pennsylvania for all women prior to undergoing abortion, specifically rejected the "trimester framework" of *Roe* "as a rigid prohibition on all previability regulation aimed at the protection of foetal life". The trimester framework was flawed, the Court held, because "in its formulation it misconceives the nature of the pregnant woman's interest; and in practice it undervalues the State's interest in potential life . . ." *Ibid.*, at 2818. The Court went on to explicitly recognise that "there is a substantial state interest in potential life

end, and a standard would be set which is permanent, predictable, and independent from any sort of judicial tampering, contrary to the results predicted by many who fear a "return to *Lochner*"[92] with any resort to notions not explicitly state in the Constitution. And while some balancing would necessarily be required in cases presenting competing constitutional rights, the clear Lockean "preference" for rights which preserve the life of the individual would give the Court and the legislature bold markers to guide them through those areas in which the Constitution has not spoken.

Getting away from abortion and sexual privacy, one would find that the application of the secular natural law tenets to other cases involving non-expressed privacy rights, through either substantive due process under the Fourteenth Amendment or a right of privacy under the Ninth Amendment, would result in reaching much the same conclusions which the Court has already reached. Thus, in preserving an individual's life, liberty or property, the secular natural law would most likely recognise, as the Court has, a right to marry,[93] a right to procreate,[94] a right to divorce,[95] a right to educate one's

---

throughout pregnancy" and not just after viability. *Ibid.*, at 2820. Based on results from a 1990 Gallup Poll, seventy-seven per cent of Americans believe that abortion, at any stage of pregnancy, is the taking of a human life. "Abortion Laws, A Report From the States" *Wall Street Journal* (9 August 1995) p. 9A.

[92] In an amusing footnote in Professor Grey's article, "Do We Have an Unwritten Constitution?" at 711 fn. 35, he submits that "the ultimate punchline in the criticism of a constitutional decision is to say that it is 'like *Lochner*'. Professor Ely has even minted a generic term, 'to *Lochner*' . . . " *Lochner v. New York* 198 *US* 45 (1904) dealt with a state statute which, among other measures, prohibited workers in the baking industry to "be required or permitted to work" more than ten hours daily or sixty hours per week. The Court held that the statute was unconstitutional because it "interferes with the right of contract between employer and employe[e]s, concerning the number of hours in which the latter may labour in the bakery of the employer". *Ibid.*, at 53. And while the Court insisted that "[t]his is not a question of substituting the judgment of the court for that of the legislature" that is precisely how it came to be viewed. The Court had expanded upon the Contract Clause to promote its own laissez-faire, pro-business, economic philosophy, contrary to the prevailing trend in the country to finally enact labour laws prohibiting child labour and instituting various health and safety measures for the protection of poorly paid, defenceless workers toiling in Dickensian conditions. (The Court, "We do not believe in the soundness of the views which uphold this law." *Ibid.*, at 61.) To have characterised the relationship of an all-powerful employer and a powerless worker in a baking factory in 1904 as two equal parties to a contract was truly a legal fiction. The four dissenting judges pointed out that indeed bakery labourers worked in overheated, poorly ventilated workplaces, constantly exposed to highly injurious flour dust, and that experts agreed that an eight hour day was appropriate. *Ibid.*, at 70 (Harlan J., dissenting). Clearly, under secular natural law thinking, such basic state action to protect the lives and well-being of workers would stand up to any possible infringement upon the property rights of the employer. Such laws could not be said to "infringe fundamental principles [of liberty]". *Ibid.*, at 76 (Holmes J., dissenting).

[93] *Zablocki v. Redhail* 434 *US* 374 (1978).

[94] *Skinner v. Oklahoma*, 316 *US* 535 (1942).

[95] *Boddie v. Connecticut* 401 *US* 371 (1971).

children,[96] a right to determine one's family make-up,[97] a right to travel,[98] a right to vote [99] and a right to association.[100] There are two other areas, however, in which the secular natural law may produce a different outcome than the Court has or would.

The first area pertains to what one could call 'welfare' rights, or the general right to be guaranteed a job (or liveable wage), shelter, food, etc. One could make a strong argument, based upon the secular natural law discussed here, that the preservation of the life of an individual, the paramount purpose of the natural law according to Locke, depends more than anything upon his being able to earn a liveable wage, have shelter and sufficient food. Locke, of course, presented his tenets against the background of the 17th century in which most persons supported themselves by means of subsistence agriculture or participation in a trade. It was assumed that an able-bodied man would work to support himself and his family; a woman, of course, tended to her marriage, hearth and children. Those who were not able were cared for by their families or, in the case of the village 'drunk' or 'idiot' (the latter most likely a person born with mental or physical handicaps), cared for on a haphazard basis by various members of the community. The Church may have provided for orphans and others who had no one to care for them, but generally, in the words of Hobbes, life was "solitary, poor, nasty, brutish and short".[101] The concept of a governmental 'safety net' is a relatively recent development. Yet, just as the Constitution is 'living', to be interpreted to best suit the needs of the current generation, the secular natural law tenets are eternal and do not bring any preconceived notions with them. Thus even though the culture in which Locke lived would not have made allowances for women to live as independently as men, for example, the natural law philosophy he transcribed can be held to support the preservation of a woman's life, liberty and property just as equally as it would a man's. That is the brilliance of the natural law: eternal truths which may be adapted to modern circumstances and modern cultures. Therefore, even though Locke would not have had in mind a notion of a welfare state, could his natural law philosophy be held to enunciate the right of the individual to shelter, food, healthcare and a living wage (whether the person works or not)? Or, put another way, do we have a natural law right to be provided with these essentials? Or is it merely a right to have equal access to or the opportunity to achieve those things? The Court has been equivocal.

---

[96] *Meyer v. Nebraska* 262 *US* 390 (1923); *Pierce v. Society of Sisters*, 268 *US* 510 (1925).
[97] *Moore v. City of East Cleveland* 431 *US* 494 (1977).
[98] *Aptheker v. Secretary of State* 378 *US* 500 (1964).
[99] *Louisiana v. United States* 380 *US* 145 (1965).
[100] *NAACP v. Alabama* 357 *US* 449 (1958).
[101] Hobbes, *Leviathan* (1659) Chapter 13.

It has ruled that there is no constitutional right to housing[102] and has upheld some state formulas for welfare payments against constitutional rights claims.[103] On the other hand, it has not upheld some state restrictions on Food Stamp schemes[104] or the application of Social Security benefits.[105] The Court has held that a defendant in a criminal case who cannot afford counsel has the right to counsel paid for by the state,[106] yet a person does not have a constitutional right to be provided with a job.[107] In deciding what liberties are encompassed by the due process liberty clause, the Court has attempted to choose those which are "essential to the orderly pursuit of happiness by free men".[108] But has the Court, as Professor Ely claims, chosen to call some rights fundamental over others based upon the members' own cultural bias?[109] Isn't it at least as fundamental to an individual's preservation of life, liberty and property to be guaranteed a living wage, food, shelter and health care as it is to be guaranteed counsel in a criminal case?

Even if we apply Locke's parameters of preserving the life, liberty and property of the individual, we must determine, as many have attempted to, in what order of preference those liberties are to be protected.[110] Clearly an individual must have life in order to enjoy his liberty and property, so it would seem that rights directly tending to the preservation of one's life would be paramount under this theory. But then which rights most directly tend to the preservation of life? Could it not be argued that the right to food and shelter would be the most important? Or the right to a minimum standard of living? It is at this point that, by looking at the wording of Locke and the Constitution itself, one can find a plausible answer. The presumption upon which the Constitution and Locke's natural law theory were based was the inviolability of the integrity of the individual and those rights which protect and preserve that integrity. Phrases referring to government were always presented in the negative: the government will not do this and the government will not do that. The idea was not to require the government to do something for the individual, but rather for the government to get out of the way so that the individual can achieve whatever he or she wants to achieve. And indeed if government were

---

[102] *Lindsey v. Normet* 405 *US* 56 (1972).

[103] See, for example, *Dandridge v. Williams* 397 *US* 471 (1970) Maryland welfare formula which granted a fixed payment to families on welfare, no matter the size of the family, held not to be a violation of the equal protection rights of larger families; *Jefferson v. Hackney* 406 *US* 535 (1972).

[104] *United States Department of Agriculture v. Murry* 413 *US* 508 (1973).

[105] *Jimenez v. Weinberger* 417 *US* 628 (1974).

[106] *Gideon v. Wainwright* 372 *US* 335 (1963).

[107] *Board of Regents v. Roth* 408 *US* 564 (1972).

[108] *Meyers v. Nebraska* 262 *US* 390, 399 (1923).

[109] See Ely, "On Discovering Fundamental Values" at 37, claiming "a systemic bias in judicial choice of fundamental values . . . in favour of the values of the upper middle, professional class . . ."

[110] See, for example, Murphy, *op. cit.*, and the numerous articles and authors cited therein.

going to provide something for one person in a particular situation, then it had better well provide it for everyone in that same situation. But primarily, as Justice Douglas stated, "[t]he purpose of the Constitution and the Bill of Rights, unlike more recent models promoting a welfare state, was to take government off the backs of people"[111] so that each person can freely determine his or her own course in life.[112]

This leads to the second area, although there are many others,[113] in which the application of Locke's secular natural law tenets could lead to a different outcome: the tumultuous topic of the right of a competent adult to die. In Detroit Michigan, a retired pathologist by the name of Dr Jack Kevorkian has gained world fame by the creation and use of his machine which has enabled over one hundred people, none of whom were imminently close to dying (and even some who were not suffering from a terminal illness), to die quickly and painlessly. The machine allows a person to take in carbon monoxide which, of course, kills the person in a matter of minutes. The advocates on both sides cite fundamental rights in their favour. Those opposed to Kevorkian (and they include the Roman Catholic Church, the Council of Orthodox Jewish Rabbis, and the state of Michigan, which has unsuccessfully prosecuted Kevorkian twice under various criminal statutes) claim, as Locke does, that an individual, just as he does not have the right to take another's life, does not have the right to take his own life. Referring to coercion or familial pressures that the ill individual invariably feels, the opposition group submits that the decision to die is not truly a competent or independent one and that, by permitting assisted suicide, one is embarking down the slippery slope of euthanasia, which would invariably entail the killing of those elderly, infirm or handicapped whose quality of life society judges not to be sufficient.[114]

Proponents of assisted suicide claim that just as one has a right to determine the course of his or her life, one has the right to determine the time and method of his or her death. And, since March 1996, the proponents have had the 9th US Circuit Court of Appeals on its side. The ruling by that court,

---

[111] *Schneider v. Smith* 390 *US* 17, 25 (1968).

[112] However, a more thorough analysis of this issue is necessary elsewhere. For just as there have been great cultural changes affecting the perceptions of the role of women and minorities in society, so could not future perceptions change with regards to the duty of everyone to support himself or herself and the obligation which government owes to each citizen?

[113] For example, can states reinstitute divorce statutes requiring proof of fault which result in making it more difficult for a divorce to be obtained? Are health care organisations which limit or prohibit access to certain types of health care denying individuals their necessary liberty rights?

[114] Opponents invariably refer to the situation in the Netherlands in which the euthanasia statutes which were originally passed to apply only to the ill elderly are now being used in defence of killing babies who have been born with severe deformities or handicaps. "Baby killers acquittal likely" *Detroit News* (6 December 1995) p. 2.

which was reported widely, held that Washington state's ban on doctor-assisted suicides violated "constitutional guarantees of life, liberty and the pursuit of happiness"[115] Although this decision was ultimately overturned, as will be discussed in the final chapter, the Supreme Court did not utilise the secular, natural law and did not go far enough in recognising a constitutional right to life.

As hinted above, under Locke's natural law tenets, those opposing assisted suicide would most likely prevail. As stated previously, the natural law maintains that man naturally seeks life and the preservation of that life, and may not undertake any activity to end that life. In addition, there is grave concern whether a decision to die can ever truly be uncoerced, as anyone who is ill and perceives themselves to be a burden to their family may subconsciously sense a desire on the part of the family to be rid of them. Also, one must truly question the mental competence of an individual who is ill, on medication, and in a depressed state of mind which invariably accompanies those who are contemplating suicide. Last, the 'slippery slope' notion is one to be concerned about, for there is indeed a fine line between a person wanting to die and a person who agrees to die because others around him feel that it is appropriate. Again, it is feared that once one ventures into quantifying the quality of life by degrees, one risks destroying a life that had much to offer, and arbitrary decision-making as to the relative value of life would become prevalent. Only by maintaining a clear standard in which *all* life is considered worth saving, says the natural law, can the value of *each* life be appropriately protected. (One need only look at the changed perception society now has of children with Down's Syndrome. Formerly left to die, it is now accepted that their lives are just as valuable and as worthy of defence as any other. Similarly, children with handicaps and disabilities are now recognised as having much greater ability to learn and contribute to the community in which they live, for the betterment of all.) And this is what Lockean natural law would require us to do.

In summary, it is contended that the open recognition of the secular natural law basis of the US Constitution and Bill of Rights, as best exemplified by the writings of John Locke, and its utilisation via the Ninth Amendment to enunciate and protect necessary rights which were not specifically expressed, especially those pertaining to privacy, would best serve the spirit and intent of the US Constitution. In addition, uniform adoption of the parameters of the secular natural law, an independent and eternal standard of right and wrong, would provide the predictability and stability so greatly needed to prevent arbitrary decision-making in adjudications pertaining to fundamental rights of life, liberty and property.

---

[115] Castaneda, "Suicide ruling sends a message" *USA Today* (8 March 1996) p. 3A, citing compassion in *Dyning, Inc v. Washington* 79 F3d 790 (ith Cir. 7996).

The *raison d'etre* of the secular natural law, as descended from Ulpian, through the Roman jurisconsults and the Medieval glossators, to the Enlightenment era of Pufendorf and the essential John Locke, is the preservation of the life, liberty and property of the individual. Through such preservation and protection, limited only by infringement upon another's rights to same, each can achieve his or her 'due' and thereby is the common good attained.

CHAPTER 8

The Thomistic Natural Law Model:
The Irish Judiciary's Full Embrace
via the Common Good

For since one man is part of the community, whatever any man is and has belongs to the community just as what any part is belongs to the whole: hence nature also imposes some loss on the part in order to preserve the whole . . . [A]ny precept concerning a particular matter [is only law] insofar as it is ordered to the Common Good [and] . . . [the good consists of] those things by which the life of man is preserved and opposite impeded.[1]

[T]he common good is not the good of the political community as such (which is a concept inherent in the totalitarian State and inimical to the protection of human rights) but is an end to be promoted for specific purposes, which include the furtherance of the dignity and freedom of every individual in society.[2]

The right of privacy is not absolute . . . You can't be required to do anything against your conscience, but that doesn't mean you have the right to do everything that your conscience allows.[3]

The Constitution of the United States is based upon the secular natural law philosophy best exemplified by John Locke, as handed down from the secular Roman jurisconsults. This philosophy has at its primary tenet the preservation of the life, liberty and property of the individual, with the underlying purpose to attain the common good by giving each 'his due'. The rights of the individual, however, are paramount and this thinking has formed a uniquely American view of the right of privacy which requires that the rights of the individual ought to be preserved and protected until the point at which that exercise infringes upon another's rights to life, liberty and property. The right of privacy is among those rights not specifically expressed in the Constitution or Bill of Rights, but arises from the notions of the secular natural law through

---

[1] Thomas Aquinas, *Treatise on Law* at 96, 4; 90, 2 and 94, 2 (emphasis added).

[2] Mr Justice Declan Costello, *Limiting Rights, Constitutionally, Human Rights and Constitutional Law* (1992) p. 178 (emphasis added).

[3] Mr Justice Brian Walsh, from an interview with the author, Dublin, 8 October 1992.

the Ninth Amendment and/or the due process liberty clause of the Fourteenth Amendment. Ideally the views of the majority or any sort of moral consensus are not to be considered in determining whether the recognition and exercise of a particular right is protected. For the primary purpose of establishing government in the United States was to protect one's unique life, liberty and property, the last defined as including one's property in one's self. Thus, rights are to be protected as widely as possible. Indeed, according to the Framers, that which is considered as the greatest threat to the individual's exercise of his rights, is the powerful authority and coecive nature of the majority. Therefore, under the US Constitution's Bill of Rights, through the due process liberty clause of the Fourteenth Amendment and the general terms of the Ninth Amendment, based upon secular natural law, the right of privacy is to be protected insofar as the exercise of that right does not infringe upon the rights of another. This much has been established up to this point.

The Constitution of Ireland, on the other hand, is based upon the Thomistic natural law as handed down from the Church fathers and canonists. The Thomistic natural law via the Irish Constitution affects the recognition and application of the right of privacy, as follows:

1. The common good, being the end of the Thomistic natural law and the primary purpose for the establishment of government under the Irish Constitution as compared with the emphasis upon the rights of the individual under the US Constitution and its secular natural law, has the effect of qualifying the right of privacy, making it a narrower right than its US counterpart, both in definition and scope;

2. Because a law, in order to be valid, must be "ordered to the common good", then rights pertaining to privacy are subject, to a certain extent, to the notions of the consensus of the Irish population, unlike, as discussed above, in the United States;

3. The notion that there is a higher, unwritten law which can always supersede any written positive law is an accurate reading of the Thomistic natural law. Under a proper reading of the natural law and the common good, this does not impair the effectiveness of the Constitution in general nor Article 28.3.3° (re: emergency legislation) but rather complements all of the articles in the Constitution, and makes them more effective in achieving the common good and protecting the rights and dignity of the individual.

In addition to the above, it is submitted that:

1. The Irish judiciary, in referring to or utilising the natural law in its opinions, ought never to refer to that which the Catholic Church maintains in its social teachings or Papal Encyclicals, which may or may not be derived from the natural law, for this has *no* place in the jurisprudence of Irish

Constitutional Law. Rather the judiciary ought to rely purely upon its own Constitution and the natural law underlying it, with the understanding that the only relation that the Irish Constitution has with the teachings of the Catholic Church is that the latter utilises, to some extent and among other sources, portions of the Thomistic natural law as well;

2. The Thomistic natural law can provide the Irish Courts with both the flexibility and permanent, independent standards necessary for stability and fairness, and as such, ought to be even more fully embraced by the Irish judiciary, with direct reference to the writings of Aquinas in order to properly understand the notion of common good and valid law.

Let us begin, however, with the general concept of a constitutional right of privacy in Ireland. It has long been recognised that, like the US Constitution, the Irish Constitution did not 'create' rights, but rather recognises their existence.[4] In fact, the Irish Constitution, through its various articles, is more explicit in recognising the existence of unexpressed rights than its American counterpart's Ninth Amendment. In the Irish Constitution, particularly under the "Fundamental Rights" articles, "[t]he State simply acknowledges that [there] are pre-existing and natural rights superior to all positive law".[5] Furthermore, "[i]t should be borne in mind that it has already been decided several times that rights which are guaranteed by the Constitution, whether specified or not, are directly enforceable in court without the necessity of introducing [positive law] to implement these rights".[6] Of these are a collection of rights which fall under the general category of the right of privacy.

Beginning with Kenny J.'s High Court recognition of a right to bodily integrity,[7] against which the Supreme Court did not dissent and which subsequent decisions have accepted, the Courts have built upon the notion of a right of privacy based on the wording of several articles and other considerations. As Professor Kelly noted, in reversing his previously critical view of the right of privacy:

---

[4] See, for example, *McGee v. Attorney General* [1974] I.R. 284 at 310. (Walsh J.)" [The Constitution] emphatically reject[s] the theory that there are no rights without laws, nor rights contrary to the law and no rights anterior to the law. [It] indicate[s] that justice is placed above the law and acknowledge[s] that natural rights, or human rights, are not created by law but that the Constitution confirms their existence and give them protection. The individual has natural and human rights over which the State has no authority." See also *Norris v. Attorney General* [1984] I.R. 36 at 46 (High Court, McWilliam, J.) where that court accepted Justice Kenny's holding in *Ryan v. Attorney General* [1965] I.R. 294 at 312-313, in which he stated that "personal rights which may be involved to invalidate legislation are not confined to those specified in Article 40 . . . " including "the right to bodily integrity."

[5] Walsh, "Existence and Meaning of Fundamental Rights in the Field of Education in Ireland", 2 Hum. Rts. L.J. (1981) 319 at 321.

[6] *Ibid.*, at 323.

[7] *Ryan v. Attorney General* [1965] I.R. 294.

It seems to me that a right of personal privacy is an obvious candidate
for recognition and enforcement, partly on its own merits, partly because it is recognised both by the Universal Declaration of Human Rights
and by the European Human Rights Convention, both of which are subscribed by this State.[8]

In *Ryan v. Attorney General*, the High Court dealt with a claim by Mrs Ryan
that the fluoridation of the water supply was a violation of her constitutional
rights under Articles 40.3, 41 and 42. After a lengthy discussion of the safety
of the minuscule amount of fluoride (1 ppm) which is actually placed into the
water, and weighing the interest which the legislature has in protecting the
dental health of citizens, the Court held that fluoridation did not infringe upon
Mrs Ryan's rights to protect her family, under Article 41.1.2°, nor did it affect
her rights to educate her children under sections 1 and 2 of Article 42. Turn-
ing to Article 40.3, however, Kenny J. in the High Court, first reiterated the
notion of judicial review.

In my opinion, the High Court has jurisdiction to consider whether an
Act of the Oireachtas respects and, as far as practicable, defends and
vindicates the personal rights of the citizen and to declare the legislation
unconstitutional if it does not.[9]

Before proceeding to Kenny J.'s, discussion of the right of bodily integrity,
and the Supreme Court's holding, let us examine the various articles of the
Irish Constitution upon which Mrs Ryan sought to rely in her claims against
fluoridation.

In that affirmation of judicial review, Justice Kenny referred directly to
the language of Article 40.3.1°, which is translated from the Irish as, "[t]he
State guarantees in its laws to respect, and, as far as practicable, by its laws to
defend and vindicate the personal rights of the citizens". (Note, however, that
the Irish itself is much more demanding upon the State, roughly reading: "The
State guarantees no interference by its laws in any citizen's personal rights

---

[8] Kelly, *Book Review: Privacy and the Law* 2 Dublin U. L. Rev. 112 at 113 (1970). "In the
second edition of my Fundamental Rights in the Irish Law and Constitution I wrote criti-
cally of the turn which *Ryan v. Attorney General* had given to the law; it seemed to me
that its result was uncertainty, together with a concealed encroachment by the Courts on
the well-intentioned discretion of the Oireachtas. In retrospect I think I took the wrong
side. As time goes on, the world's pressures on the individual become heavier, and the
interest of the legislature...in liberal law reform in the individual's interest is nearly non-
existent. The present subject under discussion (the right of privacy) illustrates this very
well. We are unlikely to get a Protection of Privacy Act, far less likely, at any rate, than we
are to get its equivalent through a purely judicial initiative launched from Article 40.3."
Cf. Justice Walsh's statement: "Courts achieve what the parliament is not prepared to
undertake." Interview with the author, Dublin, 8 October 1992.
[9] [H.C. 1962] at 312.

and further guarantees to defend (those rights) in its position/situation with the laws, to the extent it is possible.") This section, not unlike the due process liberty clause of the Fourteenth Amendment of the US Constitution ("No State shall make or enforce any law which shall abridge the privileges or immunities of citizens of the United States; nor shall any State deprive any person of life, liberty, or property, without due process of law . . .") leaves the term "rights" open, as indicated by the wording of that section itself, and the following section, which, by its discussion of rights "in particular", implies that there are other rights which are not expressed. The Ninth Amendment of the US Constitution works in a similar way, although it is more straightforward in establishing that "[t]he enumeration . . . of certain rights, shall not be construed to deny or disparage others retained by the people". The strongest language enunciating and protecting the unexpressed rights of citizens, however, is under those sections of Article 41 protecting the rights and interests of the family unit:

> The State recognises the Family as the natural primary and fundamental unit group of Society, and as a moral institution possessing inalienable and imprescriptible rights, antecedent and superior to all positive law. The State, therefore, guarantees to protect the Family in its constitution and authority, as the necessary basis of social order and as indispensable to the welfare of the Nation and the State.

There is no part of the US Constitution which compares in any way with Article 41. While it can be said that Article 40 is very similar to the secular natural law protection of individual rights, and indeed, these may be the rights to which de Valera was referring when he spoke about the secular nature of some of the rights in the Irish Constitution,[10] Article 41 is purely Thomistic natural law. It mimics the notion which is the basis of that natural law, i.e. that man, like one part of a whole, only thrives within the embrace of the family and, on a large scale, as a part of the whole community. Indeed, as has been stated earlier,[11] Aquinas did not recognise the notion of individual liberties as part of the natural law. Rather, the emphasis was upon the common good and any individual rights which were protected, arose as a secondary result of attaining the common good. Article 42, though sounding much like the holding in *Meyer v. Nebraska* (regarding the right of a family to educate its children as seen fit), also reflects the Thomistic emphasis upon the family unit, the whole over the part, in recognising the inalienable right of a family to educate children. Of the three Articles discussed here, only one, Article 42, has a clear common good qualifier. Article 40.3 has no mention of the common good, although it does allow that the State will protect said rights "as far

---

[10] See Chapter 6, p. 78 fn. 34.
[11] See Tuck, *Natural Rights Theories* (1979) p. 20.

as practicable", thus suggesting that the common good may be a limitation. Other sections of Article 40 do make mention of common good qualifiers, however, and the common good is emphasised explicitly in other sections of the Constitution, most notably in the Preamble. Again in Article 41, there is no mention of the common good, though this Article is by far the most representative of the Thomistic natural law and every other Article under the Fundamental Rights section of the Constitution has a clear common good statement: Article 43 (Private Property); 44 (Religion); and 45 (Social Directives, not enforceable). How do this collection of rights, some Thomistic in nature, some secular, come together to form a right of privacy and what does that right look like?

First and foremost, it has been established, in court decisions based upon the emphasis in the Constitution itself, that the common good dominates any adjudication of constitutional rights, whether those constitutional rights are expressed clearly or are unexpressed. As Kenny J. stated in *Ryan*:

> I think that the personal rights which may be involved to invalidate legislation are not confined to those specified in Article 40 but include all those rights which result from the Christian and democratic nature of the State. It is, however, a jurisdiction to be exercised with caution. None of the personal rights of the citizen are unlimited: their exercise may be regulated by the Oireachtas when the common good requires this.[12]

Mr Justice Kenny had essentially laid out the first part of the double limitation upon the legislature, which would be discussed more thoroughly in *McGee*: The legislature may not abandon the common good in its attempts to protect the rights of citizens. Mr Justice Kenny then went on to present the other side of the limitation.

> When dealing with controversial social, economic and medical matters on which it[s] notorious views change from generation to generation, the Oireachtas has to reconcile the exercise of personal rights with the claims of the common good and its decision on the reconciliation should prevail unless it was oppressive to all or some of the citizens or unless there is no reasonable proportion between the benefit which the legislation will confer on the citizens or a substantial body of them and the interference with the personal rights of the citizen.[13]

In other words, the legislature may not unduly trample upon individual rights in order to promote the common good. Thus the parameters for the legisla-

---

[12] [1962] I.R. 312 (High Court, Kenny J.).
[13] [1962] I.R. 313 (High Court, Kenny J.).

ture, and the courts as well, in recognising and enforcing individual rights are defined in terms of the common good: rights may not take away from or be contrary to the common good, but the common good may not be utilised to unnecessarily infringe upon rights. Mr Justice Kenny's statement is very close to what Aquinas himself wrote in describing unjust laws:

> However, laws can be unjust in two ways, one way by being contrary to human good (the good having been defined as consisting of those things by which the life of man is preserved and the opposite impeded:[14])
>
> a. either from the end as when some authority imposes burdens on the subjects that do not pertain to the common utility but rather to his own greed or glory;
> b. or from the lawgiver, as when someone makes a law that is beyond the authority granted to him;
> c. or from the form, as when burdens are unequally distributed in the community, even though they pertain to the Common Good.[15]

Thus, a law is unjust if it is contrary to the preservation of an individual's life, i.e. contrary to the substantive good, or, even if it is not contrary to the preservation of an individual's life, it is unjust if it unfairly burdens one segment of the population (and this can be rephrased in modern terms to mean "if it infringes upon the rights of certain individuals more than upon others", keeping in mind that Aquinas did not recognise "rights" as such), or is done to unfairly benefit the lawmaker or one segment of the population, or is otherwise beyond the authority of the lawmaker. In defining what is just law versus unjust law, Aquinas clearly stated that, just as individual parts are subservient to the whole (reflecting the influence of Aristotelian thought), the individual should expect to sacrifice for the good of the whole.[16] The Irish Constitution, with its overall emphasis upon the common good, and its recitation of rights subject to common good qualifiers, clearly adopts this view, and subsequently, any rights which are recognised are not nearly as broad as their American counterparts, where there is no common good limitation. Under Irish law, the individual's right of privacy, though recognised by utilising the secular natural law principles laid out in Article 40, is limited not only at that point at which the exercise of said right infringes upon another's rights, as under the secular natural law basis existing in the United States, but also is generally limited by the Thomistic natural law notion of the common good. (Note that a familial

---

[14] *Treatise on Law* at 94, 2.

[15] *Ibid.*, at 96, 4. Aquinas also stated that a law is unjust if it is against the "Divine Law," with a fleeting reference to the Ten Commandments (e.g. laws promoting idolatry are contrary to the Divine Law), but more than likely meant as a reiteration of the notion that all just laws are ultimately derived from God's law. *Ibid.*, at 96, 5.

[16] *Ibid.*, at 96, 4.

right of privacy, which would most likely arise and be protected under Articles 41 and 42, and is a Thomistic natural law concept, would be subject to the same common good limitation, as will be seen.[17]) Thus, the right of privacy in Ireland is narrower in scope and definition. In order to understand the scope and definition of the individual right of privacy in Ireland, however, it is necessary to first define what is meant by the common good. For if we can understand the notion of the common good, we can understand how it limits privacy, and then return to *Ryan* and subsequent cases.

Aquinas, in an amazingly forward-looking view of the law, stated that the common good requires an regular examination of a consensus of views:

> Whatever is ordered to an end must necessarily be proportioned to that end. The end, however, of law is the common good ... Hence, human laws should be proportioned to the Common Good. *Now the common good consists of many things. Therefore law should relate to many, with respect to persons and affairs and time. For the community of the state is made up of many persons, and its good is achieved through many actions; nor is it established for some short period of time but to endure for all time through the succession of its citizens ...*[18]

He went on to submit that the purpose of human law does not require the control of all human behaviour, as humans have differing abilities and some are more virtuous than others. Rather:

> ... human law is framed for the whole community of men in which most men are not perfect in virtue. And therefore human law does not prohibit all vices from which the virtuous abstain but *only the more serious ones from which it is possible for the majority to abstain and especially those which are harmful to others and which, if not prohibited, would make preservation of human society impossible: Thus human law prohibits murders, thefts and the like.*[19]

Therefore, the human law is properly ordered to the common good in one of two ways:

> [H]uman law does not command all the acts of all the virtues but only those which can be ordered to the Common Good, *either immediately,*

---

[17] Professor Murphy maintains that the US would do well to recognise familial rights as Ireland does and points to several US cases in which the rights of the family unit have been denigrated or entirely rejected. Murphy, "An Ordering of Constitutional Values" 53 S. Cal. L. Rev. 703 at 737-740 (1980).

[18] *Treatise on Law* at 96, 1 (emphasis added).

[19] *Ibid.*, at 96, 2 (emphasis added).

as when some things are done directly for the Common Good, or indirectly, as when legislators order the citizens to do something for good order, thus training them in upholding the Common Good of justice and peace.[20]

It would be so convenient if there was a checklist for the common good from which it could easily be determined whether a law is properly ordered to it. Short of such a checklist, however, one can draw from Aquinas's writings the following three generalised elements. Hence, a law is deemed to be ordered to the common good if:

1. It serves to preserve the life and health of humans or at the least is not contrary to the preservation of such; and, does not unfairly burden or favour a segment of the population; and, otherwise abides by accepted notions of due process; and

2. It prohibits acts or "vices" which a consensus wishes to prohibit because said vices make preservation of human society impossible; or;

3. It seeks to maintain general order, justice, or peace for the benefit of the community.

The first part of the point 1 is what has been referred to here as the "substantive common good", recalling that the good is that by which the life of man is preserved and the opposite impeded, and drawing a parallel to the "substantive due process" notion in the American Fourteenth Amendment. This section is the focal point for the entire Thomistic natural law theory, and, as such, is a required element to any acts which also fulfil the elements listed in 2 or 3 (as indicated by the conjunction *and* at the end). The next section of the first element has been deemed also to be necessary by Aquinas, as seen above, for even if an act is not contrary to the preservation of life, it is not considered to be ordered to the common good if it unfairly burdens one segment of the population or was enacted to unfairly benefit the lawmaker or a particular interest group. Last, of course, other notions of due process in properly enacting legislation in a democratic government must apply, e.g. as Aquinas has stated, a lawmaker cannot go beyond his own authority. Points 2 and 3 are derived from Aquinas' writings referred to on the previous page, and can be labelled as direct (2) and indirect (3) orderings to the common good, per Aquinas's own definitions.[21]

---

[20] *Ibid.*, at 96, 3 (emphasis added).
[21] For a brief but interesting overview of some practical applications of the Thomistic Natural Law, see Davitt, "St Thomas Aquinas and the Natural Law" in *Origins of the Natural Law Tradition* (1954) p. 26.

Other definitions of the common good are not unlike the above. Mr Justice Walsh, in one article, called it "the satisfaction (in so far as possible) of the greatest proportion of interests of all persons with the least sacrifice, the least friction, and the least waste . . . "[22] And Mr. Justice Declan Costello gave a thoughtful discussion of the common good in another article.

> This concept of 'the common good' firstly appears, most importantly, in the Constitution's preamble [citing preamble]. It is indeed one of the key concepts in the Constitution and one of particular significance [in the discussion of limiting rights constitutionally].
>
> "The notion of the common good is derived from the concept that a political community exists to provide a whole range of conditions (material, social, moral, cultural) so that each of its members can realise his or her development as a human person. Thus the common good is the whole ensemble of conditions which collaboration in a political community brings about for the benefit of every member in it. This point is made clear in the preamble to which reference has just been made, for the common good is not the good of the political community as such (which is a concept inherent in the totalitarian State and inimical to the protection of human rights) but is an end to be promoted for specific purposes, which include the furtherance of the dignity and freedom of every individual in society . . . *When therefore the exigencies of the common good are called in aid to justify restriction of the exercise of basic rights it has to be borne in mind that the protection of basic rights is one of the objects which the common good is intended to assure.*[23]

The last sentence reiterates the double-edged limitation which the common good places upon the legislature and the courts. Costello then proceeded to give a practical example of the way in which the common good can limit the exercise of rights under Article 40.3, specifically the the right of privacy, among other unspecified rights.

> The Supreme Court has concluded that it is for the courts to decide what these rights are [under Article 40.3] and the courts have fulfilled this task by declaring, for example, that the right of privacy is a "personal right" within the meaning of the article. But obviously laws may interfere with the enjoyment of personal rights (as when, for example, powers of search trench on the right of privacy) and questions arise as to the constitutional validity of such laws. Here again the concept of the common good is a relevant consideration *for unless the personal right in-*

---

22 Walsh, *op. cit.*, at 327.
23 Costello, "Limiting Rights Constitutionally" in *Human Rights and Constitutional Law* (1992) p. 178 (emphasis added).

volved is an absolute one whose exercise can in no circumstances be restricted then there has been no unconstitutional failure on the part of the State to respect, defend or vindicate the right in suit if the impugned restriction is one reasonably necessary in order to promote the common good.[24]

Here is a restatement of the absolute nature of the right to preserve one's life and health under the Thomistic natural law ("for unless the personal right involved is an absolute one . . ."), referred to here as the "substantive common good", i.e. the collective right of each person in a community to preserve his or her life and health and presented here as a necessary element to the overall definition of the common good. Costello continued on.

> The exigencies of the common good may therefore justify laws restricting the exercise of constitutionally protected rights. But there is an aspect of the common good, "public morality", to which the Constitution specifically refers.
>
> [Costello then proceeded to compare the two views about the propriety of allowing morality to be considered in the adjudication of individual rights.]
>
> [While] adherents to Mill's view [basically the American view that rights are limited only when harm to others may occur] would argue that the law cannot be used to enforce morality as such. On the other hand there are those who maintain that society has the right to make judgments on what is morally right or wrong conduct . . . whether or not the actions which are thereby prohibited cause harm to others . . .
>
> This controversy has been raised in, and authoritatively settled by, the Supreme Court, which has made clear that the Constitution permits the enactment of laws whose object is to protect the moral ethos of society [citing *Norris v. Attorney General*, to be discussed below] . . . [T]he concept of "public morality" as employed in the Constitution connotes more than the idea of a nuisance committed in public . . . [but rather] *must be understood as including the notion that there exist certain moral standards which society is entitled to protect.*[25]

Here is the other part of Aquinas's formula, as rephrased above. By prohibiting acts or vices which are a threat to the maintenance of human society itself, the common good is utilised to protect the moral climate of the society, under the understanding that the maintenance of an acceptable moral climate benefits the health and well-being of the citizens in that society just as much as

---

[24] *Ibid.*, at pp. 178-179 (emphasis added).
[25] *Ibid.*, at pp. 179-180 (emphasis added).

the protection of individual rights. Costello defined the duty of the courts, therefore, as follows:

> What has to be achieved is a proper balance of, on the one hand, the need to preserve society's moral ethos and on the other the protection of the rights of those who do not share the ethical principles which the community wishes to uphold. Differences will, of course, arise as to whether a just balance has been achieved. But the existence of differences does not, in itself, invalidate the power to legislate.[26]

Finally, in admitting that a consensus of the community is necessary in order for such laws to be enforceable, Costello cited Mr Justice Walsh's dissenting opinion in a case before the European Court of Human Rights:

> [i]f it is accepted that the State has a valid interest in the prevention of corruption and in the preservation of the moral ethos of its society, then the State has a right to enact such laws as it may reasonably think necessary to achieve these objects. The rule of law itself depends on a moral consensus in the community and in a democracy the law cannot afford to ignore the moral consensus of the community. *If the law is out of touch with the moral consensus of the community, whether by being either too far below it or too far above it, the law is brought into contempt.*[27]

Even so, Costello stated:

> [n]o matter how homogeneous a society may be there will always be members of it who do not accept the views of the majority on all moral issues . . . Unless every member of a political community has a fundamental right that laws will not be enacted contrary to his or her moral tenets . . . then the fact that some members will disagree with the moral principle which society is attempting to protect is not in itself a reason which flaws the principle (of morality legislation). If however a law restricts some recognised right enjoyed by some members of a minority group then it may well be that the legislative power now being considered had been invalidly exercised. This, of course, does not mean that the power itself is invalid . . . Tolerance of disagreement and dissent within a community is a value to be preserved. But this does not imply that when there exists a moral consensus within a community as to what is right or wrong behaviour the existence of an opposing view automatically prohibits legislation to protect the community's moral values.[28]

---

[26] *Ibid.*, at p. 181.
[27] *Ibid.*, at p. 183, citing *Dudgeon v. United Kingdom* 4 E.H.R.R. 149 at 184.
[28] *Ibid.*, at p. 181.

Or, in other words which Mr Justice Walsh stated:

> You can't be required to do anything against your conscience, but that doesn't mean that you have the right to do everything that your conscience allows.[29]

This leads us to another question re: consensus which pertains particularly to Ireland. If a community is governed, in part at least, by the consensus of the community, and the citizens in the community overwhelmingly profess a particular faith, then cannot the tenets of that faith be utilised directly in determining what the consensus of the community is for the purpose of lawmaking or judicial adjudication? The answer here is no, for several very crucial reasons. Even though the consensus of the community and the teachings of the Catholic Church may, from time to time and on particular issues, coincide, and even though the Constitution of Ireland and the Catholic Church have adopted, each to a certain extent, the natural law theory of Thomas Aquinas, the two entities are different and separate – and ought to be treated as such.

First, any official adoption of the teachings of a particular church is the equivalent of the establishment of that particular religion and, as such, is unconstitutional under Article 44. In addition, any official adoption of the teachings of a particular church would be offensive to those who do not profess that faith. Although Ireland is over ninety per cent Catholic, the rights and interests of the remaining ten per cent ought not to be cavalierly offended, especially when such offence is not necessary. (Imagine if the Irish Courts upheld a law prohibiting meat to be served anywhere in Ireland on Fridays, then you understand the discomfort and fear than many non-Catholics feel when Catholic principles are cited in the opinions of the Irish Courts. If the Court can cite one Catholic teaching, what is to prevent it from going further and adopting all Catholic tenets officially. The line between Church and State is best kept strictly maintained, as in the United States, for that reason.)

Second, the Constitution of Ireland contains legal notions other than those of Thomas Aquinas. There are secular natural law rights, and various Anglo-American notions of due process and 'law of the land' concepts, described previously, which also play an important role in defining the nature of the Irish Constitution. Similarly, the Church is governed by concepts other than Thomistic natural law. There are Papal Encyclicals, Canon Law and various treatises based upon the Biblical sources which also have been utilised to create rules and laws with which Catholics must abide. (One mentioned above, i.e. not eating meat on Fridays, is just one small example.) Ireland and the Church are not the same, and the population of Ireland ought not to be subject to the laws of the Catholic Church via the Irish Government.

---

[29] Mr Justice Brian Walsh, from an interview with the author, Dublin, 8 October 1992.

Last, acceptance of the beliefs of a particular faith ought to be voluntary, may vary in intensity from person to person and, most importantly, is a private act. A person who claims on a census form to be Catholic is stating, at least for that poll, that he or she believes in at least some of the tenets of that church. Whether that person wants the State to enforce those tenets officially is a far different matter, and indeed, many who state that they are Catholic do not support all of the Church's teachings or would not want those teachings enforced upon all via State mandate. The controversy surrounding the recent vote on divorce is an example of this. The results, which were extremely close, clearly did not reflect the religious make-up of the population. Obviously, all citizens who profess to be Catholic either do not accept the Church's teachings on divorce or accept them but do not believe that the State should adopt and enforce that view. In the United States, it has long been recognised that faith and actions pertaining to religious beliefs must be voluntary in nature. Making such activities and beliefs mandatory not only denies civil liberties, but also denigrates the very faith or beliefs the mandate intended to support. Here at least, the Irish Courts ought to follow the American way.

Hence, with the above in mind, let us return to the definition of the common good proposed here in order to define, as best as possible, a right of privacy under the Irish Constitution, with its basis in the natural law of Thomas Aquinas.

That right of privacy can be defined as encompassing any individual activity which does not denigrate the life or health of any human life; exercised to the extent allowed by the majority consensus of the community and in which no segment of the community is unduly burdened or favoured and general order, justice and peace in the community is maintained.

Here we have the absolute Thomistic "substantive common good" requirement pertaining to the preservation of the life and health of all human life. In addition, the Thomistic notion which allows government to prohibit those 'vices' which the majority of the community would want prohibited is included here, as are the other common good limitations prohibiting unfair burdens or favours for certain segments of the community, and the general requirement that the exercise of rights not be disruptive to the general order, justice and peace in the community.

Accepting the above definition, and comparing it to the American constitutional right of privacy defined here, one clearly sees the distinction. The American right of privacy essentially encompasses the individual exercise of one's rights to life, liberty and property to the extent that another's exercise of same is not infringed (and note that 'life' does not currently include foetal life). The Irish right of privacy is arguably limited in that way as well, with the inclusion of foetal life limiting it even farther. It is also limited by the common good notions of community consensus, fairness in the distribution of burden versus advantages and the general component of serving justice, order and peace for the community. These added limitations or parameters to the right of privacy would and should obviously have an effect upon the jurisprudence surrounding the Irish right of privacy as compared with the jurisprudence surrounding the namesake American right. Therefore, any value judgements concerning the jurisprudence surrounding each respective right of privacy should not be made based upon a comparison to the other's holdings, but rather upon how well each jurisdiction interprets its own Constitution in light of its own unique natural law foundation. The Irish right of privacy is rightfully different from the American right of privacy. The holdings of the Irish courts should be different than the holdings of American courts, even if the subject matter of the case is the same. For based upon each one's philosophical basis, it would be wrong to assume that the holdings would necessarily be the same.

With the above in mind, let us finally return to Kenny J. and the High Court decision in *Ryan*. There his recognition of the general notion that there are rights which are not specifically expressed in the Constitution, specifically the right to bodily integrity in that case, led to a series of holdings, very much like holdings in similar US cases, which served to recognise other rights not specifically expressed in the Constitution, and grant them constitutional protection.

> Since that time, now twenty-five years ago, a large list of further personal rights has been declared to be latent in the guarantee of Article 40.3 and thus enforceable by the courts, although none of them is specifically mentioned in the Constitution. Thus . . . [the courts have upheld the] personal right of "marital privacy" . . . the right to earn a livelihood, the right to litigate, the right to fair procedures, the right to travel outside the state and consequently the right to a passport, and the right to get married. In addition, although the Constitution recognises as a "family" only that based on marriage, the courts have also, via the same Article 40.3, recognised that both the mother of an illegitimate child and the illegitimate child itself have personal rights that go a long way towards making up their lack of standing under Article 41, which deals only with the marital family.[30]

There are two cases in particular which will be discussed here in order to discern the effect which the Thomistic natural law has upon the unexpressed right of privacy, under which all of the above listed rights generally fall and to

---

[30] Kelly, "Fundamental Rights and the Constitution" in *De Valera's Constitution and Ours* (1988) p. 169 citing *McGee v. Attorney General* [1974] I.R. 284 (marital privacy); *Landers v. Attorney General* 109 I.L.T.R. 1 (livelihood); *Macauley v. Minister for Posts and Telegraphs* [1966] I.R. 345 (litigate); *The State (Healy) v. Donoghue* [1976] I.R. 325 (fair procedures); *The State (M.) v. Attorney General* [1979] I.R. 73 (travel); *Ryan v. Attorney General* [1965] I.R. 294 (marriage); and *G. v. An Bord Uchtála* [1980] I.R. 32 (unmarried mother).

examine how the parameters defined in this book – and other Thomistic notions – apply in either case.

The first is that which Professor Kelly listed first: *McGee v. Attorney-General*.[31] There, in a holding and case somewhat similar to *Griswold v. Connecticut* in the United States, the Court found that the a married couple's decision to use contraceptives is one in which the State may not intrude. Mr Justice Walsh's opinion reiterated Justice Kenny's statements in *Ryan*, emphasising more strongly that "the individual has natural and human rights over which the State has no authority".[32] Specifically, Walsh J. stated that:

> Articles 41 (family), 42 (education) and 44 (private property) emphatically reject the theory that there are no rights without laws, no rights contrary to the law and no rights anterior to the law. The indicate that justice is placed above the law and acknowledge that natural rights, or human rights, are not created by law but that the Constitution confirms their existence and gives them protection.[33]

Based upon Article 41, the act in question which restricted the availability of contraceptives was found to be unconstitutional as "an unjustified invasion of the privacy of husband and wife in their sexual relations with one another".[34] Furthermore, with regards to Article 40, Walsh J. stated that not only does a married woman possess the personal right to use contraceptives, but that, as in this case, when a woman's health may be endangered without the use of contraceptives, the State has "the positive obligation to ensure by its laws as far as possible that there would be made available to a married woman . . . the means whereby a conception . . . might be avoided . . ."[35]

Next, Walsh J. examined the State's role as the "guardian of the common good" and, in keeping with the Thomistic parameters discussed here, recognised that "the individual, as a member of society and the family, as a unit of society, have duties and obligations to consider and respect the good of that society".[36] After reiterating the accepted notion of the separation of powers, he went on to state that "the power of the State to act for the protection of the common good or to decide what are the exigencies of the common good is not one peculiarly reserved for the legislative organ of government" and is subject to review by the courts.[37] Then he stated the double-sided limitation which is placed upon the legislature under the Irish Constitution and its natural law basis:

---

[31] [1979] I.R. 284 (Walsh J.).
[32] *Ibid.*, at 310.
[33] *Ibid.*, at 310.
[34] *Ibid.*, at 314.
[35] *Ibid.*, at 315.
[36] *Ibid.*, at 310.
[37] *Ibid.*, at 310.

> In concrete terms that means that the legislature is not free to encroach unjustifiably upon the fundamental rights of individuals or of the family in the name of the common good, or by act or omission to abandon or to neglect the common good or the protections or enforcement of the rights of individual citizens.[38]

Mr Justice Walsh examined the possible common good reasons the State could have for intervention into this "particularly private" area. After having established that the sexual practices of a husband and wife and the size of their family are something for them to decide, Walsh J. stated that any State intervention into the "matrimonial bedroom" other to protect the life of a human (i.e. to prevent abortion) would be "an intolerable and unjustifiable intrusion" into the privacy of the couple. Then, relating back to Aquinas's moral "vices" element, Walsh J. examined whether the State ought to prohibit contraceptive use in order to protect the morality of the State (and be consistent with Roman Catholic teaching) for the common good. On that issue, Walsh J. made the following statement, which would have ramifications later, and points to the major area of disagreement in the utilisation of the Thomistic natural law.

> The question of whether the use of contraceptives by married couples within their marriage is or is not contrary to the moral code or codes to which they profess to subscribe, or is or is not regarded by them as being against their conscience, could not justify State action. Similarly the fact that the use of contraceptives may offend against the moral code of the majority of the citizens of the State would not per se justify an intervention by the State to prohibit their use within marriage. *The private morality of its citizens does not justify intervention by the State into the activities of those citizens unless and until the common good requires it* . . . [T]he rights of a married couple to decide how many children, if any, they will have are matters outside the reach of positive law where the means employed to implement such decisions do not impinge upon the common good or endanger human life. It is undoubtedly true that among those persons who are subject to a particular moral code no-one has a right to be in breach of that moral code. *But when this is a code governing private morality and where the breach of it is not one which injures the common good then it is not the State's business to intervene.* It is outside the authority of the State to endeavour to intrude into the privacy of the husband and wife relationship for the sake of imposing a code of private morality upon that husband and wife which they do not desire.[39]

---

[38] *Ibid.*, at 310.
[39] *Ibid.*, at 312-313 (emphasis added).

Essentially, Walsh J. stated that the State ought not to be used to enforce the moral tenets of the Church, when the violation of those tenets does not otherwise harm the common good. Citing also to Article 44, which protects the free exercise of religion, Walsh J. reiterated that while each person has "the right not to be compelled or coerced into living in a way which is contrary to one's conscience . . . so far as the exercise, practice or profession of religion is concerned . . ." this does not mean that each person has the "right to live in accordance with one's conscience subject to public order and morality."[40] This is a clear rejection of the secular natural law theory upon which the US Constitution is based. In Ireland, under the Thomistic natural law, as correctly represented by Walsh J., one does not have the right to live as he or she chooses merely because there has been no injury to another or no disruption to public order or morality. Rather, the individual is a part of the entire community just as one portion is part of an entire living organism, and as such, the needs of the whole are superior to the needs of the part. Accordingly, the State is free to intervene in the lives of individuals for the preservation of morality when required by the common good. But when does the common good require State intervention for the purposes of protecting the collective morality? In *McGee*, there was held to be no harm to the common good by the protection of the marital right to sexual privacy. In practical terms, it would be nearly impossible and extremely awkward to enforce a ban on contraceptives. More importantly, it can be said that the majority of Catholics in Ireland, as elsewhere, do not support the Church's ban on contraceptive use,[41] and a ban on contraceptives for married couples would be enormously unpopular. Here, as in other privacy cases listed above by Professor Kelly, once it has been accepted that an enforceable right of privacy does exist even though unexpressed in either Constitution, the holdings themselves have generally reflected the popular consensus and have been straightforward to decide.[42] The majority of people understand that they themselves want to be able to travel or vote or litigate or do any of those things which make their lives their own. So deciding to pro-

---

[40] *Ibid.*, at 316-317.

[41] The fear has been that artificial contraceptive devices abort an already fertilised egg. This is true with the Intra-Uterine Device (IUD) which prohibits the fertilised egg from implanting itself in the wall of the uterus. This method has been largely abandoned and the most popularly used contraceptives are those which utilise hormones to prevent fertilisation from occurring, or male or female sterilisation. There is the other traditional notion that sex should only be an activity for procreation. This has largely been abandoned by the Church and ridiculed by all but the most arch-conservative Catholics. But see, "Contraceptive Sex is 'a Lie'" *The Sunday Tribune* (Ireland) (19 September 1993) p. 8A, in which Mr Justice O'Hanlon reiterated notions which this writer hasn't heard since the 1967 sex education talk given by her primary school nuns.

[42] Another privacy case not included above is *Kennedy v. Attorney General* [1988] I.L.R.M. 472 (High Court) prohibiting phone tapping. See generally Kelly, *The Irish Constitution* (Supp. to 2nd edn, 1987) pp. 146-169; Casey, *Constitutional Law in Ireland* (1992) pp. 309-358 for a discussion of other related cases.

tect another's right to do something which they themselves would want to be protected in doing seems very desirable and makes for what would appear to be a simple decision. With *Griswold* and *McGee*, an overwhelming majority of Americans and Irish agree with both courts' rulings and would strongly resist any notion that the State could intervene in their own sexual activities.

But in other areas in which the majority would not agree, the waters are muddied. Under the secular natural law, as stated before, the consensus of the majority has no place in the consideration whether the rights of the individual to life, liberty and property ought to be recognised and protected. Under the Thomistic natural law, however, as Walsh J. noted in *McGee*, there is a point at which the consensus of the majority must be considered so that the collective body of the community can be preserved, as required by the common good. But what is that point? If not with *McGee*, then where?

In *Norris v. Attorney General*,[43] the plaintiff submitted, among other claims, that laws prohibiting homosexual activities in the privacy of one's home were violative of his right of privacy under Article 40.3 and, as such, were unconstitutional. The High Court rejected his arguments, and plaintiff appealed to the Supreme Court. There the Court, in a 3-2 decision, ruled against the plaintiff. The topic of the State's interest in protecting and promoting community morality for the common good, however, was aggressively debated, with references to the controversial Wolfenden Report and the theories of John Stuart Mill. O'Higgins C.J., though relying on quite inaccurate information,[44] held for the majority that "the State [has] an interest in the general moral well-being of the community and [is] entitled, where it is practicable to do so, to discourage conduct which is morally wrong and harmful to a way of life and to values which the State wishes to protect". In summarising, the Chief Justice, placing further emphasis upon outdated notions of homosexuality, stated that the State's interests were paramount.

> On the ground of the Christian nature of our State and on the grounds that the deliberate practice of homosexuality is morally wrong, that it is damaging to the health both of individuals and the public and, finally,

---

[43] [1984] I.R. 36.

[44] The Chief Justice attempted to distinguish between congenital and acquired homosexuality. Today it is generally acknowledged by scientists and psychiatrists that homosexuality is always congenital – a person is born homosexual just as a person is born with a tendency to be left- or right-handed. He also referred to the unhappiness and depression homosexuals typically suffer. This, however, has been shown to be due to society's ostracism of them rather than the homosexuality itself. In addition, his inference that homosexuality can be 'caught' from another is inaccurate, as is his premise that homosexuality is inimical to marriage. Under that line of thinking, anyone who chooses to remain unmarried is a threat to the institution of marriage. *Cf. Commonwealth of Kentucky v. Wasson*, 842 S W 2d 487 (Ky. 1992), discussed above p. 109, fn. 74 in which all the above is scientifically supported.

that it is potentially harmful to the institution of marriage, I can find no inconsistency with the Constitution in the laws which make such conduct criminal. It follows, in my view, that no right of privacy, as claimed by the plaintiff, can prevail against the operation of such criminal sanctions.[45]

Attorney for the plaintiff, the former President Mary Robinson, argued that the holding of the European Convention on Human Rights ought to be applied to the case in support of the plaintiff's claim. The majority – consisting of the Chief Justice and Finlay and Griffin JJ. – was joined by one member of the dissent, Henchy J. in holding that the rulings of the European Convention do not form a part of the domestic law of Ireland.[46]

Putting aside any discussion of the accuracy of the notions upon which the majority's opinion was based, the ruling established that here was a limitation upon one's right of privacy based upon the morality of the majority of the community. The State could rightfully infringe upon the private activity of two consenting adults in order to protect the moral well-being of the community and serve the common good. The Court essentially stated that married couples (and now unmarried heterosexual couples[47]) have a greater zone of privacy than do homosexual couples because the activity of the homosexual couples is contrary to that which a majority consensus finds acceptable and thus such activity denigrates the moral well-being of the community, contrary to the common good.

If one accepts the notion that a shared morality is necessary to the maintenance of government, in accordance with the theory put forth by Lord Devlin,[48] and the "one body" notion so important in the natural law theory of Thomas Aquinas, then the State's interest in protecting that shared morality is an integral part of promoting the common good. Indeed, an interesting development in New York City lends credence to this view. In the past, New York's police authorities generally spent most of their time and attention attacking major crime activities: murder, rape, robbery and the like. Minor crimes such as vandalism, loitering and panhandling were ignored. The result was that both major and minor crime persisted and the generally fearful quality of life

---

[45] *Norris v. Attorney General* [1984] I.R. 36 at 65 (O'Higgins C.J.).

[46] *Ibid.*, at 65. But see *Norris v. Ireland* [1991] 13 E.H.R.R. 186 in which the European Court of Human Rights held for Mr Norris and the laws in question were repealed by s. 14 of the Criminal Law (Sexual Offences) Act 1993.

[47] The Health (Family Planning)(Amendment) Act 1992 permits the sale of contraceptives to single persons aged seventeen and over.

[48] "[I]f society has the right to make a judgement and has it on the basis that a recognised morality is as necessary to society as, say, a recognised government, then society may use the law to preserve morality in the same way as it uses it to safeguard anything else that is essential to its existence." Devlin, *The Enforcement of Morals* (1965) p. 11.

continued unabated. A new administration was voted in a few years ago, however, which employed the notion that all crime ought to be punished, especially minor crime, under the view that persistent exposure to petty crime sets the negative tone for the moral atmosphere of the community. Panhandlers, loiterers, vandals, con artists, subway thieves, etc. were all arrested and charged, and homeless persons, many of whom are mentally ill persons released from institutions, were placed with proper authorities, as a practice of "zero tolerance" was put into effect. The results were astounding. Not only has petty crime virtually disappeared, but the incidence of major crimes has dramatically decreased. Citizens in New York, feeling safer and more confident about their city than ever, claim that the new atmosphere emphasises correct, civil behaviour on every level.[49] Although this is a far different situation than that presented by the practice of homosexuality in the home (i.e. panhandlers and the like have a direct negative impact upon the community at large and cause physical harm to others), the effect of the policy put in force shows what can happen when certain previously non-compliant persons are required to conform to a moral code of conduct supported by a consensus of the community.

Crucial to any enforcement of majority moral standards is *the utilisation of accurate scientific and sociological data concerning the group or persons in question*. With *Norris v. Attorney General*, the Court arguably relied upon information which was incorrect in finding that all homosexuality is harmful to the community. It would have more truthful for the Court to have merely stated that homosexuality ought to remain a crime because the majority of people in Ireland feel that it is immoral. This, however, in and of itself is not sufficient to criminalise the private acts of any person or group. As Walsh J. stated in *McGee*: "The private morality of its citizens does not justify intervention by the State into the activities of those citizens unless and until the common good requires it."[50] Even if there is a clear consensus in the community as to what constitutes acceptable behaviour, *"where the breach of it is not one which injures the common good then it is not the State's business to intervene"*.[51]

Indeed, there have been many instances in our histories in which the majority have held beliefs which were not based upon right and wrong but rather upon prejudice and stereotypes grown out of misinformation and ignorance. This is why the enactment of laws merely to protect a particular community standard can be inimical both to individual rights and to the common good. For if the rationale behind the prohibition of a particular private activity is not based in unbiased fact, and if there is not required an actual "injury to the common good" resulting from the activities the actor, the law's infringement upon the actor's civil liberties is no more than arbitrary discrimination and the

---

[49] See "Values matter more than money" *USA Today* (3 April 1996).
[50] [1974] I.R. 312. (Walsh, J.)
[51] *Ibid.*, at 313 (emphasis added).

common good notion will have been subverted. Returning to the original question, therefore, which asked at what point should the majority's notion of right and wrong be considered in lawmaking, the proposed answer is this: the morality of the majority may be considered if, and only if, the acts to be punished have been independently and factually proven to cause harm – or an imminent risk of harm, whether that harm be physical, psychological or mental – either to one of the parties to the activity or to the community at large. Then and only then may the opinion of the consensus be utilised as a factor in determining the outcome of the adjudication or the contents of proposed legislation. By requiring a palpable "injury to the common good", the court and legislature can fairly balance the protection of individual rights, on one hand, with the requirements of the common good, and the double-edged limitation which the Thomistic natural law places upon the right of privacy and all rights recognised by the Irish Constitution, can be best honoured in a predictable, non-arbitrary manner.

More specifically, requiring evidence of palpable injury to the common good in the adjudication of so-called 'victimless' crimes would aid in distinguishing between activity which is truly harmful, and thus necessary to prohibit and that private, consensual activity which others merely find distasteful. A keener examination of many so-called 'victimless' crimes would also result. There has been much evidence recently uncovered which shows that prostitution, for example, is not as 'victimless' as many would have it appear. The prostitute herself suffers great psychological and emotional trauma, as well as injury from venereal disease and other sexually transmitted illnesses, at the very least. Similar claims can be made of exposure to pornographic material in the home. Again, though it has been maintained that this is a private affair not subject to State intervention, there has been evidence that excessive exposure to denigrating pornographic material causes deep psychological damage and bears a relation to inappropriate and often criminal overt sexual activity, such as indecent exposure or rape. Similarly, it has been proven that children of divorced parents suffer a higher rate of mental illness, depression and other psychological and social ills. It is this type of evidence, sufficiently substantiated, together with the backing of the consensus of the majority, which could correctly lead to the prohibition or regulation of such private activities in order to promote and protect the common good. Distinctions would and should be carefully drawn based upon evidence of harm, and the nature of the activity in question, so that only the most limited intrusions upon the privacy of the individual are made when necessary. But when it *is* factually necessary for the common good, those regulations ought to be enforced and protected. As Henchy J. stated in his dissent in *Norris*:

> It would not be constitutional to decriminalise all homosexual acts, any more than it would be constitutional to decriminalise all heterosexual acts. Public order and morality; the protection of the young, of the weak-

willed, of those who may readily be subject to undue influence, and of others who should be deemed to be in need of protection; the maintenance inviolate of the family as the natural primary and fundamental unit of society; the upholding of the institution of marriage; the requirements of public health; these and other aspects of the common good require that homosexual acts be made criminal in many circumstances.[52]

For under Thomistic natural law and the Irish Constitution, reflecting the continuously ebbing and flowing symbiosis between the common good and individual rights, it can be said that *only when individual rights are fairly protected is the common good promoted and only by promoting the common good can the rights of all be fairly protected*. In the context of this relationship, based upon the independent touchstones provided by the Thomistic natural law, the right of privacy in Ireland is recognised, protected and preserved.

---

[52] [1984] I.R. 104. (Henchy J., dissenting).

CHAPTER 9

Further Developments in Ireland: a Turn away from the Natural Law

> Everyone seriously engaged in science reaches the conviction that
> the laws of Nature manifest a spirit which is vastly superior to Man,
> and before which, with our modest strength, we must humbly bow.[1]

There are many issues pertaining to the right of privacy which will arise in the future and with which the courts of Ireland and the United States will have to contend. Even now, privacy topics are making news in both nations.

In the US, the right to die is one which is regularly discussed in the newspapers as court rulings and medical studies are handed down daily. Though the US Supreme Court heard this issue in its Autumn 1996 term[2] and found that a right to die is *not* and unexpressed, constitutionally protected right under the Ninth and Fourteenth Amendments and thus *not* applicable to the states via the Fourteenth Amendment, the Court failed to look closely at the underlying purpose and philosophy of the Constitution and recognise that self-destruction is something, as Locke would state, which no man has the power (naturally speaking) to do, i.e. act contrary to the preservation of his own life. The Court did recognise that it would be opening a nightmarish Pandora's box in finding a constitutional right to die and that such a ruling would certainly lead to a perverse panoply of cases seeking rulings in issues pertaining to competence, quality of life, intent, etc. (Not dissimilar to what followed *Roe v. Wade*). Yet the Court did not lean on the secular natural law which would have provided it with great assistance and stability in deciding this crucial, fundamental issue and unfortunately did not achieve ultimate natural law justice when it failed to hold that there was a constitutional right to life.

In Ireland there have been three major holdings concerning privacy which have arisen out of the holding in *McGee*: the right to obtain an abortion if the life, as opposed to the health, of the mother is in danger; the right to obtain information about abortion; and last, the right to die a 'natural death' in a case which may be initiating the slide down the slippery slope of euthanasia in Ireland. Their overall effect appears to be a turn away from the natural law.

In the *X* case, in which a 14-year-old girl sought an abortion after becom-

---

[1] Albert Einstein, 1936.
[2] *Washington v. Glucksberg* 117 S. Ct. 2258 (1997).

ing pregnant as a result of rape and was found to be suicidal as a result of the pregnancy, the Court *via* Finlay, CJ., concluded that "the proper test to be applied is that if it is established as a matter of probability that there is a real and substantial risk to the life, as distinct from the health, of the mother, which can only be avoided by the termination of her pregnancy, such termination is permissible"[3] under the Constitution. Protests which arose after the High Court's ruling, overturned by the Supreme Court, were as short-sighted as they were acrimonious. The failure to even examine the philosophical basis for Mr Justice Costello's thoughtful and careful decision indicated that those who protested were merely promoting their own agenda, and not seeking to understand the entire tragic issue in its natural law context. Similarly, the Irish Supreme Court could have found support in Aquinas as well, if it would have looked. For Aquinas allowed for a notion of "exceptionality":

> However, it sometimes happens that some precept . . . is not useful for a particular person or in a particular case because it either hinders some greater good or even causes some evil . . . it would be dangerous to leave this judgment to any individual, except perhaps in the case of a clear and sudden emergency . . . Consequently, he who governs a community has the power to dispense from a human law that rests on his authority, so that when the application of a law to persons or cases fails, he can grant permission that the law be not observed.[4]

In rare situations, such as in the *X* case, the Court would have been justified in making an exception to the laws prohibiting abortion as allowed by the above. Note that Aquinas did not allow for the alteration or denial of the natural law, but rather submitted that human law could be dispensed with when necessary. As has been stated, one tenet of the natural law is absolute: the preservation of life; and it is this absoluteness which gives any legal system truly based upon the natural law its integrity. By relying upon an independent standard of right and wrong, as opposed to a positivistic approach in which 'the good' varies from legislature to legislature, the government and the society remain stable: the essential building blocks of that society are protected and allowed to flourish. If one accepts the allegation that the young mother was indeed suicidal and the continuation of the pregnancy would have resulted in her death (it was noted throughout that it would be nearly impossible to prevent a suicide) and thus the death of the foetus as well, then the 'greater good', under the application of the natural law, would be the abortion of the foetus. It is better to save one life than to lose both lives, and in terms of the result, the decision is consistent with the natural law because it does not denigrate the value of the

---

[3] [1992] I.R. 51-52.
[4] *Treatise on Law* at 97, 6. See also discussion in Chapter 3 (around fn. 45-49)

foetus relative to that of the mother. Both are viewed as having equal value. In the *X* case, a most unfortunate and unusual situation, the outcome was consistent with the natural law in that it served to save one life.

Having stated that, however, it must be noted that Finlay C.J. did not rely primarily on the tenets of the natural law in his opinion, but rather upon a section of the opinion in *McGee* written by Walsh C.J. which has been cited as the primary reason for the need to enact of the first paragraph of Article 40.3.3° in 1983 by the electorate.[5] In that particular section, Walsh C.J. stated:

> In this country, it falls finally upon the judges to interpret the Constitution and in doing so to determine, where necessary, the rights which are superior or antecedent to positive law or which are imprescriptible or inalienable. In the performance of this difficult duty there are certain guidelines laid down by the Constitution for the judge. The very structure and context of the Articles dealing with fundamental rights clearly indicate that justice is not subordinate to the law. In particular, the terms of section 3 of Article 40 expressly subordinate the law to justice.[6]

Up to this point, it seemed that Walsh C.J. was leading to the conclusion that the natural law, with its absolute notions of justice, especially that pertaining to the right to life, is superior to all positive law and must be the paramount guide in adjudicating all cases coming before the Irish courts. But a few sentences later, he shifted direction:

> According to the preamble, the people gave themselves the Constitution to promote the common good, with due observance of prudence, justice and charity so that the dignity and freedom of the individual might be assured. *The judges must, therefore, as best they can from their training and their experience interpret these rights in accordance with their ideas of prudence, justice and charity.* It is but natural that from time to time the prevailing ideas of these virtues may be conditioned by the passage of time; *no interpretation of the Constitution is intended to be final for all time. It is given in the light of prevailing ideas and concepts.*[7]

Absent was any reiteration of the tenet stated so absolutely only six pages previously which held that: "[A]ny action on the part of either the husband and wife or of the State to limit family sizes by *endangering or destroying human life must necessarily not only be an offence against the common good*

---

[5] See, for example Binchy, "Marital Privacy and Family Law" 65 Studies (1977) p. 330.
[6] [1974] I.R. at 318 (Walsh C.J.).
[7] *Ibid.*, at 319 (emphasis added).
[8] [1974] I.R. 312 (Walsh C.J.) (emphasis added).

but also against the guaranteed personal rights of the human life in question."[8] In other words, the preservation of human life is an absolute, not subject to any human law or whim, or interpretation "in light of prevailing ideas and concepts". Perhaps Mr Justice Walsh's statements on pp. 318-319 of the *McGee* decision were not intended to disavow the absolute right to life language of p. 312, nor his assertion two pages previous to that, stating that there indeed are rights without laws, rights contrary to the law and rights anterior to the law[9] within the context of a natural law system. The fact remains, however, that the language of "judicial interpretation" and "prevailing ideas and concepts" expressed by Mr Justice Walsh was picked up and utilised by the Irish Supreme Court in cases which followed *McGee* in order to justify decision-making which did not directly rely upon the natural law basis of the Irish Constitution. And the first of these was *The State (Healy) v. Donoghue*, cited in the *X* case to re-affirm Mr Justice Walsh's statement in *McGee*:

> In my view, this preamble makes it clear that rights given by the Constitution must be considered in accordance with concepts of prudence, justice and charity, which may gradually change or develop as society changes and develops and which fall to be interpreted from time to time in accordance with prevailing ideas ... In other words, the Constitution did not seek to impose for all time the ideas prevalent or accepted with regard to these virtues at the time of its enactment. Walsh J. expressed this view very clearly in *McGee v. The Attorney General*.[10]

The notion that judges could interpret the tenets of the Irish Constitution "in accordance with prevailing ideas" was relied upon by Mr Justice Finlay to justify the Court's examination of the factors surrounding the young mother's life and rule that the life of the unborn child could be aborted if it were established that an inevitable or immediate risk to the life of the mother existed, and, in the case at hand, such a risk did indeed exist.[11] There was no examination of the natural law, nor, as cited by many commentators, no real examination of other options whereby suicide by the young mother could have been avoided, suggesting that the majority was more interested in the result than in how it arrived there.[12] While the ultimate ruling could have been consistent

---

[9] *Ibid.*, at 310.

[10] [1976] I.R. 325 at 347 (O'Higgins, C.J.) cited in [1992] I.R. at 51-52 (Finlay C.J.).

[11] [1992] I.R. at 52 (Finlay C.J.).

[12] See, for example, Hogan, Whyte & Kelly, *The Irish Constitution* (3rd edn, 1994) p. 803, "The failure of various judges [in the *X* case] to tease out these issues ... does leave the impression that, in some respects at least, the foundations for the majority decision could have been dug more deeply ... Be that as it may, the ruling in *X* eased the dreadful predicament in which the young defendant found herself and stemmed the tide of international criticism ..."

with the natural law (assuming, as stated above, that the life of the mother was truly at risk), there was no examination of it, and hence no conclusions based upon it and its clear, stable guideposts.

Once the Irish Supreme Court ruled that an abortion is permissible under the Constitution when there is an inevitable or immediate risk to the life of the mother, it admittedly opened a door through which a host of other issues would immediately follow. That first issue was the right of a mother in the aforementioned situation to information and to travel abroad pursuant to obtaining an abortion outside of Ireland.

> The *X* case however established that . . . termination of the life of the unborn is permissible if it is established as a matter of probability that there is a real and substantial risk to the life, as distinct from the health of the mother and that that risk can only be avoided by the termination of her pregnancy . . . Once the termination of the pregnancy is permissible, the mother has the right to all relevant information necessary to enable her to have the pregnancy terminated . . . [and i]n such circumstances, the mother would have the right to travel outside the jurisdiction to avail of such services to secure a termination of the pregnancy.[13]

If this is the direction which the majority of the citizens of Ireland wish to go, then that is one matter. If the citizenry wish to be governed in a manner consistent with the natural law basis of the Irish Constitution, however, then it must seriously examine this opening of the door to overseas abortions which is entirely at odds with the natural law.[14] What the Supreme Court has done by making the above ruling is expose itself, and the legislature, to all sorts of arbitrary, bio-ethical rule-making similar to that which the US Supreme Court must still deal with in the aftermath of *Roe v. Wade*: when is the life of the mother truly at risk? What proof is required to show that only by termination of the pregnancy can the mother's life be spared? How does the government prevent abortion information from falling into the hands of a mother whose life is not at risk? Can the government still prevent any woman from travelling to obtain an abortion? What liability does a doctor face if s/he falsely certifies that a mother's life is at risk? Irish men and women must also ask themselves whether they are ready to take the American road upon which third trimester abortions, illegal by law unless the woman's life or health is at risk, are routinely performed by doctors who will certify such in order to perform another fee-for-service procedure. And, in the larger picture, what is

---

[13] *The Regulation of Information Bill 1995* [1995] 2 I.L.R.M. 81, at 98 (Hamilton C.J.).

[14] A statement made by Mr Justice Brian Walsh in an interview with the author, 8 October 1992, was strangely prophetic, "If our belief tells us that we must protect the life of the unborn child, is it alright to say 'Go to another country to have the foetus done away with?' It's very hypocritical. Would we accept someone packing up his granny to go to Holland to have her done in? It's murder no matter where it's done."

lost is the independent notion of right and wrong and the non-arbitrary guide-posts of the natural law. The Court, like its American counterpart, could eventually become rudderless in deciding this and other issues, and the twin dangers of legal positivism and relative morality could eventually dominate adjudication, rather than examinations of the effect upon the common good with the ultimate emphasis upon preservation of life, as mandated by the underlying natural law. If the Irish people wish to have their courts and legislature follow the natural law path, then it should question quickly the consequences of this ruling.

The third ruling which suggests that the Irish Supreme Court is moving away from the absolute protection of human life which the natural law requires is another unfortunate case involving a young woman: *In the Matter of a Ward of Court*.[15] There, the Supreme Court upheld the lower court ruling which allowed the family of a woman who has been in a "nearly permanent vegetative state" with "a degree of cognitive function"[16] for over twenty years to stop feeding the woman via a gastrostomy tube and allow her to die. As in the *X* case, what is equally disconcerting about the ruling here from a legal standpoint, along with the immediate case at hand,[17] is the effect the ruling will have upon future situations involving questions of the 'quality' of the life of one who is not as able as others and whether certain kinds of human life are to be more ardently protected than others. In addition, the Court will find itself stuck in another quagmire of bio-ethical questions: What is considered 'ordinary' versus 'extra-ordinary' care when medical care and capabilities are advancing yearly? How does one correctly determine the wishes of the patient? Even if one can ascertain a patient's wishes, are such wishes ever made without outside pressure or influence? At what point in the continuum of the "nearly permanent vegetative state" is one considered a candidate for death? Should the Court even be examining the 'quality' of a person's life at all? And what constitutes 'artificial' feeding? Once again, a wicked Pandora's box has probably been opened.

In summary, the Irish and American Courts should examine, rely upon

---

[15] [1995] 2 I.L.R.M. 401 (Hamilton, C.J.).

[16] The patient successfully pulled out her nasogastic tube on hundreds of occasions. ("she seemed to find this distressing") and had a "minimal capacity to recognise . . . the long established nursing staff and to react to strangers by showing distress. She also follows or tracks people with her eyes." *Ibid.*, at 412. The Supreme Court accepted the finding that though the woman would probably never get better, she was not considered terminally ill. All other organs functioned normally.

[17] "The question here is not whether you have a right to die, or even rather you have the right not to have your life prolonged, but whether you have the right to have yourself killed. And in a case like this, how can one know what the patient truly wants anyway? And what do you put as the cause of death on the death certificate?" Interview with Mr Justice Brian Walsh, 15 May 1996. See also, "Court understanding of 'ordinary' care flawed" *The Irish Times* (29 July 1995); "Determining precise scope of right to die" *The Irish Times* (29 July 1995).

and celebrate the natural law bases of their respective constitutions. The natural law in both countries can provide each nation with a permanent, eternal standard of right and wrong and enable justice to be meted out in a predictable manner while allowing for variabilities in human experience, knowledge and growth. The law, and our lives, ought never to be subject to the whim of legislation, even if that legislature has been duly and properly elected by the majority of the citizens in that country.[18] Certain rights, especially the right to life and those liberties pertaining thereto, are too important and necessary to be subject to the arbitrariness of man.

---

[18] Mr Justice Walsh pointed out in an interview with the author, 15 May 1995, that "Hitler did nothing contrary to the existing law of Germany". The fact remains that an act can be promulgated by properly elected legislature, appropriately representing an electorate in which all competent adults are allowed to vote, and that act can be entirely repugnant to human life and the natural law. "Law is rooted in a series of objective value judgements about morality or justice, or it is about nothing." Lord Hailsham, "Modern Reflections on The Natural Law" A Commemorative Lecture given to the Canon Law Society of Great Britain and Ireland 19 October 1978 (London).

Bibliography

BOOKS

Barker, E (ed., trans), *The Politics of Aristotle* (1958).

Birks, P & McLeod, G (trans), *Justinian's Institutes* (1987).

Braudel, F, *The Structures of Everyday Life: civilisation and capitalism 15th–18th centuries*, Volume 1 (1979).

Burt, R A, *The Constitution in Conflict* (1992).

Casey, J, *Constitutional Law of Ireland* (1992).

Chubb, B, *The Politics of the Irish Constitution* (1991).

Chubb, B, *The Constitution and Change in Ireland* (1978).

Coogan, T, P, *De Valera* (1993).

Cooke, J E (ed.), *The Federalist* (1961).

Cox, A, *The Court and the Constitution* (1987).

Crowe, M B, *The Changing Profile of the Natural Law* (1997).

Cunningham, N, *In Pursuit if Reason: the life of Thomas Jefferson* (1987).

de Toqueville, A, *Journey in Ireland, July-August 1835* (1990).

Devlin, P, *The Enforcement of Morals* (1965).

Dwyer, T P, *De Valera: the man and the myth* (1991).

Ellis, P B, *The Celtic Empire* (1990).

Ely, J H, *Democracy and Distress* (1980).

Farrell, B (ed.), *De Valera's Constitution and Ours* (1988).

Finnis, J, *Natural Law and Natural Rights* (1980).

Finley, M I, *The Legacy of Greece* (1981).

Finley, M I, *Ancient Slavery and Modern Ideology* (1980).

Forde, M, *Constitutional Law of Ireland* (1987).

Foster, R F, *Modern Ireland 1600-1972* (1988).

Frazer, J G, *The Golden Bough* (1922).

Gay, P, *The Cultivation of Hatred* (1993).

George, R (ed.), *Natural Law Theory, Contemporary Essays* (1992).

Harding, A (ed.), *Origins of the Natural Law Tradition* (1954).

Harding, A (ed.), *Natural Law Theory, Contemporary Essays* (1992).

Hart, H L A, *The Concept of Law* (1961).

Hart, H L A, *Essays on Bentham, Jurisprudence and Political Theory* (1982).

Henley, R J (ed., trans), *The Treatise on Law (being Summa Theologiae I-II, QQ. 90-97) by Thomas Aquinas* (1993).

Herm, G, *The Celts* (1975).

Hogue, A, *Origins of Common Law* (1966).

Jowett, B (ed., trans), *The Republic by Plato* (1992).

Kammen, M, *A Machine that would go of Itself* (1986).

Kauper, P & Beytagh F X, *Constitutional Law: cases and materials* (1980).

Kelly F, *A Guide to Early Irish Law* (1990).

Kelly J M, *A Short History of Western Legal Theory* (1992).

Kelly J M, *The Irish Constitution (with supplement)* (1984, 1987).

Laslett, P (ed.), *Two Treatises of Government by John Locke* (1964).

Le Goff, J, *Intellectuals in the Middle Ages* (1993).

Levy, L & Mahoney, D (eds), *The Framing and Ratification of the Constitution* (1987).

Litton, F (ed.), *The Constitution of Ireland, 1937-1987* (1988).

MacNeill, E, *Early Irish Laws and Institutions* (1935).

Malone, D, *Jefferson and his Times*, 5 Volumes (1951).

McDonald, F, *Novus Ordo Seclorum, The Intellectual Origins of the Constitution* (1987).

McIlwain, C H, *The Growth of Political thought in the West* (1932).

McKenchnie, W S, *Magna Carta, A Commentary* (1905).

Morgan, E, *Inventing the People: the rise of popular sovereignty in England and America* (1988).

O'Reilly, J (ed.), *Human Rights and Constitutional Law* (1992).

Osborough, W N (ed.), *Essays in Honour of J M Kelly* (1994).

Richter, M, *Medieval Ireland, the Enduring Tradition* (1983).

Rouse, W (ed., trans), *Great Dialogues of Plato* (1956).

Rutland, R, *James Madison, the Founding Father* (1987).

St John-Stevas, N, *Life, Death and the Law* (1964).

Scanlan, A (ed.), *Natural Law Institute Proceedings, 1947* (1947).

Schwartz, B, *Super Chief: Earl Warren and his Supreme Court* (1983).

Shattner, A J, *Family Law in the Republic of Ireland* (1981).

Smith, J M (ed.), *The Republic of Letters, The Correspondence between Thomas Jefferson and James Madison, 1776-1826* (1995).

Stockton, D, *The Classical Athenian Democracy* (1990).

Tuck, R, *Natural Rights and Theories: their origin and development* (1979).

Van Doren, C, *Benjamin Franklin* (1938).

White, G E, *The American Judicial Tradition* (1976).

Wills, G, *Inventing America: Jefferson's Declaration of Independence* (1978).

Wills, G, *Explaining America: The Federalist* (1981).

Wills, G, *Cincinnatus: George Washington and the Enlightenment* (1984).

Wood, G, *The Radicalism of the American Revolution* (1992).

ARTICLES

Berger, R, "The Ninth Amendment" 66 *Cornel L. Rev*. 1 (1980).

Berns, W, "Judicial Review and the Rights and Laws of Nature" *S. Ct. Rev.* 49 (1982).

Beytagh, F X, "Privacy in Perspective: the experience under foreign constitutions" *U. Tol. L. Rev.* 449 (1984).

Beytagh, F X, "Equality under the Irish and American Constitutions: a comparative analysis" *Ir. Jur.* 56 (1983).

Binch, W, "Pluralism Religious Freedom and Marriage Law" 45 *Doctrine & Life* 71 (1995).

Brandeis, L, "The Right to Privacy" 4 *Harv. L. Rev.* 193 (1890).

Brennan, W, "The Constitution of the United States: contemporary ratification" 27 *S. Tex. L. Rev.* 433 (1986).

Caplan, R, "The History and Meaning of the Ninth Amendment" 69 *Va. L. Rev.* 223 (1983).

Casey, G, "Man and His Nature" (Unpublished., 1980).

Casey, J, the Judicial Power under Irish Constitutional Law" 24 *Int. & Comp. L. Quart.* 305 (1975).

Clarke, D, "Emergency Legislation, Fundamental Rights and Article 28.3.3° of the Irish Constitution" *Ir. Jur.* 217 (1977).

Clarke, D, "The Role of the Natural Law in Irish Constitutional Law" *Ir. Jur.* 187 (1982).

Costello, D, "The Natural Law and the Irish Constitution" *Studies* 403 (1956).

Cox, A, "The Role of the Supreme Court: judicial activism or self-restraint?" 47 *Maryland L. Rev.* 118 (1987).

Crowe, M B, Human Rights, the Irish Constitution and the Courts" 47 *Notre Dame L.* 281 (1971).

Davitt, T E, "St Thomas Aquinas and the Natural Law" in Harding, A (ed.), *Origins of the Natural Law Tradition* (1954).

Delaney, V, "The Constitution of Ireland: its origin and development" 12 *U. Tor. L. J.* 1 (1957).

Duncan, W, "Can Natural Law be used in Constitutional Interpretation?" 45 *Doctrine & Life* 125 (1995).

Ely, J H, "On Discovering Fundamental Values" 92 *Harv. L. Rev.* 5 (1978).

Grogan, V, "The Constitution and Natural Law" *Christus Rex* 8 (1954).

Grey, T, "Do we have an Unwritten Constitution?" 27 *Stan. L. Rev.* 703 (1975).

Grey, T, "Origins of the Unwritten Constitution: fundamental law in American revolutionary thought" 30 *Stan. L. Rev.* 843 (1978).

Heuston, R, "Personal Rights under the Irish Constitution" *Ir. Jur.* 205 (1976).

Hogan, G, "Procedural Rights under Natural Justice" *Ir. Jur.* 107 (1979).

Hogan, G, "Natural and Constitutional Justice – Adieu to Laissez-Faire" *Ir. Jur.* 309 (1984).

Hogan, G, "Free Speech, Privacy and the Press in Ireland" *Pub. L.* 509 (1987).

Kenny, J, "The Advantages of a Written Constitution incorporating a Bill of Rights" 30 *N. Ir. L. Quart.* 189 (1979).

McWhinney, E, "The Courts and the Constitution in Catholic Ireland" 29 *Tul. L. Rev.* 69 (1954).

Meese, E, "The Supreme Court of the United States: bulwark of a limited constitution" 27 *S. Tex. L. Rev.* 455 (1986).

Murphy, W, "An Ordering of Constitutional Values" 53 *S. Cal. L. Rev.* 703 (1980).

Nolan, M, "The Influence of Catholic Nationalism on the Legislature of the Irish Free State" *Ir. Jur.* 128 (1975).

O'Donaghue, N, "The Law beyond the Law" 18 *Am. J. Juris.* 150 (1973).

O'Flaherty, H, "Some Aspects of the Law, the Constitution and the Courts in Ireland" 51 *Australian L. J.* 74 (1977).

Quinn, G, "Legal Change, Natural Law and the Authority of Courts" 45 *Doctrine & Life* 97 (1995).

Temple Lang, J, "Neglected Aspects of Fundamental Rights" 1 *Dublin U. L. Rev.* 83 (1969).

Temple Lang, J, "Private Law Aspects of the Irish Constitution" *Ir. Jur.* 237 (1971).

Walsh, B, "Existenc and Meaning of Fundamental Rights in the Field of Education in Ireland" 2 *Hum Rts. L. J.* 319 (1981).

Walsh, B, "Constitutional Jurisdiction in the Context of State Powers" 9 *Hum. Rts. L. J.* 1 (1988).

Index